GRANDMA LEONE'S

MEMOIRS

(1880 TO 1910)

AMAZING JOURNEY
OF THE NEELY PIONEER FAMILY

Leone Neely Mayouck

MANUSCRIPT PREPARED BY GRANDDAUGHTER
PAULA EISENMAN PASCOE

Library of Congress Catalog Card Number: 2005901824

ISBN 0-615-12819-X

First printing May 2005

Published by
Fox Island Press
PO Box 599
Fox Island, Washington 98333

Edited by Georgia McDade

Illustrated by Lance DuBois

Cover design by John Fosberg

Printed in the USA by
Reischling Press, Inc.
Seattle, Washington

FRONT COVER PHOTO
Grandma Leone in Her Wedding Dress on June 10, 1910

BACK COVER PHOTO
Neely Family in Chicago Park in 1907
Left to right
Back Row: Marie, Leone, and Laura
Sitting: Henrietta, Bill, and Helen

For additional copies of this book contact Fox Island Press.

FOREWORD

My grandmother, Leone Neely Mayouck, wrote this autobiography. She recalls memorable life events and presents day-to-day living situations of her Neely pioneer family. She wrote that she "set the stage in the first four chapters of this book by introducing characters that had some direct bearing upon the Neely family." In Chapter Five, Grandma Leone was not yet nine years old when Baby Helen arrived in 1893. She noted, "Perhaps my book should have started at this point because Helen was the youngest of the five Neely sisters with whom these memoirs are mainly concerned."

This is Grandma's document, the story of the Neely family in her words. There may be a clearer way to present passages she wrote. However, as her granddaughter, I respect her story and made changes only when absolutely necessary and never added content. Some mistakes in grammar do occur, but it accurately reflects the way her characters talked. Punctuation mistakes could also exist.

The original typed onionskin pages were too light to scan and put into our computer, so I had to take the time to enter the manuscript manually. The good news is that making corrections, copies, or changes of any kind was easier. A problem for me was the lack of a discernible order of the chapters. After much reading and re-reading, I began to see groupings. I took the liberty of naming chapters, and then I was able to decipher the four distinctive parts of the book. Another issue was Grandma's use of family nicknames, by which she and her sisters often called each other. Since all of the family members she presented have died, I elected to change all the nicknames to the true names of the Neely girls. It was at this point the chapters took on an entirely new meaning for me. I could actually hear Grandma and most of my aunts talking.

As Grandma noted, "I have kept to the true names of places and have endeavored to use the various expressions of each included individual." Further she indicated, "This book is a true relating of the history of at least one pioneer family that started life in Michigan's lumber regions."

Grandma Leone had asthma throughout her life. In her later years she became further troubled with Parkinson's disease, which caused her body to shake. I was in first grade when doctors gave her six months to live. In fact, it was seven years later in 1955 that she died! I truly believe it was her will to tell the Neely family story that extended her life. Doctors advised her to move to a drier climate, so she did. My grandfather purchased a small trailer to tow and drove her to the Phoenix valley. Although Grandma shook badly from her illness, she managed to spend time writing in small secretary spiral notebooks. (*See sample page in Appendices section*). Her physical illness did not affect her memory; Grandma's mind was very clear during the time she wrote. She hired women--probably living in the same trailer court--to type copies from her handwritten notes on her Underwood manual typewriter. My mother passed both Grandma's typewriter and the typewritten chapters of this book to me in hopes that I would some day be able to get it published.

It was 2002 before I was blessed with a summer when I could focus on getting the book together. For Christmas 2003 I was able to give each of my immediate family members a spiraled 8 ½" by 11" copy of Grandma's Book. Cousins were able to download the chapters from a website.

Since working with Grandma's Book, I've become aware how important true historical documentaries are to both libraries and historical societies. Staff members of the Arenac County Historical Museum in AuGres, Michigan; the Historical Society in Bay City, Michigan; the Historical Society in Edmonton, Alberta; and the library in Bradford, Ontario, all gave unselfishly of their time to help me find photographs, census verification, and early historical information about each of their respective towns. Their assistance helped me as I was preparing the manuscript. And it furthered my desire to continue searching for more information about the areas where Grandma and her sisters had lived.

Finally, a good number of friends and extended family members have also indicated an interest in having a copy of Grandma's Book. It is for these reasons I decided to publish Grandma's memoirs of the amazing journey of her pioneer family.

JOURNEY OF THE NEELY PIONEER FAMILY

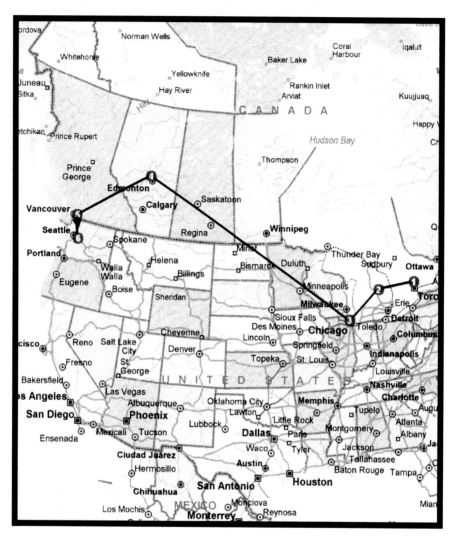

1. Robert and Julia live in Bradford, Ontario: 1850's – 1880's
2. Neely family homestead near AuGres, Michigan: 1884 – 1903
3. Neely family relocate to Chicago: 1903 – 1907
4. Neely sisters move to Edmonton, Alberta: 1907 – 1909
5. Two Neely sisters try Vancouver, B.C.: 1909
6. Three Neely sisters settle in Seattle: 1910

Robert and Julia Neely on their wedding day in 1875: Robert was
25 and Julia was 15. They were married in a small town near
Bradford, Ontario

Descendants of Robert and Julia Neely

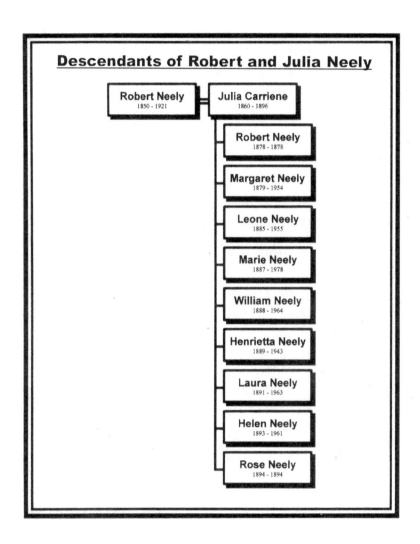

Robert Neely
1850 - 1921

Julia Carriene
1860 - 1896

Robert Neely
1878 - 1878

Margaret Neely
1879 - 1954

Leone Neely
1885 - 1955

Marie Neely
1887 - 1978

William Neely
1888 - 1964

Henrietta Neely
1889 - 1943

Laura Neely
1891 - 1963

Helen Neely
1893 - 1961

Rose Neely
1894 - 1894

Table of Contents

Part I - The Farm (AuGres - 1880 to 1899)

Chapter 1   - NEW FRONTIER   1
Chapter 2   - THE INDIANS!   6
Chapter 3   - A FIRE   9
Chapter 4   - LIFE IN AUGRES   14
Chapter 5   - NEELY FAMILY   18
Chapter 6   - GRAPEVINE ACCIDENT   23
Chapter 7   - RIFLE BOOM HOUSE FESTIVITIES   26
Chapter 8   - MOTHER'S GUIDANCE   28
Chapter 9   - MOTHER'S FAILING HEALTH   31
Chapter 10 - COUSIN YOUNG   34
Chapter 11 - TRAVELING SALESMAN   39
Chapter 12 - LIFE WITHOUT MOTHER   42
Chapter 13 - MARIAN COLE'S INFLUENCE   47
Chapter 14 - CHANGES IN THE NEIGHBORHOOD   51
Chapter 15 - MINNIE'S VISIT   55
Chapter 16 - FATHER'S NEW WIFE   59

Part II - The Break (Bay City, Saginaw, and Detroit - 1899 to 1903)

Chapter 17 - LEONE'S ESCAPE AT AGE FOURTEEN   66
Chapter 18 - THE ABBOTS   75
Chapter 19 - BAD WORK EXPERIENCE   82
Chapter 20 - CAPTAIN GILBERT'S WIFE   86
Chapter 21 - TRAVELS WITH MRS. JACOBUS   94
Chapter 22 - LIVING WITH THE MINNERS   100
Chapter 23 - SUCCESSFUL NURSES TRAINING   109

Part III - A New Life (Chicago - 1903 to 1907)

Chapter 24 - LEONE'S INVITATION TO RELOCATE   125
Chapter 25 - NEELYS IN CHICAGO   132
Chapter 26 - NEELY MEN'S DEPARTURE   140
Chapter 27 - LIFE IN CHICAGO   143
Chapter 28 - FUN WITH HOUSE GUEST JANE HALL   151
Chapter 29 - SMALLPOX SCARE   156
Chapter 30 - SOCIAL TIMES   161
Chapter 31 - FAMILY VISITS   174

Chapter 32 - NEELY MEN'S SECOND DEPARTURE   178
Chapter 33 - VISIT FROM CAPTAIN JIM OF AUGRES   181
Chapter 34 - BACKYARD AIRSHIP EXPERIENCE   183
Chapter 35 - DAY'S BOAT TRIP WITH BERNIE   187
Chapter 36 - VISIT FROM MAYOR OF AUGRES   193
Chapter 37 - BOARDER EMILY DALL   197
Chapter 38 - SISTER MARGARET'S FAMILY   200
Chapter 39 - ABOARD CAPTAIN MARKHAM'S BOAT   205

Part IV – The Move West (Edmonton, Vancouver, and Seattle - 1907 to 1910)

Chapter 40 - MOVE TO EDMONTON   213
Chapter 41 - GUEST HOUSE/HOTEL OWNERSHIP   222
Chapter 42 - NURSING HOME MANAGEMENT   230
Chapter 43 - FINAL DESTINATION   235
Chapter 44 - THE FUTURE?   240

Part V – Epilogue   249

Appendices

Appendix A - LIST OF BOOK'S MAIN CHARACTERS   268
Appendix B - JULIA NEELY'S OBITUARY   269
Appendix C - NEELY HOMESTEAD (1884-1903)   270
Appendix D - SETTLEMENT OF HOMESTEAD (1903)   271
Appendix E - DREXEL AVENUE APARTMENT (1907)   272
Appendix F - LEONE'S WEDDING INVITATION (1910)   273
Appendix G - ORIGINAL MANUSCRIPT PAGE (1954)   274
Appendix H - LETTER OF THANKS (JUNE 2000)   275
Appendix I - ACKNOWLEDGEMENTS   276
Appendix J - TRIBUTE TO GRANDMA   277

Part I

The Farm

AuGres

1880 to 1899

Chapter 1
NEW FRONTIER

Julia was but a schoolgirl when the handsome Robert Neely first came into her life. He was tall, had dark hair, and smiling roguish Irish eyes; however, his ready wit and humor was met with the disapproval of her parents. Undaunted, Robert devoted himself to both her mother and father, while he courted their daughter. Sweeping aside her objections to his arbitrary way, he disarmed the little French girl, too youthful and too much in love to be very discerning.

In three months they were quietly married in the next village. After a few days, they came home and received the family's blessing. They took up their residence in the town of Bradford, Province of Ontario, Canada, where Julia had spent her young life. Here they lived four years; two children, Robert and Margaret, were born to them. Julia was fairly happy here except for a little grave where they placed the remains of their infant son, Robert.

The beautiful baby, Margaret, was a solace to her. However, Robert left them to go out into a new part of the great universe and seek his fortune. His letters came regularly with money enough to maintain his wife and child in their modest home. Time drifted into years. The village gossip had just concluded Julia was a deserted wife when a letter came for her to join Robert in the New World. She was to meet him at Bay City, Michigan. They would journey from there to Point AuGres, a French settlement. This would be their utopia where wealth awaited them. Friends and relatives alike turned out to see Julia off. At twenty-two years of age, the dignity of motherhood rested lightly upon her untroubled face. She was looking forward happily to rejoining her Robert. Little Margaret tripped lightly by her mother's side, too young to understand what "going to the States to live" meant.

However, she did understand something of unusual importance was taking place. She joined her mother in tears when it came to parting with her grandparents. Poor Julia, she little dreamed the good-byes would be for a lifetime. They waved from a window as the train pulled out, gazing wistfully to one another as the distance separating them grew wider.

Robert met them at Bay City, much to Julia's delight, and together they finished the trip by boat. They had a good reason for selecting the boat trip. It was the only method of travel available. There was no railroad and at that time, not even a stagecoach. Even the gullible Julia began to be apprehensive as with the passing of each hour it became more apparent they were going to a most remote and inaccessible place. They had arrived to board ship at seven o'clock that morning. Evening found them still sitting on a plank with nothing in sight to indicate a village. Julia would have liked to take her sleeping child and go home, but this was obviously quite impossible. She tried to bear her lot with patience. The old, slow half-steamboat and half-sailboat, grease-soaked, and smoke-begrimed, plied its way through Saginaw Bay and finally made a stop at the village of AuGres. The little lumber town looked gray and uninteresting to Julia. Her husband Robert had proudly driven Julia to the hotel where they spent the night. He had previously not mentioned the oxen, keeping them as a surprise for his wife. To say Julia was surprised would be putting it mildly. She had seen an ox team at times passing, but had not been sufficiently interested to give them a second glance, and now she was supposed to look pleased!

The next morning, the ox team plodded along the rough trail that served as a road. Robert walked some of the way when the oxen sweated and blew too much from hauling the heavy wagon loaded with their few household supplies, bales of hay, and the family luggage. What chilled Julia most was that Robert seemed happily a part of all this, fitting in so naturally with this pioneer way of life.

When she first saw the log hut with its door of rough boards, she mentally compared it with the nice little home they had owned in Bradford on a pleasant street. Robert had cut away trees and brush to make room for their new home, a crude shack of meager dimensions. The dismal little lumber town of AuGres now looked like paradise compared to this point in the stark wilderness where Robert had built their home.

After resting a few days, Julia decided she would persuade Robert to move away from this creepy woodland where wild animals roamed the forest and threatened their lives. When she attempted to do this, however, she uncovered the harsh, unselfish nature of the man she married. Neither tears nor threats moved him.

Julia was by nature a calm person. However, she soon realized she was like a moth, caught in a net of her own weaving. She must think out a solution to her problems. She could not go back to her parents. It was futile to consider this. She must take the tangled threads of her life and make the most of them.

Robert made a lot of boastful remarks about how they would make a "tidy little fortune off these 160 acres of virgin timber." He had been the first man to swing an axe in it. After the land was cleared, he insisted, "They would have this rich soil for a farm."

Julia patiently pointed out he would be an old man when it was cleared. Trying again to convince him of the futility of clearing the land, she asked, "What use would a farm be without a market?"

Robert retorted, "That would come."

Julia realized it was hopeless to point out to him that it was not a naturally strategic location and it was too remote from the city. This argument just made him quarrelsome, and there was nothing to be gained by quarreling.

Soon, Robert began the task of cutting especially selected timber to build a log house. Each log would have to be tall and straight. This house when completed would be his masterpiece. As the young wife watched him, she grew more desperate to make an escape from the bitter loneliness. In the vast timberland there was only the creaking of giant trees buffeting the wind. The howl of wolves would break the stillness in the land of shadows and frosts, where a living must be wrested from the stark wilderness by sheer physical force.

Robert seemed to have the necessary skill and endurance to accomplish this. He would work a few days a week on the Rifle Boom where they purchased the logs cut by the few settlers in the area. He was flattening the four surfaces of each log to a smooth nicety with a broadaxe and adze. Julia half hoped this task might be done by spring when they would welcome a little stranger, but she knew this was in vain. There were logs to cut for market and extra work for Robert on the log drive in the spring.

Julia thought the long, dreary winter would never come to a close. For six months all the women she saw were of the Indian tribes, friendly, but Julia shrank from them. She had read Fanny Kelley and other books on Indian history, and she could not trust Indians.

Little Leone was born that spring in the log cabin. She was large and strong, and this worried her young mother a little. Margaret had been such a tiny infant, dainty and cute with dark curly hair. This new baby was such a practical looking little creature with pale, straight hair.   Comparing them, Julia wondered if the environment had any influence on this. She recalled the hours of bitter weeping, and yet, here was such a happy baby. She even asked Mrs. McKege, the midwife, what she thought about this. However, the lady could shed no light on the subject.

That summer they had a nice little garden, as well as a little hay to help feed the ox team, Buck and Bright, and their cow that Margaret had named Cherry. Julia helped with all of the outside chores as well as with the demands of the two children. She quickly became so very busy that there was not much time to grieve the reality of her situation.

During these first years, there seemed to be nothing left of her former life. Robert had been the great lover, but now he was a far cry from that. She had known nothing of the woods in her girlhood. This Michigan woodland blossomed forth a wonderful fairyland of wildflowers. The small harmless wildlife had never been hunted and was rather tame. In a short time they would take food from the hand of their new friends.

While the troubled young mother tried to become accustomed to the big new baby, Margaret saw nothing unusual about this new sister. She would play happily with her when permitted.

With the hot days of midsummer came the regular seasonal closing of the boom. This did not prove a signal for Robert to ease up on his relentless driving force and become even for a time a cheerful husband again. No, not him. He redoubled his efforts and turned full force to the construction of his new house. Confronted with the problem of putting the cedar logs that would form the walls in place, he brought out his dependable ox team, Buck and Bright. Familiar with all the tricks of his trade, he soon put the first few logs in place and cornered them to smooth perfection. But as the walls grew higher, Robert realized he must invent some method of getting the logs up there. He had neither men nor the proper tools at hand. By making successive loops of wire, he formed strong links to hold his several pieces of steel chain together, thus forming one chain long enough to reach over the top of the building. He would hook the ox team on this, and they would slowly lift each timber up the skids until it rested on top. There with his trusty cant hook, Robert would cant it to a correct angle. This went well while he could look across the building to watch the progress of the log, but the building grew in a few days to a point where this could no longer be accomplished.

It was then Julia came to his assistance. She first tried driving the ox team, but this proved to be somewhat of a failure. Taking a pike pole, she decided to try to guide the timber, and she had Robert show her some things that could be done with it. She was young and agile. Robert warned her if the timber slipped to be on guard and be careful not to get injured. After that she worked with him every day until the walls were up.

Then Robert made good with his boast. As log houses go, it was a masterpiece in craftsmanship. The thick walls made ample protection from the sun of summer and the storms and frosts of winter. Even Julia experienced a little thrill of pride.

Robert had procured the small amount of lumber he required by hauling logs to a mill. He split cedar shingles by hand and shaved them with a drawing knife to a smooth finish. Because he did not have them, he was obliged to buy finish nails for the shingles. The windows and doors were factory made. The interior was finished in solid hardwood, the finest in the land. Most of it was hard maple, planed and polished; its snowy whiteness reflected the woodworker's skill. Even the floor was solid hard white maple, and its natural beauty reflected like stainless steel. If the house had been located where there was promise of a future, Julia could have been happy about it. However, she felt there was no such promise here.

They lived in the new house during Leone's second summer. Julia was relieved to find this new baby was of an independent disposition. She could amuse herself for long periods, and then drop to sleep. However, the young mother found herself not so well. She was not suffering, just weak. She slowly learned she must muster all her strength to feed the creatures that made up the little farm.

The winter was cold, long, and merciless. Both Robert and Julia were pleased to have the protection of the sturdy new house. A beautiful warm spring seemed to play an apologetic role for the savage preceding winter.

Then early summer turned over a new page for the struggling young couple. A third baby daughter was born. She was quite the opposite of Leone in looks and disposition and surely not the counterpart of Margaret. No one worried about that, for this was not a well or strong baby. Most of little Marie's waking hours were spent wailing dismally. Medical advice was not conveniently available, and the warm summer months were upon them. The baby's delicate and wasted little body was made comfortable, and she was taken to a doctor. It was through his foresight that the inexperienced young mother recognized convulsions. She had also learned something could be done for this most discomforting condition. On a much later date, Marie suddenly closed her eyes and appeared as though dead. Others followed this terrifying experience. The child did not grow normally as time passed, and she made no effort to walk, talk, or show natural reaction to life. Leone loved this delicate little sister and remained steadfastly by the frail girl's side.

When the little invalid was two years of age and Leone four, Bill--a welcomed baby boy--was born. Henrietta, the fourth daughter, arrived a year later. This daughter was beautiful, fair, and normal. However, Leone's sympathies remained with the little and frail Marie. Margaret could have the newest pretty little blonde.

Chapter 2
THE INDIANS!

"The Indians are coming!"
"No! They can't be!"
"Look out the window!"
Margaret's dark brown curls quivered a little as she hastily turned to obey the command. She had known her sister had seen the Indians before her own eyes rested upon them. She was only trying vainly to adjust her thoughts to the terrifying reality. Tall, straight, and menacing in their approach to the Neely home, the braves advanced first in the line of march, a few small arms dangling from their belts. The squaws followed, some burdened with great loads of baskets made of splints from the green timber.

Margaret's heart throbbed wildly. She found their appearance most alarming.

The two younger girls, pale and trembling, joined their sisters. Leone began removing their wraps and whispered, "Let us try not to look frightened. It will only make the Indians bolder to see that we are afraid. I do not think they will harm us, only take our food."

Margaret turned from her survey at the window, white and shaking, "You are afraid yourself," she said weakly.

Leone tried to smile reassuringly as she acknowledged what was so obvious. "I am more than afraid." With a rather sorry attempt at playfulness, she added, "Let's try to play pretend."

"Let's hide," faltered Marie, her arms clinging tightly about Henrietta, the youngest of the group.

"We cannot do that. There is no place secure from them. If they found us scared and hiding, our situation would be worse," Leone advised.

Margaret agreed quickly, "No! No, we must not try that, but what will we do? I cannot face them!"

"You must!" said Leone convincingly. "Mother and Dad would expect you to. You are the oldest. I will help all I can."

The time was late winter. A light snow had fallen. Their parents had taken Bill and gone to town for supplies. There was a hint of early spring in the air, at a period when the red man was still something to be reckoned with in the State of Michigan's early history. The terrified girls formed a little group at the doorway when the Indians came on the front porch. The uninvited guests stomped the snow from their moccasins as they crowded upon the doorstop and pounded loudly for admittance. Margaret timidly opened the door slightly and peeked out. The door was pushed rudely from her trembling fingers. The youngsters hastily maneuvered themselves out of the way in fear of being trampled by the crowding intruders as they came rushing in.

"Where your father?" a big fellow demanded. "Me know him, Robert Neely. He buy basket. Me, John Pepa. Where he go?"

"He is out getting the cow," said Margaret as bravely as her dry lips would permit.

"Where your ma? She gettum cow too?" his sharp penetrating eyes upon her. "Me seeum track go village."

Leone, true to her promise, attempted to help. "That was Mr. Peary's track," she interposed.

The burly red man turned his piercing gaze to her. "Mr. Peary track," he mimicked, "go, no come. White girl lie. Pa, Ma both go to village. You buyum John Pepa's basket!" At this juncture, as though pre-arranged, the squaws began showing the attractive features of their rather nice baskets while the braves, numerous enough to swarm the entire premises at once, were soon in possession of the several loaves of bread baked by Julia Neely the previous day. Some cooked meat was following the wake of the bread. The milk

7

crocks, which contained the milk and cream so necessary to the family's subsistence, were lifted like cups and quickly emptied by the unwelcome guests.

"How much do you want for this basket?" Margaret asked meekly.

"Me takeum meat," The girls turned to look in the direction he indicated. Through the window could be seen the red men now making off with the meat supply taken from the little storage building adjoining the house.

He showed her another basket. "Me takeum flour, this basket."

Leone went to the pantry and removed the scale from its hook. In the meantime Margaret uncovered the barrel where the flour was kept and was busy dipping the powdery mass into a milk bucket to be weighed as Leone returned and hooked on the scale. The glance they exchanged told volumes as they went to work knowing that regardless of the weight, they could only stop shoveling flour when John Pepa permitted. They found the activity to be somewhat of a relief as they tried to reassure their two frightened younger sisters.

The Indians soon showed signs of terminating their visit. A small number of them began forming a line at the gate, as they had taken everything they wished in the way of food. What they did not consume on the spot had now disappeared amid the bags made from skins and in the baskets that the women members of the party carried.

John Pepa placed in the center of the room some baskets of his own selection. The girls understood him to mean that he considered this good value in return for all the plunder that had been so ruthlessly taken by his followers.

He grabbed the flour from Margaret's reluctant hands, threw it into a bag, tossed the bucket back, slammed the door with a bang that shook the house, and with that the Indians were gone. Relieved of the ordeal, the girls all started sobbing at once. Pressed close to the glass window, tear-wet faces watched the departure of their recent tormentors who followed one another in a single file down the lane, their bright colors flashing in the sunshine.

A few hours passed before Robert, Julia, and little Bill Neely came home to the distressed family members. Robert was a hard and stern man. Had he been present when the Indian put in his appearance with a number of his tribe, it is safe to say that John Pepa would not have presumed to have been quite so bold in his daring visit. The young parents looked about in deep concern at the apparent wreck of their once neat little home. Their children were terrified, and to the parents' great dismay, the little store of supplies had been ruthlessly foraged. Robert Neely looked at his empty shelves bitterly; the gentle Julia clasped her daughters to her in deep gratitude. Losing their food was a major calamity, and to this there was no question.   However, Julia's heart was filled with thanksgiving that the villainous red men had only frightened the girls and had not done them any harm.

Chapter 3
A FIRE

Robert's sister, her husband, and children moved from Canada to the village of AuGres to make their home. This marked a great event in the lives of the Neely family members. Their Aunt Rita-- tall, stately, and very charming--proved to be the answer to Julia's long suppressed hope for family ties. The Neely children also enjoyed visiting their new cousins and loved their Uncle Walt Rennol as only he should be loved. He was a very exceptional man.

The lives of Julia and Rita paralleled one another in many respects and drew the two young women into a very close relationship. It was indeed an auspicious influence that brought the two families closer together.   Activities of all persons in the community were touched closely by the hopes and ambitions in the lives of their neighbors. Some were more interwoven than others, either guided by trend or circumstance. This was particularly true when the Dan Peary family became a part of the community. Dan Peary's sister was the wife of Joe Rennol, brother of Walt Rennol. Joe and Rhoda, as they were affectionately known, joined the colony the previous year and soon became a very important part of it. With no children of their own, they gave generously of their time and talent. All of the families eagerly looked forward to the arrival of the Pearys.

Dan Peary's wife, Marcie, proved to be a gentle, frail little lady. The woman's fine features bore traces of past suffering. Dan was big and very jovial, and you knew instinctively his popularity was assured. There were four nice children, two boys and two girls. An important member of their household was Mrs. Peary's mother, Janet

Babie. Slender, she stood erect, had silvery white hair, and a flawless complexion. She was one of the favored ones, who never intruded, yet had the enviable ability of appearing when needed. She took care of both the household chores and children. Also, because of Marcie's poor health, Janet had the responsibility of caring for another child permanently crippled in childhood. This interesting family took up quarters in a neat log house, which had been abandoned by a former neighbor. It was located adjoining the Neely farm.

Along about this time Robert Neely, a horseman at heart, purchased a team of horses. Feeling the reins once more in his hands was a source of pleasure for him. The Peary family purchased Robert's ox team. The Neely children were all pleased that Buck and Bright would be near enough that they might see the beloved animals.

One morning when the Pearys were nicely settled in their new home making plans for the future, a great shouting took place accompanied by the clanging of tin pans and the pounding on saws, and the piercing sound of a shrill horn. It was an alarm that carried far on the quiet country air. The cry of "Fire!" soon brought assistance.

The blaze was just starting on the roof. The fire fighters fought valiantly. The only firefighting equipment at hand was a few buckets, shovels, axes, and a couple of ladders. This was no match for the demon fire, working with the able assistance of a brisk wind on the dry cedar. In a short time the nice log house was a smoking mass of cinders. Only help rushing in saved the home furnishings.

There was but one casualty. Poor Leone suffered a broken nose. She had been standing with a group of children where they were told to stand to watch the unusual spectacle. A small object of some weight was thrown violently from an upper window. It carried further than calculated, striking Leone. Julia, with the aid of neighbor Scotty, who had some experience and was relied upon in the community for such emergencies, fixed the damaged member as best they could. In the absence of adhesive, they improvised with the white of egg as the principal ingredient. It seemed to be a fair job, and they hoped it would leave no permanent disfigurement. In the confusion that followed, the injury was almost forgotten, except by Leone.

Storage must be found for all the household goods and a place for the family to sleep. The Neelys' barn was pressed into service, and a great hauling and carrying took place following necessary sweeping and dusting. It was fortunately a very warm summer, and everything was able to be undercover by nightfall. The day was spent when the moving was accomplished. The weary workers turned their attention to the beds. It was decided by agreement of the parents involved to put all the children including the four Neely girls out in the barn to sleep. Marie had improved greatly, and she was proud to sleep in the barn as one of the gang.

A meeting of the adults concluded that the greater part of this temporary confusion would remain with the Neely family. It would simplify matters if the Pearys could remain with them. Rhoda and Joe would also come each day. Rhoda would help with the overcrowded household; Joe would wield the ax or saw to help with the task of building another house. There could be no hope of duplicating the house that burned for such long straight timber of even size was not to be had where they could take it free of charge. A lesser house would fill the emergency. They would push the work on it as fast as possible. They must take into consideration it was midsummer and the season when crops must be cared for and stock wandered far afield requiring more attention.

While all this discussion was taking place, Dan sat silently; his usual cheerful personality was darkened with despair. He had come to this country a stranger, in a strange land, his obligations much heavier than his slender means could provide. With the help of these good people, his family was comfortably housed and his prospects of providing for them were on a par with his friendly neighbors. Then fate struck leaving his hopes in a mass of embers. He was at the end of his resources without a board or a nail for a new house or the wherewithal to purchase them. The generous neighbors whom he was imposing upon had even turned their children out in the barn to sleep. If that weren't bad enough, the blood stained bandages on Leone's face reminded him of the final disaster his woes had brought his neighbors.

Aware of his bitter disappointments, Rhoda and Julia went to Dan's side and seated themselves. They talked long and earnestly, their words carrying conviction. The women insisted that the families could conquer this disaster and that this was not the time to be distraught. Dan listened and slowly regained confidence, faith in

11

God, faith in himself, faith in his friends, and faith in this new country.

It was slow hard work that summer. They cut the logs back where the limbs dipped low and heavy, where little or no breeze could reach. The dependable oxen team, Buck and Bright, did their share of hauling out the timber. Hitched to Robert's wagon, they hauled a few large logs for lumber to a small mill leaving a tithe of the lumber in payment for the sawing.

In six weeks the Pearys were gleefully moving into their new house. Buck and Bright headed the procession pulling bravely on the load as they wound their way down the long familiar lane. Julia watched from a window as the last of the household goods moved down the road. The entire group of children followed them.

Rhoda, who had elected to remain where she felt she could do the most good, came and stood by Julia's side. Both young women smiled contentedly. "It has been wonderful," Julia said thoughtfully, "to live so closely with so many persons almost strangers, and not have a rift. Both Marcie and her mother are very sweet and tolerant women."

Rhoda turned warm, admiring eyes upon her. "You are not so bad yourself, you know," she said gently. "I could not express my gratitude to you and Robert. It is too deep for words."

"Don't think of it again, Rhoda," replied Julia. "You would do as much for me. However, one thing troubles me—Marcie's health. She is very delicate."

"Don't worry about her," admonished Rhoda. "She understands her limitations and knows how to take care of herself. Besides, Dan is devoted to her. You and I will probably be laid to rest long before her."

Some time passed, but Julia and Scotty were both quite anxious concerning Leone's shattered nose. The two had awaited results of a slow healing process. When the bandage was finally removed, they were both slightly dismayed to find a small ridge Leone called a little hump marking where the cleavage had been. Everyone seemed to agree that this would improve with time, and Leone assured everyone that it was still a good nose. With that, there was relief in her mother's voice and a smile as she tenderly tilted the wistful little face and pressed a kiss on the wounded member. "In this short time, I hoped that it would not mar your looks. However, I would feel worse if it had changed your disposition."

12

"Leone is such a good child," she told Scotty.

His retort was, "Robert says she is too stubborn."

"She is determined," Julia clarified. "And I hope that she keeps that spirit."

Scotty stood a moment, studying Leone. Watching her brought a habitual grin to his face. Then he offered solemnly, "I believe she will. She is an unusual child."

The Pearys' new home was built close to the charred foundation of the one that burned near the border of a small clearing. This furnished a break in the woodland adjoining the highway, which was appreciated by the occasional traveler.

Leone liked the forest, its deep shadows, cool fresh greens and soft mossy carpet and earthy smells that intrigued her childish fancy. On her way for a special errand, she trotted briskly along with her limp hair damp on a flushed forehead and a sunbonnet hanging forgotten on her neck. She passed the Pearys' house, then the Half Mile Woods before she finally approached the home of one who could trace her origin to bonny Scotland. This was where the beloved Katherine and her good husband, Malcolm, lived. Their two sons were gifted musicians, furnishing the music for most social functions throughout the countryside. Katherine was no longer young in years, but she remained delightfully young in spirit. All the children would bear witness to that, foremost among them, Leone. She was eager to show her friend the progress her wounded nose had been making. As she ran along, she found it very encouraging to cautiously place the tip of her finger on the spot where the bandage had been. On her arrival, the child rushed to Katherine's quick embrace. The embrace was followed by an examination worthy of such an occasion as a battered nose.

Katherine and Leone then settled down to spend an afternoon that Leone loved. She helped to shell peas and wind the ball of strips of cloth that would be made into the popular rag carpets. Katherine worked busily beside her on the loom in the production of the finished product. Then the two enjoyed a wonderful lunch together. It was the end of a perfect afternoon when Leone tripped her way homeward. The Mother Hubbard dress she wore was billowing in the breeze about her slim little legs.

Chapter 4
LIFE IN AUGRES

The once very tiny community in which the Neelys lived was showing signs of growth. A small number of settlers had moved in, most of them French Canadian families. They had taken timbered land and were hopefully undertaking a struggle with adverse circumstances and elements that showed no favoritism. To build a home and then manage to make a living for their families from this wilderness was indeed a challenge.

New settlers met a glad hand and a hearty welcome from their prospective neighbors. Some of their properties had abandoned shelters, but they could scarcely be called a home. Nonetheless, they had to be pressed into service. Tents were also borrowed and set up for occupancy.

All the neighbors were summoned on an appointed day, and, if need be, they provided dinner for a hungry crew. Being summoned together on behalf of a family or some project was called a "bee." No swarm of busy bees worked with more industry, cheer, and harmony than these hardy pioneers. Julia looked with modest pride on the men of her race as represented in this little, but strong, industrious, and honorable community. She slowly came to understand now what strange impulse of fate had directed their destiny to a place she had first seen as devoid of future promise.

The Rifle Boom Company, owners of the local area, began advertising the land. They assured their reading public that the land was cheap, but they did not promise more than it had to give. The land had been logged of the choice timber, and thick tall brush. Second grade trees and many huge stumps rendered the land very difficult to clear. Hand tools and ox teams were all new owners could afford to assist with the clearing process.

However, giant strength was vested in the resourceful young bodies of the pioneers, and their valiant hearts beat in unison with humble ambitions. All they asked was for a living for their families. Conditions soon became not so harsh as they had been in those first few years, and working together they had softened many a blow.

It was not within Julia's nature to mourn for what might have been. Faith prompted her to make the most of what fate provided. She had long since started a nice little dairy. She was often first to present newcomers with a fine young animal, which they could use for beef or a cow in the near future. With the addition of a few hogs and chickens and the assistance of her children, she had a prosperous little farm underway. Most of the bitterness from cruel disappointments of earlier years had drained out of her heart, leaving but a memory. Her time and energy were now devoted to the work at hand.

Robert devoted himself to his timber in winter, but when summer came he took care of the planting, harvesting and clearing more of the land. By the time his children were large enough, he saw to it that they picked up small rocks and sticks from the new land, pulled weeds, and gathered vegetables after he dug them up.

Robert laughed at the neighbors who called his girls "pea soups." He happily continued to announce the arrival of new family additions with his, "Another frizzy top pea-soup in town." Julia would smile her slow, sweet smile and refrain from making any comment, for Robert never failed in his duty as a good neighbor. He made it a point to seek popularity, and he was always jovial and smiling with his neighbors. He liked to dance and was the leader in all the neighboring festivities. If Robert attended a ball in the village hall, the dancers sat by the wall until his arrival. He would quite probably announce in all solemnity that he had come to dance, not sit, and with an apology would turn to leave. Knowing he was a leader, the dancers would not let him get far, and Robert loved to be begged to take over. He would promptly be hailed as a "jolly good fellow," and then the music would start. Once the band started playing, he had plenty of assistance to keep the ball rolling.

Sometimes a step dance was played, and always one couple, Robert Neely and Mrs. McLem, a lovely young woman with hair of red gold and eyes of Irish blue, came forth. The McLems had been friends of the Robert Neelys for many years. The two families did not get an opportunity to meet very often, and it was always gratifying to Robert to have occasion of matching steps with this charming lady from the land of his birth.

Robert's activity as a good neighbor was just as obvious at work as at play. He would bring his tools, wagon, plow, and oxen team, and then help at anything and everything that required doing.

On one memorable occasion, an important bee was called for a man recovering from a long illness. His children were small, and very little had been done for the coming crop season. The organizing committee, determined to have a good response, promised a keg of beer and a dance in the evening. It was no surprise when there was a full turnout. The women who came fixed the food, sewed garments for the man's small children, and planted the garden after the men had prepared the soil. Besides working the ground, the men patched the roof of the man's house and fixed his fences. Robert Neely, who took pride in his smooth plowing, kept a steady pace all that day until the work was done. It was a busy day for all, but when evening fell, the festivities marked the close of a wonderful day.

Julia noticed with some misgivings Robert's frequent return to the beer keg, and it was at moments like this that Robert repeated his well-worn tall story. He had what he called "knocked off work for the day" as dusk was falling. Looking over by a little planting of late turnips, he saw a nice plump deer grazing on the green turnip tops, so he quickly ran into the house to get his gun. However, by the time he had returned, the deer had gone. Deciding there was still sufficient light to see the animal's tracks, Robert followed them as quietly as possible. While in pursuit, he heard the beat of hoofs, the crackling of brush, and other sounds that he attributed to the deer. Robert hoped that the deer might stop to browse and then he would overtake it. However, too soon it got dark, so he concluded that it was best to go home. After groping around in the darkness for a time and making no progress, Robert decided that it was useless. He could be compelled by force of circumstances to remain in the woods until daybreak. With the aid of a lighted match, he located a tall stub of a tree, a place of safety from the bears and wolves. Hiding his gun carefully in the bushes, he prepared to climb. At the top he figured that he would have reached a place with a fair amount of safety. Once he climbed to the top, however, and attempted to sit down, he found the stump to be only a shell. The inside had rotted away, and Robert tumbled down inside the tree. His hair slowly began to lift as he soon realized that there was some sort of creature in there with him! Striking another match, he saw two small cub bears. This wasn't so serious, but what about the mother bear? How long would it be before she would put in her hazardous appearance?

Robert tried bracing himself against one side with his hands while he climbed the other side with his feet, but he was soon convinced he was tiring himself and would only be easy prey for the old bear. Just as he was getting out his dependable pocketknife, he heard the bear sniffing and growling at the base of the stump. Her suspicions thoroughly aroused, she was not long in going up.

Meanwhile, the prospective victim was thinking fast. To the best of his knowledge, a bear always came down backwards, so he put up a hand and felt for her short tail. He was right! Grabbing the bear's tail with his left hand, he drove the knife to the hilt into the animal's rump with a mighty thrust of his right hand. Giving out a howl of rage and pain, the old bear started back up again. Robert went along with her, but it was a manner not to be envied. At the top he let go of the tail and cut a further slash in the bear's skin when he withdrew the knife. He knew the habits of the bear would prompt her to stanch the flow of blood with leaves and grass before going back after her prey. Robert lost no time in sliding to the ground, securing his gun, and putting the distance between himself and the old bear.

The applause and cheering after hearing Robert's story, of course, called for another round at the beer keg, while Julia urged him to take them home as the children were very tired. However, the celebration went on, and when they finally got underway, Robert was no longer responsible as a driver. The children took their places seated on the clean straw in the back of the wagon, while Julia occupied the spring seat with the smallest child in her arms. She was not afraid because she knew that the well-trained oxen, when given the word, would head for home and their well filled mangers.

Robert could not be persuaded to ride, but walked behind the wagon. He was under the impression that he was driving and would holler out at the animals, "Hee, haw, get up there." Then they would hear him singing. The rhymes were of his own composition: "I take it rough, I take it rough, with nothing to defend me. I must struggle along through life. Poverty, did I ever offend thee?"

The oxen plodded along with their passenger load, slowly increasing the distance between them and their master. The animals were unyoked and munching in their stalls, and the children were in bed when Robert came tumbling over the threshold.

Chapter 5
NEELY FAMILY

Just before Christmas a new baby girl arrived for the Neely family. She was named Laura. It was said they should name her at once so that they could find her. A tiny thing, she scarcely weighed four pounds.

Julia's health gave way with the event of this morsel of humanity. She found she could not go about her work on the small projects she had undertaken. The family needs demanded her responsibilities be kept up. She knew from experience no help could be expected of Robert. He would keep up the fences and do the farm work. But the feeding of the cattle, caring of the milk, eggs, and making butter, and must all be done by the children.

By the time her sixth birthday was approaching, Marie was a little larger, but still very frail. She would take a few steps by clinging firmly to some dependable hand. Little was known in that day of the physical needs of children or what special vitamins they might require. Marie seemed desirous to solve this bewildering problem for herself. When a fine young beef was made available for the family meat supply, she ate her portion and asked for more. They dubiously gave her all she begged for, and the child promptly started to gain in size and strength as she continued to eat unusual amounts of the tender juicy beef.

Leone, at age eight, learned to help with many useful things about the farm while remaining Marie's steadfast companion. One evening Julia was delighted to find her invalid daughter taking steps on her own. She did so without assistance, as she reached for slices of raw turnip piled on a chair seat, which were being cautiously moved out of reach by the ever so patient Leone. After this achievement was successfully completed, the weeks passed, and the child gained substantially. With increased activity, her tiny form soon showed some promise of normalcy. Her gloomy, pinched little face with its sad eyes would sometimes give back a faint amused smile. Julia began to feel the undying hope in her heart revive.

Margaret helped with the farm work, driving the horses and caring for them when necessary. Leone was hardy and quick. Her strong little hands could milk a cow as quickly and well as a man.

Marie was small for her years, but strong and Leone's shadow. She was learning to milk a cow under Leone's careful tutelage. It was cold work for her tiny hands. Leone would plead with her not to work very long at one time because her fingers might become frozen.

Margaret and Leone had started to school. There was no school in their own district. The school they attended was three miles away from their home. Most of the time they walked, but sometimes they would run. It was well that they were strong and agile. When they reached home, the cattle, hogs, chickens, cows, and babies were all needing their attention. They were busy children.

Julia crept slowly around. The children must be clothed, food prepared, and baking done. She planned for them and did all her feeble strength permitted. She grieved for them more than they would ever know. And most of all she prayed for them.

There was a gnawing fear at her heart that she would not live to rear her children. There were times when the call of the Grim Reaper did not seem so far away. Julia continued to make the best of her life. But the thought of life for her children without her brought a shudder. Regrets were in vain. She must place her faith now in the mercy of the Divine Lord and trust his infinite wisdom.

Time passed. Julia did not regain her health. There were days when she could be about, showing some of her former zeal. This enabled her to attend to the business end of her venture. The larger part of this consisted in the sale of beef stock. She would be exhausted after such effort, looking so pale and ill. The girls would redouble their endeavors to have everything in order on such days.

They were a cheerful, smiling, and hard-working group of youth. Julia regarded her family with great pride. On the twenty-sixth day of March, one spring, Baby Helen arrived. She was little and cute, but not as small as Laura had been at birth. That young lady, now two and one-half years of age and in her own estimation a very important person, let it be known Baby Helen met with her entire approval.

Leone was just nine years and ten months older than Baby Helen, as her father promptly dubbed her. Leone loved to care for Helen and learned to bathe and dress this new little sister when she was but four days old. This was done, of course, under the watchful eye of the nurse. Leone was herself but a child, yet she recognized the superiority of this brave woman. Leone saw her as a Florence Nightingale in civil life who buckled on her armor and went bravely forth without assistance to new duties whenever the call came. Her successful and meritorious career took her at times deep into the woods to some remote cabin and then perhaps the village or the next town, among the rich and poor alike. It was her ear that caught the first sound of the awaited infant cry. Sometimes she was well paid. More often she received nothing but gratitude.

There was no doctor in the entire community town or country to assist or dispute her rights. Leone recalled studying about royalty. Jeanie Markam, a handsome, regal woman with a sweet smile, surely stood as a queen among her kind.

Since Baby Helen had favored them by putting in her appearance in the early spring, the overworked children had an opportunity to absorb the extra work by degrees and help smooth some of the problems. Leone would tuck the baby in beside her mother when she was forced to be out working with the stock, and Margaret would be with her father. Marie was eight years of age. She was not so large in size, but a Trojan for work. Henrietta was small yet and helped in the house, especially in the cool months.

Leone's busy brain was always at work, even as her hands quickly clicked the knitting needles during the evening. A daring plan even though in an embryonic state had long been taking shape in her scheme of life. It was nevertheless a very definite plan to make her escape from this treadmill life of slavery. More than that, the plan included liberty for her sisters and Bill.

Sometimes when tears appeared like great painful blisters on her mother's face, Leone would be sorely tempted to explain to Julia the great plan. Then she would fear that Julia might not find the disclosure encouraging. Her mother in her great anxiety for the children might warn their father, and nothing must happen to weaken the success of the scheme.

The warm, inviting spring weather arrived, and with it came the tasks of putting out great loads of fertilizer, followed with plowing, and then planting.

Julia could only offer help in preparing the noonday meals. She would fix vegetables and do some few other items of help. Margaret would hurry into the house to prepare the dinner and then go back out to help her father, who found it difficult to drive and hold in place the crude homemade farm implements at the same time. The clumsy marker must remain right in line to make the rows straight for Leone and her crew to plant the hills of vegetables. When in full operation, this was some process. Leone went first with a huge hoe.

20

She would swing it with a heavy chop in the soft earth at the point where the marker crossed the line. One chop did the trick; then Marie dropped five kernels of corn or cuts of potatoes as the circumstance might be with Bill following with a box of pumpkin seed. If they were planting corn, little Henrietta was bringing up the rear with another hoe, pushing the soft earth back over the seeds. The amount of ground they would plant in a day was incredible.

It seemed to Leone that the long, sunny days of spring flew past, charged with many heavy tasks and twice as many lighter ones. Her deft fingers flew; her strong, slender body was untiring in devotion to the delicate might of humanity, Baby Helen. In the warm, bright days of summer working in the garden or fields, she pulled the old battered buggy to the end of the row. It was there that the baby played or slept as she wished. Frequently Leone would work short pieces of the planted rows. In this way she could be near the baby and talk to her while her strong brown hands jerked the weeds and shook the mellow soil from their roots.

Occasionally, she sang to the baby, placing the blanket on the warm earth first, and then the little pillow. Baby Helen would flutter her tiny hands from this vantage point, while Leone worked up the rows. Meanwhile, unfolding her great plan to the baby, Leone would smile then as she thought, "If Helen could understand, I could not trust her with this great secret." Marie was the only one in whom she could place such confidence as yet. She had early learned to have faith from her mother. The burden of her prayer now was for the success of this plan.

Summer came along, bringing harvest to garner. The Neely children took on the task with the same enthusiasm and earnestness that they did everything else. Julia often grieved for her girls pitching the heavy hay crop. However, this did not trouble Robert.

Leone mounted the big hay rake that year for the first time and drew a rein over the mettlesome Hamiltonian. He yielded his strong will easily to the child's gentle hands. She enjoyed seeing the green windrows take shape in the field behind her. Only on her first try did she meet troublesome difficulty. The hay was heavy and inclined to cling slightly to the heavy tines that gathered the crop. She could not lift the trip quickly enough with one hand to drop in the catch, thus dragging the hay. At the next windrow, giving a little tug on the rein, she grabbed the trip bar with both hands. It moved easily to a point where the catch dropped in mechanically to trip the fork. The wise animal soon understood what was required of him; he must pause slightly while crossing the windrow. Very soon Mack was doing this without prompting.

Leone was proud of the horse. She liked to see his long legs step off so rapidly, not attempting to trot, but just moving at his fast, tireless walk. She laughed gleefully and then called out, "Macky, Old Boy, we know how to work together." She quickly added, "The entire field will be gathered tonight."

The yellow and brown butterflies fluttered by in the golden sunrays to the music of the locusts and songs of the birds or the drumming of a distant partridge. All of these wonders of nature soothed the girl's restless spirit. Leone was but a child, but one with adult ambitions. She was confident that she could make a success of her daring plan. She would dream, and always a dream brought success, sometimes riches, but never failure.

Aided by a warm fall, the Neely children spent long days in the field helping their father harvest the tuberous parts of the crops. Tons of potatoes were sorted on the ground and hauled direct to Saginaw Bay to be loaded aboard Captain David's small sailboat for shipment to the city. Great piles of them were also stored in root cellars to await better prices the following spring. Tons of other tubers such as carrots and turnips were also stored to help feed the stock during the long winter months. Sometimes a man was employed a short time to help with this task. However, this laborious work was usually done by the faithful Neely children under the driving force of their father who always urged them to greater efforts.

School did not start early in September as is now the rule. Most of the children in the area had to help harvest the fall crops. A September start would have brought a necessary light roll call. However, a more essential issue had to be considered. The school district's finances would not permit hiring a schoolteacher nine months of the year. This contingency aided the Neely sisters in keeping abreast with their schoolwork. Marie was still rather small, but sturdy. She had done her part through the summer and fall harvest and now milked three cows night and morning. She would start the school year with her sisters.

Julia improved in the cooler months and was able to dress and move her poor tired body about her home. This was the occasion for great rejoicing with the children. They all got great pleasure out of a special "feasting." Henrietta would usually be the one to begin the process of roasting a small slice of raw potato on top of the stove. The other Neely girls would follow her in this activity. The girls named the tasty morsels "moon potatoes." While she enjoyed this time with her children, Julie was not deceived. She knew the sands of her life were running low, and she was grateful for each day allowed her.

Chapter 6
GRAPEVINE ACCIDENT

Spring was early that year, with its soft winds and melting snow. This was Leone's favorite season. As it lengthened into the warmer days, she loved to meander slowly along the abandoned wood road within the inviting shadows of its restless inhabitants as they reached a friendly greeting to one another in the leafy bower overhead.

Removing her shoes, she would dig pink toes into a green mossy knoll with its crop of early spring flowers forming a beautiful shroud from a useless heap of unsightly roots that once in the dim past were anchors for one of nature's proud creations, a tree. That tree now lay where it had fallen, but it still contributed to the beauties of spring as it reposed in a shady glen draped in ferns, flowers, and mosses.

"However, nature can let you down," thought Leone. She smiled as she recalled her own little bout in which she had come off a sad second best. It had occurred only last fall near the end of this road where Margaret and Leone were gathering wild grapes to replenish the family jelly supply. The grapes grew in abundance at the top of the young trees where the fruit had gone seeking sunlight. Leone was doing the climbing and reaching for the ripe grapes. She was seated in a friendly loop of grapevine where both hands could be employed. She had become somewhat indifferent to her perilous position, when the vine suddenly parted company with the tall slender tree that had been leaning for sometime! She made a quick grab for the trunk, but she did not get a grip strong enough to hold. She found herself suspended from its top and bent over the road at a sharp angle, with her strength near the breaking point from shock.

She looked down to consider the best place to land, and her gaze encountered the horrified expression of her sister's upturned face.

"You will have to jump," Margaret pleaded. "Lower yourself as far as you can, then slide down into my arms. I will catch you."

That was a big threat to Leone's peace of mind. Margaret would be hurt, and it was no time for an argument. Leone looked hastily about, assuming a calmness she did not feel. "I see a block of wood," she shouted. "Roll it over here and stand on that and you can reach me." In her excitement, Margaret did not question the distance. As soon as she was out of the way, Leone jumped.

It may have been a good jump, but it was surely not an agile landing. A badly injured ankle was the result. Margaret was grieved, bandaging the suffering member with the aid of an apron, to the best of her ability. Margaret could not bear the thought of leaving poor Leone alone in the woods while she went for help. She was afraid that bears would come. The fear was in vain, Leone pointed out. Bears were not hungry at that time of year.

Clinging to one another, the older girl striving to make up the loss of a supple foot for her sister, they managed to arrive in a nice little field where Margaret felt she could safely leave her helpless sister. Then she dashed home for the little play wagon. The Neely children all turned out, even to the youngest member, while Julia waited anxiously. When they arrived home, Baby Helen was seated triumphantly in the wagon with the helpless Leone. Although happily unaware of its gravity, the baby realized there was something of unusual importance taking place.

There followed for Leone some weeks of discomfort that amounted to suffering at first. When a member of his family was in distress, Robert Neely could be kind and thoughtful, and he now showed this unusual part of his character. He was very considerate of Leone. She was soon sufficiently recovered to limp out and help with the milking. However, the pain she experienced from that little miscalculation urged caution and, more important, made an indelible imprint upon her life. There was nothing in her plans that allowed time for such misadventure.

Having enjoyed loitering beneath the maples where the mandrakes grew and May apples were to be found, Leone arose and stretched her long, slim body. She continued sauntering, finally coming out at the head of the old drainage ditch. She could not fail to admire the tangle of willows that grew on its banks. They were troublesome things and had to be cleaned away at times to permit unobstructed flow of the swamp water. The willows did have, however, a certain wild beauty all their own.

She strolled slowly, her shadow falling upon the remaining pools, as the moisture dried away from the drain in the warm sun. Here was to be found hundreds of aquatic small life, tiny fish, and many different sizes and colors of tadpoles. Leone gazed upon the tadpoles' plight with regret. They were doomed to a slow, torturous death as the water continued to evaporate. They were already experiencing the discomfort of their impending fate as the receding puddles forced them into cramped quarters. The ditches were taking on an evil odor from the stagnant water, which in turn was attracting flies. Leone looked at this with a wry face. It is sad they do not drain Mudd Lake she thought unhappily as she approached the meadow. She could not see her horse Kit on the far side. Sighting her at once, the mare came trotting proudly up, displaying her foal. It was six weeks old, but she never tired of showing it off. The girl reached up a hand to pat the mare gently on the neck, "You proud old thing and no wonder." The colt came to nuzzle by her other hand. Kit whinnied softly. Nothing's strange about loving horses, thought Leone. They are intelligent creatures. This little lady knows me, and she is only a baby.

Leone looked around for Fleet, the yearling colt. "What are you doing over there? You look dumpy." She called, "Come here."

Fleet answered on a plaintive note, trotting slowly to her side. Looking anxiously at the shiny coat, Leone's gaze dropped to the slender foreleg. There she saw moisture. Hair on the slim fetlock was dripping blood. Nothing must be permitted to dim the prospects of those swift legs at the starting post some day. The girl's practiced hand glided over the smooth skin, to the shoulder--no injury. Then she found a gaping hole in the sensitive flesh somewhat hidden under the bay's foreleg. It if healed properly, it would not disfigure the beautiful creature. The flies were at their deadly work. Leone took the colt by the forelock, leading her along the path to shelter.

Bill was dispatched in haste for the local veterinarian. While not a doctor, he knew his horses. He found the puncture had gone through, but it was a clean cut. With good care and vigilance on the flies, Fleet would be as good as new in a short time.

Leone put an arm about the colt's neck. Fleet nickered softly in response. "You were jumping again, you naughty! Have you gone into conspiracy against my time? I just love to stroll in the woods and commune with nature for an hour, and sometimes even I need recreation. How will I indulge in such extravagance now?" The colt's head dropped and reached for petting. Leone laughed. She thought, Fleet knows my taunts are tender and is not alarmed.

Leone realized that all her spare moments must be put to caring for Fleet. The hours spent on other important tasks would have to be shuffled as well to gain more time for a few days. Nature proved an able ally. The wound soon healed, leaving a scar that would pass unobserved.

Chapter 7
RIFLE BOOM HOUSE FESTIVITIES

That winter was the beginning of more social life for the colony. The Rifle Boom House where the men were quartered during the spring log drive was the scene of some pleasant dancing parties. The huge dining hall was roomy enough for this purpose, as square dancing was the order of the times. The guests did not worry about the floor, even though it was only fair for such activity. The building loaned an atmosphere of gaiety to such gatherings, located at a strategic point well out on Saginaw Bay. The smooth ice reflected the evening's moonlight.

High-pitched voices of the approaching merrymakers, many in song, were carried afar. The accompaniment of sleigh bells could also be heard as the horses trotted over the shining surface. The rhythmic beat of hoofs added a harmonious note, while their shadows seemed to flash as they held the pace, all this forming an important part of the evening entertainment.

Robert Neely was well up in front on such occasions. He now proudly held the reins over a team of high steppers that would take a notable place amid any equine group.

A lover of better horses, Robert had hopes of greater achievements, looking forward to such a moment. There had been a foal in that spring. The following spring there would be another.

Julia was never with Robert in his moments of triumph. This did not trouble her. She much preferred to remain with her small children and insure their safety. Her health would not permit her to participate in the Rifle House festivities. Margaret and Leone accompanied their father. The older girl, with her beautiful brown curls and merry youthful manner, was popular among the younger set.

Captain David's young people were growing up and filled a prominent place in the social life of the younger set. William had grown tall and impressive in appearance and played the violin and harmonica, and he was a popular and amusing caller of the dance. He was the author of the rhymes he used, and they were, for the most part, a take off on someone or something familiar to all, such as "Alamin-shoepac, up through the Arenac, all the way to Dowagiac, bring my shanty back." Shanty referred to the occupation of a fisherman that included himself and others. They would spear fish from a small shanty through a hole cut in the ice. A heavy gale of wind could come up and carry the fishing shanties and equipment some distance along the smooth surface of the ice. This was considered fun when the group of shanties would start playing tag. It was not so amusing, however, when the breeze arose to a dangerous velocity.

The residents of Point AuGres found themselves learning to frolic and enjoying the sensation. The parties kept up until every house in the community, with the necessary space, had been hosts for an evening.

Neelys' party gave them an opportunity to present their cousin, Young Rennol, and his pretty sisters Eileen and Mabel. Young, a musician and caller of the dance, was also a clever amateur entertainer,

Julia was at her best. She made it a point to be rested and took an active interest in the comfort and pleasure of her guests. Most of the mothers were like her, still young, their rights crowded into the background by the care of children and the haunting anxiety of making a living until they had forgotten how to snatch a little pleasure for themselves.

She thought caustically that while this life hadn't necessarily trapped them, it had surely wrapped up its victims. Then she turned with the subtle care of a confident hostess and went to see that the little ones were put to bed. Young, ever the faithful ally of his Aunt Julia, assisted with his unassuming efficacy during the serving of refreshments. Mrs. Duran sang old ballads; so sweetly alluring was her caressing voice.

There was unanimous agreement that Neelys' party was the most successful of the season. Julia gave a little sigh of victory. She had enjoyed the brief experience, too.

Chapter 8
MOTHER'S GUIDANCE

Julia reclined pale and listless amid pillows. So much of her time was spent thus. Even the bed looked tired in all its cruel homeliness. A bag had been filled with cornhusks from the corn grown on this remote farm that held her prisoner throughout the years. The bed was refreshed each day by some strong, willing hands that dipped deep into it for the purpose of a vigorous stirring of the clean selected husks. Atop this was a feather mattress that would be tossed with much billowing, shaking, and smoothing. The beautiful, dainty pillows were an apology for the wretched mattress. Sorted goose feathers plucked from Julia's own geese were soft and downy. They made up in a measure for much of what the bed lacked. Plumped into shape, the bed was soon ready for another day of pain, marked by patience and smiling endurance.

Julia decided to have an earnest talk with Leone one evening. Her second oldest daughter had taken the youngest child in her arms and was rocking and singing softly.

"Leone, I have been going to talk to you and have been rather slow about it until today. The doctor remarked that you do too much for the baby. You are spoiling her and harming yourself."

"How is that, Ma?"

"It is not necessary to rock her. You have fixed her nice with everything she requires. Put her in bed and rest yourself. After doing a man's work in the harvest all day, you need rest."

"But Ma! She would not like that and would cry."

"She would soon go to sleep, and after she finds you will not rock her, she will not expect it."

"She must know by this time that I like to rock her just as much as she likes to be rocked."

"But Leone dear, I have noticed it is affecting your posture. You do not stand erect as you did. The doctor remarked about this today. He said it was too much for any ten-year-old child. You should be playing."

Leone turned to her mother, her eyes shining with scorn. "The doctor," she said contemptuously, "should grab a bucket and milk seven cows twice daily and work a long day in the harvest field and help do a lot of chores, then take my only joy away from me." Holding the baby closer, she sat down in the large old-fashioned rocking chair and sang louder and more firmly than usual. When she had placed the baby in her bed for the night, she came to help her mother.

Julia turned to her. "Sit down, Leone. We will not light the lamp yet. I like the gathering dusk." She paused a moment as her daughter seated herself and then continued. "Your father says you are stubborn, Leone."

The girl was silent a moment, then answered meditatively, "I guess I am."

"I think it sounds better to say determined," her mother went on. "And this can be a virtue. Call it stubborn and it can still be a virtue."

"He does not mean to compliment me," the girl asserted bitterly.

"I know, dear," Julia's voice was low and tender. "We must not talk in riddles. I want you to understand me clearly. I am pleased that you have this strength of character. I am not going to live very long, and you must carry on my plans."

"Oh, Mom! What makes you say that? We could not live without you."

"I'm saying it because it is true," the low, gentle voice went on. "I shall remain here a while. Death is only the inevitable fulfillment of the law of God. We must not rebel against it, just be prepared as best we can. You must carry on my work. Listen closely, Leone."

"Margaret is older than I am, Ma."

A slow, tender smile lighted the beloved face on the pillow. "My beautiful Margaret," she whispered softly. "You must try to understand, Leone. Margaret is almost a young lady now. She is very attractive and will marry young, and she has not your determination. And I have chosen you." Both were silent a few moments while the shadows deepened. Then the soft voice continued. "I'm not asking you if you will do this. I am charging you with a commission of carrying out my most cherished wishes." Again there was silence, fraught with meaning.

Leone arose, arranged the pillows in a more comforting position. Seating herself on the bed, she took one soft wasted hand in her own strong clasp. "I'll do my best, Ma."

"Do you have faith, Leone? I have tried to teach you. I wonder sometimes how well I have succeeded."

"Oh yes, Mama. I have faith in the Divine Will. I was going to say perfect faith, but I realize we could never be perfect, especially in faith."

"Have you confidence in yourself, Leone?"

"Yes, Ma, too much perhaps."

"And you believe in your country?"

"Oh yes, Ma! It's the best country in the world."

"Then my dear child, you are already prepared to carry out my wishes. I do not want fame or beauty for my children; let that fall where it may. But I do want them to have faith: Faith, first in God, faith in themselves, and faith in their country. Those who believe in the law of God and the law of man just naturally live good lives and merit heaven when they die. There can be no higher reward than this, no matter what fame or wealth we attain. It is more or less transitory; in a few years all may be forgotten in this world, while treasures laid up in heaven remain to our credit for all times."

Leone directed her gaze to her mother, her face white, her eyes shining bright and eager through the gathering dusk. She spoke earnestly, "Ma, you are everything a good mother should be and a good business woman besides. Do you doubt when you think of leaving us?"

"Doubt the wisdom of God, Leone? That could not be. I would have no faith if I had any doubt. As dreadful as this calamity seems to be, it will be to the children's advantage in the end. Just keep the faith, and it will be for the best."

"I was keeping the faith, Ma, but what you tell me creates such a conflict in my thoughts. I wanted to hear you say that I was right." Leone wiped the tears from her eyes. She put a lighted match to the lamp wick as the younger members of the family came rushing in.

"Let us fix, Ma. Leone, you're slow."

In the evening of the following day when Leone had prepared Helen for the night, she asked, "Can I rock the baby, Ma?"

"Yes, Leone, but don't overlook what I said about your posture. Try to spare yourself a little."

"How could I do that, Ma?"

"Don't run so much and work so hard. You are a strong child, and it is very important that you remain so."

Chapter 9
MOTHER'S FAILING HEALTH

Julia's apparent improvement fostered hope in the hearts of her children. However, the situation proved of short duration. Brave and unwontedly quiet, she made a determined effort to dine with her children as usual. But it was evident to the anxious family that her strength was slowly ebbing as she became more wraithlike in appearance each day.

A Dr. Eastman moved into the community, taking up his residence near the shores of Saginaw Bay. The man had sharp features, keen gray eyes, gray hair, and a slow step. His genteel dignity inspired confidence. His slender hands seemed almost transparent, but his grip was one of steel. He had retired from active participation of his profession. However, he became interested in Julia, the brave, young mother. Her condition promptly took an upward trend under his ministrations, but he promised them nothing.

The girls put tender clinging arms about their mother as they aided her; when strength failed her, she would be obliged to return tired to the bed. Then came the unfailing little jokes, the cheering giggles as they did the little preparations each night. Baby Helen would have the leading role in the performance. Henrietta was their outpost on such occasions, watching for their father. Even with this precaution, Robert sometimes surprised them; his heavy step and harsh, churlish voice would bring a rude termination to these fragile little moments of bliss. Broken by his crude shout, "Get to bed, children, get to bed," there promptly followed a wild scurrying for the stairway. If their work was not finished, Leone would linger to complete it, then tiptoe quietly after her sisters. Julia's prayer, softly breathed, followed in their wake.

Robert remained steadfast in his method of preparing the soil for planting and cultivating where horses were required. Invariably, Margaret must drive for him. This left the vast number of jobs for the other children. During harvest time they rushed downstairs to his call as though the house was on fire at four o'clock in the morning, even earlier, if the heavens threatened rain.

These occasions left their mother unattended for hours. It was at times like this that their good friend and ally, Mrs. Markham, could be depended upon to comfort and care for the frail Julia. Dr. Eastman also remained earnestly at work trying to alleviate her suffering and to give her a little more time with her children. He met with some degree of success. The strong heart that beat for the courageous Julia had the will to live.

The summer passed, and the following winter, and, as fate willed it, another year.

As the hot days drifted into the past on the dying summer breeze, it was known that Julia could not long survive. Even Dr. Eastman bowed his venerable head admitting defeat. The fragile thread holding her to life did not separate for many weeks. After everyone had ceased to hope, it was the month of February when the word went around: Julia Neely was dying.

Devoted friends came from far and near to offer their assistance. There was no confusion. They did not speak to one another within doors, and they moved about with bated breath and gentle steps. They brought with them all necessary food, well prepared. The table was spread again and again. There was always plenty to go around.

Leone crept softly in at times, kneeling by her mother's side. She would press the pale cold hands with her own warm clasp, as though striving to put life in them. The children appeared to be unknown to their mother who lay in a deep unmoving coma for many days.

One morning the watchers who kept the night vigil went to breakfast, and Leone was left alone to watch for a short time at Julia's bedside. The mother and daughter were scarcely alone when the pale eyelids fluttered. A weak-returning pressure on her hand indicated to Leone that her mother was conscious. Kneeling by the bedside, she bowed her head and caught the faint whisper. "Leone?"

"Yes, Ma."

"Are we alone?"

"Yes, Ma."

"Do not call them." The words were faint. Leone leaned closer, listening intently. She could scarcely speak. "Do you remember your promise child?"

"Yes, Ma. I will always remember."

The dying eyes brightened a little. She smiled faintly. Leone was striving to catch every word.

Julia asked, "Will you ever regret it?"

"No, Ma. I only want to be found worthy of your trust."

"Do your best, Leone. That is all. I am going now, child. I am tired." She gave a soft, little sigh, and her head dropped. Leone could see that her valiant spirit had left her.

The girl placed her back on the pillow, smoothed the bed somewhat, and repeated a short prayer. She peeked out cautiously. The others were about breakfast. She waited a little while before calling out.

The moment she had so fervently wished for, of being alone with her mother, had been granted. The rest lay with a dim distant future. There were important things to be done that would find many kind and willing hands, hands glad to be of some service. That was death, but life is different. You fight out the battle of life alone.

Leone went out past the breakfast table, out beneath the pale stars, still faintly luminous in the cold, early dawn. She raised tearless eyes to the Big Dipper. The angel of death had just taken their beloved mother. Silent and sure, he came and was, as ever, invisible. Robert's sister, Rita, had been with them often and long when the clouds hung the lowest. She was there at the end to stay until the angel of death departed with the beloved Julia.

Julia's mortal remains were laid to rest in the old cemetery on a frosty, dismal day. Hampered by snow and ice, the funeral cortege moved slowly and it extended for more than two miles. They were all the dear people she loved. The family, friends, and neighbors of Standish, Omer, Tonkey Road and several other towns were represented on that long, sad journey. Julia Neely had gone forever from their midst.

Don't bury her too deep or drop any stones on the cover;
Perhaps she may smile in her sleep, at our kiss on the grass above her.
Oh, Lord; with her earliest breath she was given to Thee when born
And now she has passed through Death's dark gate and left us here to mourn:
Beyond the dark and silent river, we will be united forever.

(Lines taken from Julia's obituary)

Chapter 10
COUSIN YOUNG

One day in early fall, Robert Neely accompanied Captain David on his little sailing vessel. The boat plied its way through the gentle swells of Saginaw Bay, dependent upon the intermittent breeze to billow the canvas and furnish power for motion. The morning winds had been favorable for an early start and gave promise to a spirited trip when the light wind dropped to fitful gusts. They soon lay almost becalmed. Frequently nature was more lavish with her gifts, and the men would be kept alert looking for squalls and the general safety of the little craft. However, the approach of this gentle night engendered no such hope. Seated on the deck above the little galley, they watched the necessarily slow progress. The twosome would while away the time with an exchange of stories that each would declare was a personal experience. This inexhaustible oratory could, and often did, go on for hours.

During the harvesting of the farm crop, these trips were of frequent occurrence. Two hundred bushels of Robert Neely's good potatoes now lay in the snug little hold beneath the vessel's hatch on their way to city markets. This method of disposing of the crop was in use for many years. On arrival in Bay City, farmer Neely would promptly become a businessman, casting about for an opportunity to sell his load to the best advantage.

Robert had no anxiety about the farm during his absence. In her lifetime, Julia, with the aid of the children, had taken care of the living creatures they kept. The animals helped bring them a livelihood. Now, as taught by their mother, Margaret maintained the household, and Leone took charge of the feeding and caring of the livestock; both were assisted by the younger children. Their father's absence created no concern for the children.

However, this particular day was being anticipated as one of special importance to the Neely family.

Their cousin Young, now grown to young manhood, was expected to arrive from the small village of AuGres to remain a few days at the farm. Sure enough, about noon, he came into sight, sweating and puffing beneath the hot rays of the noonday sun. He had valiantly pedaled some six miles of heavy sand road on his trusty old bike. His eager hosts saw him coming the moment he emerged through the Half Mile Woods at Knight's Corner.

The smaller members trotted off promptly to meet him. By the time he arrived, they were waiting at the end of the long lane that led to the farmhouse.

Glad to dismount from the uncomfortable perch and stop the unwieldy bike, Young stepped to the ground in his graceful fashion. He placed the wheel in charge of the admiring Bill while he stretched his cramped legs. With the rakish straw hat that adorned his head set at a sharp angle, Young scampered along with the youngest Neely girls clinging to each hand. His handsome boyish face seemed to smile all over at once. His clothing bore that different air with no apparent effort of the wearer.

Young's presence was always hailed with delight by the Neely children. They hastened to bring him cold water from the deep well and a seat to rest on in the shade of the old oak tree as they plied him with questions. Always a suggestion of the Great World beyond seemed to emanate from him. Gifted in music, he traveled with members of his band to neighboring cities. He and his musician friends had brought back the laurels on some few such journeys. A talented linguist, interesting and amusing, he was his cousins' hero and never lacked an appreciative audience when with them.

He called to Bill to bring the saddlebags. The little fellow removed them from the bicycle with impatient fingers, gazing speculatively at their bulging sides. Their contents were found to consist of the usual amount of dainty sweets and treats sent by their thoughtful aunt. Margaret and Marie prepared a picnic lunch, topped with tea and some of the delicious cakes.

Young's visits had always been an event. Yet throughout the merrymaking, he appeared strangely distraught at odd moments. Leone finally remarked, "Young, you are tired wheeling all them miles through the sand. Lie on the grass and rest a while."

Stretching out, he laughed about this, obediently and lazily. "The wheeling did not affect me nearly so much as not sleeping last night."

"Not sleeping!" gasped Leone. "This is good. Tell me more."

"There is little more to tell," he added lamely. "Ghosts is ghosts. I visited with Mrs. Ames last evening. She convinced me there was more to this ghost business than appears on the surface." He promptly launched out on a story, both eloquent and descriptive, of some spiritual phenomenon, his earnest voice carrying conviction.

35

Leone shuddered. "You will have me going creepy any minute. You need a guardian to protect you from innocent old ladies. Go to sleep for a time; it will do you good." She tossed him a small pillow. "I must go out and feed the new calf."

"Shall I help you?" he asked.

She grimaced. "You need rest. Your nerves are shattered."

He submissively reached for the pillow. The crooked little smile on his face deepened. "Guess you're right, Leone, I am in bad form." Placing the pillow beneath his head, his hat shading his eyes, he was soon oblivious to his surroundings.

Ghosts aren't bothering him much, thought Leone.

Later when the shadows lengthened and the heat died out of the day, Young and the children cantered through the meadows. Mounted bareback on the fleet colts, they watched with interest a great flock of wild geese following their leader, as they winged their way to migratory places and safety for the winter. The wild fowl taking to the air was like a barometer to the little community. The season might be warm, but instincts of the birds could be relied upon to give out no false warning. Summer was on the wane.

The happy group of young people gathered to a late supper with zestful appetite. The boys had gathered butternut and acorns from the woods. When the meal was cleared away, they prepared to shell quantities of nuts and be entertained by the versatile Young.

Bill hurried out to bring another basket of wood and returned in some alarm. The basket empty, he declared something was troubling the sheep.

"What made you think that?" asked Leone anxiously. "At such a distance, you could not hear them unless they were bleating."

"That is just what they did do, bleat," her brother said decisively.

This brought the girl to her feet in haste. She took the extinguished lantern from his hand, applying a match to the wick as quickly as possible. About to rush from the room, she took notice of the fact that not one member of the group had made a move to bear her company. "Who is coming with me? You come, Bill."

"Not me, Leone. You know I don't like the dark. I'd stub my toe."

"Your toe? What about the poor sheep? You come, Young."

"No, not me, Leone. It might be a ghost. I would not go if I were you," he added.

"And why not?" she asked scornfully, feeling a little furious.

"You could not do anything about it if it were dogs, and it is dangerous for you to go."

"I could try to do something. That is more than I can do standing here. You are a bunch of cowards."

"Oh don't be so rough on us, Leone. The night is darker than a stack of black cats."

She waited no more. Going hastily out past the milk house, she called to the dog Carlo. He ran along by her side, down the familiar path, through the garden to the old barn where the sheep sought shelter at night. There they were, the entire flock, eight head, lying close together. They seemed to fill all the space, sleepy-eyed, chewing their cud, and not a sign of any disturbance.

Leone raised the lantern, looking carefully about in the shadows.

Carlo waited patiently. She knew there had been nothing strange about, or Carlo's keen nose would be sniffing inquisitively.

She turned to retrace her steps, wondering what could have caused a noise with a sound like the bleat of a sheep and so startled Bill.

Strolling leisurely now, her mind free of anxiety, she listened to the sounds of the night. Young's fanciful description was something fitting, she thought. No moon, few stars were visible, a tree toad's call, shrill and distant, the low of a calf, the cheerful chirp of a cricket, a call of wild geese resting for the night at Mudd Lake. Leone raised her eyes to the dark heavens. Her thoughts drifted back to the afternoon, when a large flock had winged its laborious way, ever striving to obey the call of the wild.

There were many small-winged insects in this peaceful place. The fireflies, so much a part of Michigan's summer darkness, with the soft glow of their tiny sparklers, had yielded and were gone to quarters for the winter.

The girl shrugged off a shiver as she lifted the latch of the old gate leading into the garden. As it opened, the gate emitted the customary loud squeak. The bizarre sound was startling in the dark and near silent night. Leone smiled. She could not recall having noticed it on her way out, hurrying along, and intent on rescuing the sheep. No one knows better than I that squeak has been there many a day, thought Leone. Such observations are what make cowards of us, she soliloquized, as the gate closed with a clang.

Moving along the garden path, she raised her eyes and thought she saw what appeared to be something lying on the ground by the old drainage ditch. The something was overgrown with willows in the background, darkened by the overhanging gloomy shadows. She could not be sure there was an object. Leone shifted her line of vision for a moment as a test, and then she looked again. The white object appeared to have grown larger. And what was it she asked herself in startled amazement. Yes, it surely was moving! The night was cool. She could feel a tremor pass through her strong, young body. Scarcely pausing, she leaned a little, reaching for a long, slender, black ash pole, one of several Bill had placed to be the support for his scarlet runner beans. Withdrawing this from its upright position in the soil, Leone placed the large end conveniently under her arm, allowing the rest to trail. It could be useful in the strategy she had in mind.

The terrifying object had assumed much larger proportions. She lifted the lantern high. This did not aid in solving the mystery. The darkness was so intense, and the rays from the lantern were feeble. She was approaching very slowly, weighing every move, as she watched in fearful fascination the white mass moving easily in the darkness.

She was obliged to keep a firm restraint on herself to prevent admitting her fear and making a dash for safety through the barnyard, throwing caution to the winds and depending upon her sure and nimble feet.

Again the dog was the deciding factor. He kept pace with her, close at her heels, paying no attention to what was creating such pandemonium within her own breast. This was an argument, which convinced her to go on. Carlo could be canny when danger lurked.

She continued to move slowly, and the distance between her and the dread apparition steadily diminished. With a sudden movement, she set the lantern on the ground. She then grasped the beanpole with both of her strong hands and swished it through the air at a terrific speed, landing a well-directed blow at the white mass. She had time to repeat the retribution before a startled young man could divest himself of the clinging sheet to allow freedom for a hasty and inglorious retreat. Leone instantly was aware of the ghost's identity when his voice rang out, "Leone, it's me." The girl laughed shakily and went back to Carlo and the lantern. Patting the old dog's head, she confided, "You saved my reputation, ole boy. I can see now there was a most elaborate plan that was well executed to brand me as a coward. I turned the tables all right, but I must admit I do not like having struck Young. Maybe this experience will cure him of such future follies."

She reached the house and threw open the door. There was the group standing about the kerosene lamp and Young with his shirt off. The rest of her sisters were gathered close, and they were gazing in sympathetic dismay at two angry looking red welts on Young's back. Bill was in the background grinning. He looked at Leone as she entered the room and did not try further to suppress his uproarious amusement. "I warned him, Leone, that he would get the worst of the encounter. Now just look at him."

Leone went directly to the cupboard for a bottle of ointment and approached Young ruefully and apologetically. As she applied lotion to the welts, she offered, "I am sorry, but you should have had an illuminated sign on you saying, 'This is Young.'"

Her cousin looked at her, his eyes full of mirth, "You little devil. I'll bet you knew it was me all the time. But I must admit I got just what was coming to me. And I might add, that stuff is soothing."

Chapter 11
TRAVELING SALESMAN

Leone was hastily preparing a variety of nice young vegetables for the evening meal. The family would be coming very soon from the fields, vociferous for their supper.

Carlo gave a warning bark, which always meant that a stranger was approaching. Leone raised her eyes while her nimble fingers made the peelings fly. A good-looking, well dressed young man was coming through the garden gate. He spoke pleasantly to Leone, informing her his name was Edward Cherney. Opening a large book he carried, he started to explain its numerous merits.

Leone smiled, as she hurriedly continued her task. "You are wasting time explaining the book to me. My father is down at the far end of the hay field. He falls for all the salesmen. Tell him about it."

The young man paused with a brief laugh, "We are both young. Is a little time so important?"

"It is to me. Especially right now. I quit work in the field in time to have supper ready, but when I came up, the pigs had rooted a hole under the fence, escaping from their pen, and were doing a lot of damage. I was obliged to put them in and fix the fence, and that is making me late with supper."

"I am sorry I did not come along sooner to help you with the pigs."

Leone paused a moment and looked at him. Then she placed the pots on the stove. "You don't know much about pigs. All I had to do was take a bucket of feed, open the gate, and call, 'Here Piggy, Piggy,' and they all came running. While they ate the feed, I fixed the fence. They are so destructive, but I could not leave them out even for a short time."

"Well," he said calmly, "If supper is late, your father will not be angry when he finds out about the pigs."

"You don't know anything about my father either," she said cryptically.

He closed the book with a slam. "I have walked many miles today, am worn out, and I must confess that I am very hungry. I will hasten to the field and try to engage your father in conversation, hoping to win him to allow me to stay here tonight."

"You might try delaying him at least until supper is ready," Leone offered. "Your brain is still working good," she assured him, taking the heavy book. Placing it on a shelf, she accompanied him down the path to a point where he could see her father in the distance, and he moved briskly away.

While Leone went back to the now steaming food, she was intrigued by the strange young man and wanted to talk with him. He made his living from industry, maintained in that great outside world. Who knows but some slight bit of knowledge would be added to her meager store that would help guide her footsteps to a place where she, too, could make a living in a place that was now closed to her.

She knew he would spend the night at the farm. That was a foregone conclusion. Robert Neely was never known to turn away from his door any wayfarer in search of a night's lodging. And many there were, thought Leone. She recalled one old Indian, traveling by dog team one winter, who refused to sleep in a bed, assuring his host, "No good em bed." He brought from his sled a nice soft fur skin and wrapped himself in it as he lay on the floor by the stove.

All he wanted was a bucket of water and a dipper. He grunted his satisfaction when this was conveniently placed near his hand.

The following morning, the water was gone. So was the Indian. He had quietly let himself out at an early hour. An empty water bucket was the only evidence of his orderly presence.

As thoughts of a former guest flashed through her mind, Leone made some rapid preparations for the comfort of a new one, whom she was pleased to welcome.

When the family came up from the field, Robert had unhitched the team, and was walking behind them, in animated conversation with Edward Cherney.

Supper was ready and on the table by the time they were prepared to seat themselves at the festive board, as their congenial guest called it. Such abundance of perfectly fresh vegetables and home-cured meat was seldom his good fortune to have placed before him. And he did the repast ample justice, with an occasional slight grin or glance exchanged with Leone. He welcomed the good fellowship over the delayed supper.

When Leone took her milk bucket to go forth for the evening's milking, the young man joined her.

She learned more about the book he was selling. It was the final edition of Dr. Chade's book for the home. Her father would buy a copy, and a part of the purchase price would pay for his overnight stay.

They talked on many subjects, but chiefly about the great outside world. Edward Cherney's pleasing manner left an inspiring impression when she bade him good-bye. His visit gave her renewed determination to go out into that new world.

It was midsummer. More than a year had passed since that cold February day when all that was mortal of Julia was placed in the dark frosty breast of Mother Earth. When spring came, her children made an effort to plant flowers on this barren spot. Leone's pathetic idea was to use the wood cradle that their father built. It had rocked them all in infancy, with the exception of Margaret. Baby Helen had now outgrown it. They filled it with rich soil, planting many flowers. Robert hauled it down and set it deep into the ground on their mother's grave, where it gave mute evidence of their love.

They were learning self-reliance as the young family members shuffled their way through the stubble that was wet with dew each morning. Leone served as leader of the little group. The children were targets for both the summer's sun and hot winds as they worked day after day at slavish tasks. While not earning anything, they were developing strong physiques. Meanwhile, the disturbing factor, fate, moved a little closer.

Chapter 12
LIFE WITHOUT MOTHER

Julia's children resumed their way of life with its burdens. She left instructions for each one to take his or her own place quietly, to do their work well and to play when they could.

She left her wishes with Leone: "Any time you are puzzled as to what I would do, read the Ten Commandments of God. Never show any disrespect to religious papers. The written word of God should not be thrown carelessly where it will be trampled on, or otherwise shown disrespect. Food must not be wasted. It is bestowed on us by divine will to feed all creatures. If you have only a few crumbs left from your lunch at school, toss it over the fence where the birds will find it. When you dress, do not have one stitch laughing at the other. That means, do not think you are dressed neatly with some buttons off your coat, or if you have soiled shoes."

There was nothing in these proverbs to surprise Julia's children. They had lived by them all their little lives. There was not much for Leone to do about it except remind them, if need be. Their mother had told them to go on just as if she was there, and they were doing just that.

The girls welcomed the sunny days of spring that brought the green grass to the cattle. There were now five horses to feed. Robert decided an allotment of feed was necessary. He determined that the horses must always have the lion's share. They were a fat group of horses, showing the result of too much feed, while the cattle did not have enough to eat. However, soon the horses lost weight, and then they had no resistance to the cold. Leone attempted to point this out to her father, a move that met with complete failure. He refused to admit there could be any fault in his feeding plan.

The horse barn was some distance from the cow barn. However, the girls succeeded in taking enough grain from that reserved for the horses to save some of the favored cattle. If their father would not allow the animals to be fed properly, they resolved to find some way to dispose of the animals that were left.

The cattle must grow fat on the summer pasture before anything could be done. The sisters found they must be more determined that spring with their school work. They had lost so much time from school, but the affairs of the farm were equally important.

Nothing went quite as well without their mother's careful planning, and with their father's lack of cooperation. The days became warm at an early date that year, and the winters that inundated the land each spring were also not so deep that year. Nature seemed inclined to help them as they bent to tasks at hand.

It was near the close of the school term one day when Leone, playing in a game of ball during recess, looked over on a field neighboring the school grounds. She was startled to see the Neelys' colts playing. The ponies had evidently broken out of their pasture, and a neighbor's colt was with them. Fleet was wearing a halter with no lead strap. Leone could think of nothing at hand strong enough to serve this purpose. The drainage ditches on both sides of the road were drying down at this time of the year and were producing the usual swarms of flies. It was well known to Leone that it would be a fight all the way to take the colts back home, but she could not leave them. They were three miles away from their own pasture and could outdistance any of the other horses if they had an even start.

Asking her sister to explain her mission to the teacher, she went after the colts. Fleet came running to Leone's call. The girl petted her while she took a firm grip on the halter. The colt yielded gently at the start, and Leone made the most of this. She would leave them at the first barnyard with a fence that would hold them, but it was two and one-half miles away.

As soon as they were on the road, the flies started on their deadly work. Fleet was two years old, tall and strong. The other two colts were yearlings, fast and full of life. They were running wildly about, sometimes ahead, then falling behind, whinnying, kicking, and jumping. Bunches of willows grew rank and tall at the side of the ditches. The two colts running loose would dash into the willows to brush the flies off. This disturbance of the bushes would bring forth more swarms of flies. The two yearlings would kick almost in the girl's face. She was obliged to look sharp to avoid the sharp hoofs. Fleet reared frequently, taking Leone off the ground in a vain effort to dislodge her clinging hands.

43

Leone, however, was not to be shaken off. She tried coaxing and then scolding the colt. This proved to have a slightly soothing effect for a time. However, it was the warmest part of the day, and the air was crowded with flies, big flies and little flies. They lodged in Leone's eyes, nose, and throat. Together with inhaling clouds of dust, she was soon too choked to speak. The violence of this exercise also took its toll.

Fleet was not faring much better. Her lathered body bore the evidence, but she kept up the battle. All Leone could do was hurry along as fast as circumstances would permit, and hope that she would have sufficient strength for the ordeal. An endurance test it surely proved to be.

At last, Katherine saw her coming and had the gate open. After making the gate secure, she seated Leone in the shade of the lawn and brought water, bathing her face and hands, and provided a glass of cool water for her poor parched throat.

Then while the girl rested, Katherine called her son to go and tell Robert Neely to come and get the colts and take Leone home. Robert arrived with Mack hitched to their horse cart, and he had a lead strap for Fleet. He tied the colt behind the cart and helped the exhausted girl to a place in the seat.

Katherine and her son talked excitedly of the extraordinary feat that Leone had accomplished. Robert laughed, "It sure was lucky she saw them colts. Nobody else could catch them, and once she got a hand on Fleet, she's so damn stubborn, she would get them home if it killed her."

A better happening that year was when Leone got the lead in the school play. She found this a very agreeable experience. It was quite an elaborate affair, all things considered. There would be a small crowd from town on the big night. All the members of the cast were doing their utmost to make the performance a success. There was a very popular teacher in charge. The companion lead was taken by one of that year's graduates, a very nice tall boy. He seemed to be gifted with a certain amount of art as well as diplomacy. He took his part seriously, and was also helpful in setting the stage and assisting in other ways. Leone proved very efficient and found herself getting more deeply involved each day with the complex details of the program. The district school had but one instructor and the pupils were divided into ten grades. Needless to say, the teacher was a busy woman and welcomed competent aide.

The time came when the last rehearsal had come to a harmonious conclusion. This was done so perfectly, it brought the light of victory to the eyes of the young people who had worked so tirelessly. Their new show went down in history as one of the best as set by the standard of the times, attracting a large and enthusiastic crowd. Leone wore her first long dress on that memorable occasion. It trailed on tall grass behind her, with just the right amount of swish as she moved with her ear tuned for the faint sound. This was a thrill known only to the very young.

The Neely sisters welcomed the close of school that year. The water had receded from the fields, and the girls were all prepared to finish the planting of the crop. Quite a large part of this task had been taken care of. Many seeds in the garden were showing nice little green rows.

Baby Helen could come out where the girls were at work in the fields or garden now. She would cling to Henrietta's hand during the day and then ride back home piggyback on Leone's shoulders. If Leone showed any reluctance for this pastime, the baby would promptly call out in a plaintive little voice, "Kiea, me, Leone, kiea me," and Leone would dutifully carry Helen home. Sometimes the other girls scolded her.

"Helen is getting too big to lug around," Henrietta told Leone, one day. "That is something you could spare yourself."

Leone looked affectionately at the tiny elfin creature, running barefoot in the soft soil. Her sister's gaze followed Leone's.

Henrietta extended her hands to the baby who ran to her happily.

Lifting Helen to the older girl's shoulders, she said, "Here you are, softy."

Leone winked and responded, "Two softies." Turning to talk a moment, Leone tenderly patted the little legs. "And she must go even longer than we do without a mother."

"Not if Dad has any luck," Henrietta answered, gloomily.

Leone's bright face promptly took on a droopy expression. She retorted, "Dad is going to find himself a wife at the rate he is going. He will surely find someone, but he will not find a mother for his children. A woman worthy the name would not take the job."

"You're right, Leone."

"Do you know where he is gone now?"

"He went to Gladwin. There's a lovely woman living there. Aunt Rita tells me that she has three sons. She would not marry father."

"She sure would be looking for trouble if she did," Henrietta said sarcastically.

"I hope she keeps him interested for a long time. It will keep him from hunting elsewhere."

About that time the baby grabbed Leone's hair by one of the long, heavy braids. "Gette up, horsy. Gette up."

Leone laughed. "That is the signal I have been waiting for, I guess," she said cheerfully, moving off with the happy child. As they neared the house, coming through the large gate leading from the barn, she saw a well dressed man standing on the small bridge that afforded a crossing of the drainage ditch. His back was turned to Leone, and he appeared to be waiting. As he approached, he turned and saw her and came forward to meet her. It proved to be the venerable, old, Dr. Eastman. He greeted Leone cordially enough, but then he added in a severe tone, "I told your Mother to forbid you to carry that child. You are very much overworked for your age as it is without lugging that big child unnecessarily."

Leone put the baby down as she answered, "My mother said you told her I should not carry Helen so much."

"And why, may I ask, don't you mind what you are told, and not be doing that which will undermine your health?"

"Ma did not insist that I obey the order to the letter. I enjoy caring for the baby, and I make her happy."

The sinister look faded from the pale blue eyes of the older gentleman, and a gleam of amusement was shown instead. "Your mother was a wise woman, Leone, I must confess, and it pleases me to say that you are looking better. You have grown taller and walk erect with natural grace. This is more noticeable now, since you have outgrown those despicable short skirts. I did not think of this until I saw you in the school play. I wondered at first what you had done for yourself."

About this time Leone experienced a little wave of gratified vanity that continued until she listened further, as the doctor became reminiscent. He said, "I never will forget what a homely, awkward child I considered you to be. I realize now it was mostly them short skirts flapping about your hips and you had such a gangling form."

I shall have to get him off this subject, she thought. With him reflecting on a lady's shape right in her presence, I could have a peeve. Aloud she said, "I'm sorry, Dad is not here."

"What is this rumor about him? Hunting the country over for another wife?"

"Looks like it," Leone assented. "He is gone a lot."

The doctor made a despairing gesture and responded, "I gave him credit for having more sense."

They moved along as they talked and came to the shady spot in the lane where his daughter waited with a horse and buggy. She had been visiting with the other Neely girls. The doctor gave his horse a quizzical look, grabbed a hold of the large bushy tail and exclaimed, "Daughter, this horse is falling away. I see now that he has lost weight."

"Did you drive down here to figure that out, Dad?" his daughter asked.

"No, but have I become such a replica of the absent-minded professor that I could be driving a horse that was falling away, and not even know it?"

The dignified old gentleman standing there, holding the horse's tail with such a humble self-accusing expression on his face was too ludicrous for the girls to control their amusement entirely. His brow wrinkled as he dropped the horse's tail and jumped into the buggy. The doctor seized the reins, and drove rapidly away, calling good-bye as he did so. The doctor's daughter turned a laughing face as they moved off.

Chapter 13
MARIAN COLE'S INFLUENCE

The hot sun poured its silent, wilting rays upon Leone and her little group of youthful helpers. The tender green vines of the young potatoes grew limp and jaded looking, as they vigorously cut the weeds and tilled the soft, mellow soil about the thrifty shoots.

Marie said to Leone firmly, "Look at Bill. He has been playing there in the sand for over an hour, not helping a bit." The girl stopped, her hoe in midair, and let it drop slowly to the ground.

"I see him, the poor little fellow. He was evidently not intended by nature to be a farmer."

"Or anything else," answered Marie, unreasonably. "You will have to talk to him. What if Dad catches him playing?"

"Oh, he will look out for Dad." She called accusingly, "Bill, why don't you go to work for a change? After all, you are the man of the crowd."

"Poor pay," called back Bill, as he slapped the ground with sharp blows of a short stick. "Besides that, I'm busy."

"What are you doing anyway?" called Leone curiously.

"Getting even with this toad."

"Getting even with a poor, harmless toad? What do you mean?"

"Oh, they are not so harmless, imposing their nasty, old voices and calling it singing," and he struck the ground a few more welts.

"Uncle Watt says to let anything sing, even a mosquito, if it wants to cheer the world," shouted the previously silent Henrietta, from across the green rows.

Leone laid down her hoe. "Bill Neely!" she said sternly. "I'm going to see what you're up to," as she strode, threateningly toward him. "If you are really abusing a poor toad, you will be called sharply to order. Where is the toad?" she asked reaching his side. Then as she looked at the almost buried object, Leone exclaimed, "Well, of all things! Is that really a toad?"

Bill was beginning to look remorseful. "Leone, you always were chickeny. Don't dig him up. He looks sort of juicy in spots. It will just make you feel bad."

"Make me feel bad! How do you think the poor toad feels?" She sank to her knees on the soft earth and started to remove the soil with her lean, brown hands.

"You'll be sorry, Sis," cautioned the youngster.

"Now, what is this? Your dirty, bare foot! No toad? You had that all planned to fool me."

The boy laughed loudly and then lay on his back putting up his two soiled feet. "It's fun to fool you, Leone. You are such an easy mark." He had been sitting, crossed leg, with his one foot buried in the soft soil, without being noticed by his sister, who was bent on rescuing a toad.

She smiled, indulgently, her gaze lingering on the beloved only brother. "Pitch in and help now, Bill," she said persuasively. "See all Henrietta has accomplished, and she is younger than you."

"Too young to know any better," he called after her retreating form, as she hurried back to her work. His mischief accomplished, he picked up his hoe and cheerfully started to work in a manner that boded no good for the offending weeds.

That evening Robert announced to his children that they would have houseguests, their Aunt Rita and a Mrs. Cole from Gladwin, whom he had visited. He would drive to her home, and she would accompany him to Standish, where his sister, Rita, now lived. Rita would join them and come on through to the Neelys' farm, for a week's visit. The girls looked forward to this with pleasure. They always were delighted to have their Aunt Rita with them, and they expected to like Marion Cole. Many nice things had been said of her, and thus it proved true.

The woman was charming, tall, and slender, but also rather frail looking. The children, without exception, liked her. She had a sweet singing voice and a nice collection of fine old hymns. Robert would accompany her on the harmonica. Some very pleasant hours were spent in this way. During this visit, their Aunt Rita showed the girls how a special method of canning was done, something they found pleasant and profitable.

Robert refrained for the time from driving his children at their work, and showed himself how a gentleman should act toward his family.

Henrietta watched as he walked down the garden path with Mrs. Cole, his head bent in close attention. There was a little furrow in her forehead, as she turned toward Marie whose face was flushed from exercise and streaked with sweat and dirt. "Mrs. Cole is a nice lady. Her influence on Dad may linger when she is gone. He sure is a lot more thoughtful and kind since she is here."

Her sister looked up with a dark frown as their father dropped behind his companion and motioned to the two girls to get to work. They had been out in the cool, early morning to strip the suckers from the sweet corn that served for the family use.

"It would take more influence than she has to change Dad," Marie answered scornfully.

The girls missed the pretty lady when she was gone. Later that fall, Robert went back for another little visit with the lady of his dreams, and, wonder of wonders, he planned to take Leone with him.

Circumstances at the AuGres farm had changed. There were only two cows on the place now, and one of them was dry. The income would not be missed this year because they had the money from the sale of the stock. Leone's milking job, that had been gaining greater proportions each year, was no more.

Robert Neely was not a good manager, but he was a good traveling companion. Their mode of travel to Standish, if judged by the standards of today, was not very modern. The bay gelding, Mack, was hitched to their little road cart. Leone did not mind as she had sat many long days on the iron seat of a hayrack.

Ace Secord's place, where travelers stopped to refresh themselves and their steeds, had long intrigued Leone's curiosity. She had heard the place referred to by many persons who had passed that way. Leone looked at this landmark in wonder and studied it as she gazed in silence at the charred stumps, rough boulders, and dry grass that surrounded it. She was inclined to look with favor upon this remote old refuge for the traveling wayfarer. The place was actually impressive. This was much more so after Mack was provided his oats and a drink of cool water and Leone and her father had a nice dinner at the Inn.

When they arrived at the home of Marion Cole, the gentle lady came out to greet them herself. However, it was very noticeable that she had failed in health since her visit with the Neelys. Leone met her three sons for the first time. They greeted the guests cordially. Included in this enchanting group was a young lady friend who was taking care of Mrs. Cole. The next few days proved to be a new experience for Leone, an atmosphere of youth and enjoyment with a predominating male influence.

Robert fell easily into his natural role of the great lover. He was not daring, but rather suave. It was quite evident that he brought happiness to the beautiful lady of his dreams. The faint flush that outlined her delicate features, and the light that came into her brown eyes at his appearance told the story. Leone looked on in silence and awe. She had witnessed the approach of the Grim Reaper, but she felt no pang. The decision could safely rest with Divine Providence.

The days passed all too soon before the travelers found themselves on their way home through the tinted autumn woods. They saw a deer and many smaller animals, mostly squirrels, putting away a winter store of nuts. Leone watched with delight as their little furry bodies scurried through the thick carpet of leaves. She happily enjoyed the long drive. They allowed Mack to keep his own pace. When the road was heavy sand, he would hold to his fast, tireless walk. When the road was not so rough, he would shake his proud head, toss his heavy mane and seem to enjoy doing a fast trot. Robert and his daughter arrived home in the early evening. Leone was glad to step down from the awkward seat. She was forced to admit that the sheepskin cushion had become a little tiresome.

Every spare moment for the following week was well filled with exciting talk as Leone related every detail of the trip and visit to the rest of the waiting family.

Chapter 14
CHANGES IN THE NEIGHBORHOOD

Later that fall when the harvest was about all cared for, there came a hasty message for Robert from Gladwin. He obeyed the summons alone. After a few days, he came sadly home with the grievous news that Marion Cole had gone to the Great Beyond.

Leone experienced a chilled feeling as tears welled in her eyes. There were questions she would like to ask while her father was in this intimate mood, but the sob in her throat prevented it, and the opportunity did not come again. Her unanswered thoughts were so intangible, she wondered sometimes if they could be put into words. Life as you lived it seemed so incomplete at times. It brought a feeling of frustration that sometimes lingered and never became quite clear.

Harvey Curr made a visit to the Neelys in the early winter. The young people had fun playing in the snow and sleigh riding as Robert proudly showed his fast horses. One night they went to a party in town. The children were sorry to see him leave. He did this with a promise he would advise his older brother to come and help Robert cut timber through the winter months.

Leone was happy over the prospects of her father cutting timber that winter. She knew he would be restless unless involved in some occupation that would hold his interests and the driving force of his nature would be an asset. The ring of the cross cut saw as sawdust flew from the fresh green logs was the answer to this need. And there would also be a little money after the men were paid. The extra money would see the family safely through the pressure of planting season the following spring.

The wood chips, moss, and bark lying about on the glistening snow delighted the children. Temporary roads, skid ways, and hauling equipment were again a part of their lives. Often they waited at the end of the long lane to enjoy the fun ride back home on the empty bobsleighs through the woods; this would be the return trip after the logs had been hauled to Saginaw Bay to market. Loose ends of the chain were worn bright and shiny from contact with the ice and snow as they came trailing behind the sleigh with a little clattering, somewhat musical sound that delighted the children. Uncle Watt sometimes helped with the hauling. He was always cheerful and happy, joining in their make-believe games.

Laughter from the children would be ringing through the trees as they jumped off the sleigh in the soft snow. Sometimes there would be an echo of the joyous young voices as they scampered about on a gum hunt from the area's scarce tamarack trees. The gum with a tang all its own was the only gum known to the Neelys. They had learned a little hot water process to put it through. Leone studied out a method of coloring some of it. The Neely children chewed this gum with more pleasure than experienced in later years when they purchased beautiful wrapped gum over a counter.

Leone was always looking toward the future. Any time she glanced back over the past, it was to glean something from the experience to use in the time that was coming. Something loomed ahead at this juncture that was quite unexpected by Leone---marriage for her sister Margaret. Their mother had said Margaret would marry young. Leone had listened to this possibility with indifference. There had been so many tragically important matters to consider at that time. Now, confronted with this possibility, it frightened her. The young man who gave rise to the alarm in Leone's wise little head was Norman Curl from Gladwin. Norman worked industriously making the chips and sawdust fly as he cut timber. However, she could also now admit to herself that he was a most acceptable gentleman who would assure the future of one Neely sister. Leone had arrived at this phase of consideration before the young couple themselves appeared to be aware of the bond of love that was growing between them. Robert was happily unconscious of it, and Leone kept her observations to herself. The Neelys' near and popular neighbors, the Peary family, moved to a location a mile closer to the village. Their new house was commodious and more suited to the needs of their large family, and it also had a greater area cleared. Lea Peary, Dan Peary's bachelor brother, would also make his home with them. He was a very popular member of the community, a type that friends appealed to in emergencies. There always seemed to be dollars in his pocket for a small cash loan or contribution to a worthy cause. More often than not, he was in the solemn line of pallbearers or best man at a wedding. The girls all loved him, but he remained a bachelor.

A family named Tallon from the city of Saginaw now occupied the log house that had belonged to the Peary family. These people were not popular with Robert Neely. There was a ruling from him for his household in regard to them. They were to be respectfully tolerated if they called, but no return call was to be made. Association with them was something to be avoided.

However, the two families were soon quite well acquainted, and the rule was not strictly adhered to. The girls in passing would stop at times to chat a little. If this came to their father's attention, he would remind them of his ruling.

There was one son, Fred, who seemed to babble incessantly. Among the subjects he selected to chatter about most were his Uncle Henry and Aunt Minnie of Saginaw. The girls did not pay much attention to this apparently aimless talk. One day he reported his uncle was on the sick list. However, the following day he announced his Aunt Minnie was looking for a new husband since his Uncle Henry had died.

Henrietta, listening to this disclosure, looked at him in astonishment.

"Fred, you are a victim of hallucinations. Only yesterday you were saying your uncle was sick."

"He may not have been dead then. He died yesterday," the boy insisted.

"Died yesterday?" she repeated tartly. "Your aunt would most certainly not be looking for a new husband until after the funeral at least."

"And why not?" he asked. "You don't know Aunt Minnie. She's a fast worker when it comes to getting husbands."

Christmas was celebrated very quietly that year. They all went to the local schoolhouse where the neighborhood Christmas program was presented. The following day the girls prepared a nice dinner. Norman Curl joined the family circle for their simple festivities. The kindly young man was slowly sweeping aside any misgivings Leone might have had.

Robert was not at home on the eve of the New Year for the first time in their young lives. The girls felt privileged to watch the old year out and the new year take a bow. While they did not miss the opportunity, Bill became sleepy about ten o'clock. After yawning and rubbing his eyes a few times, he decided it was all foolishness anyway. He proclaimed that the new day would be like any other day, and he would look at it in the morning. Having made this declaration, he retired to his room. The two little girls were sleepy also, and did not require further inducement to give up the party. Bert Peary, who was sawing for Robert that winter with Norman, had also joined the girls.

In any spare moment she had, Leone could be found working with her knitting needles. The dry good store at AuGres paid her one-dollar for knitting four pairs of men's heavy socks. She felt she had to keep the stitches mounting. Bert sat near, slowly reeling off the yarn. He took a boy's mischievous delight in teasing Leone.

"I would not like to be near you a few years from now," he warned.

"What difference will a few years make?" she asked.

"You will be a regular old crab with all that knitting. You're beginning to look funny now."

"Look funny?" Henrietta quickly came to Leone's defense.

Bert replied, "Looking at you would make anyone look funny."

Henrietta was standing guard over a pot of taffy boiling on the old elevated stove, a flush on her fair young face from the effect of the heat waves thrown off by the dependable little stove.

Bert cheerfully turned his banter. "Your face will be redder than it is now if you let that taffy run over into next year, " he warned.

She took watchful eyes off the taffy long enough to level a glare at him.

Ten minutes before the old wooden clock struck the hour of twelve, the group let themselves out into the darkness and quiet of midnight. After pausing a few moments to accustom their eyes to the pale light, they then moved down the path. Leone silently took note that Margaret and Norman were walking at the end of the line hand-in-hand.

Bert reached for the lantern Marie carried, but she refused to relinquish it.

"I would not trust you with anything so precious."

"Now what harm could I do with that smoky old lantern?"

"Fall down and break it," was Marie's quick retort.

Bert was further amused to arrive in the barnyard. "Hey, Norm," he called. "This was all contrived by Leone to show us the cattle on their knees at midnight."

Norman admitted he had never heard that one before.

"Sure thing," Bert assured him. "Bossies do that every New Year's."

Leone opened the barn door. The stock were sleeping quietly on their straw beds. It was warmer in the barn, but cold enough to see the moisture of the animals breathing. "Well, that theory is exploded," Bert offered earnestly, as though he had half-believed his own fable. It was just after they had a good laugh that Norman took out his watch and announced to the group that it was the dawn of a new year.

Chapter 15
MINNIE'S VISIT

One day late that January, Bill came on the porch carrying an arm full of wood. As he stomped the snow from his shoes, he threw the door open and called to Marie, "I just met Fred. His Aunt Minnie is going to invade this district next week."

"Invade is the correct word," his sister retorted. "She is pretending to visit her brother, but in reality she is searching for a new husband."

"The worst of it is, she might find one."

"Oh, Bill, don't be so pessimistic. That is way out of all sense of reasoning."

"Well," he said slowly, "there is a catch here."

Later, the babbling Fred announced his Aunt Minnie had arrived, with war paint on and out for conquest!

Although the Neely family tried to remain indifferent, they listened to this information with some misgivings. This apprehension increased as the days went by although there was no apparent move on the part of the Tallons to promote the widow's suit.

Their father was away from home every evening. His children, however, had no way of knowing how he was spending his time.

The absence of the chatty youth, Fred Tallon, was a suspicious circumstance and furthered the thought that the widow might be more subtle than she had been given credit for. Robert's family was quite helpless about this suspected impending disaster. Even worry was futile.

One afternoon Bill joined the girls when they were indulging in a brief chat. They were grouped about the old family stove, which served the dual purpose of cook stove and heater and proved a comfort, if not a beauty of its own. Their faces glowed from recent contact with the frosty air and the enthusiasm of youth. They cheerfully made room for Bill.

"Got some bad news for you girls," he said with his usual abruptness.

Not inclined to regard him very seriously, they all greeted this with a smile.

"You can laugh if you want to, but it may be on the other side of your face if my surmise is correct. When I came home from the Pearys just now, I stopped at the Tallons. I saw Dad there shining up to the widow."

"Not really?" Marie retorted. Then she queried, "You saw the widow?"

"Yes, they were in the yard. I saw her very well. In fact, too much of her."

The girls all eagerly quizzed, "You did?" "What does she look like?" "What did she wear?" "Is she slim?"

"Had something on, the stripes going round, looked like hoops on a barrel, about that slim too." Bill paused for a meditative moment, "This is just what she did look like, a butter tub walking, not tall enough for a barrel."

The girls giggled merrily, but their brother stood grim and tight-lipped.

Helen came to his side and tugged on his hand, "Does she use face powder?"

"You might call it a face powdered. Looked like a huge hunk of taffy to me that someone had just rescued from the flour bin. And she has a little darning like cotton tacked on for hair and now you have her photo," as he snapped his fingers with a jester of finality.

Leone looked with concern reflected in her eyes at the gloomy boy. "You paint a most unattractive picture. What were they doing that caused your anxiety?"

His voice was low and dead level when he answered, "Feeding the chickens."

Leone laughed in spite of the resolution she had just made to respect his mood. "Dad, helping to feed the chickens? No wonder you felt our cause was lost. If it were not tragic, it would be humorous. The widow has him tamed all right."

The strangely mature look did not leave the little fellow. Without a smile he stood and then spoke as though in answer to a challenge. "That woman came into this community for no other purpose than to harpoon Dad. I think she must be good at it too. I understand that he would be her fifth husband."

"He would hardly go to that house to pick out a wife. He has forbidden us to go there," Henrietta reminded them.

Bill offered, "Yes, but Dad has a very different book of rules for himself than the one he expects his children to follow. Just wait and see," his voice still sounding flat. Their brother leaned down, picked up his mitts, and went quietly out into the clear winter sunshine. His step was slow and deliberate.

His sisters looked at one another in dismay. Marie was the first to speak.

"The calamity has fallen. We have been expecting it from some quarter for a long time, but it's a shock anyway. There are things in life that are worse than death," she ended gloomily.

"I wonder if she will move right in on us?"

"She will come over on a tour of inspection first; you may be sure of that," answered Leone much more cheerfully than she felt. She picked up her mitts from their warming place by the old stove. "I cannot say much for our prospects, but I can for the way we are going to take it." She concluded, "It will be with courage and dignity, like we have done many times before. And never permit her to influence us to do anything we consider wrong."

The girls echoed her confidence as she opened the door that admitted a sharp blast of wintry air. "The wind seems to be lifting," she called as she hastily closed it. As Leone turned to go down the steps, she met the two persons who in all the world she had the least desire to see, their neighbor, Mrs. Tallon, accompanied by a woman that fitted perfectly Bill's rough sketch of Aunt Minnie.

Mrs. Tallon greeted Leone in her usual jolly, disarming manner, introducing her sister-in-law, and together they joined the girls.

57

Leone felt as if she were leading an invasion into the peace and security of their home.

A very few moments sufficed to convince the family that this was the inspection trip Leone had foretold. The thinly veiled air of proprietorship could come only from the most ill-mannered of persons, reasonably sure of her position.

In spite of their cool reception, the unwelcome callers removed their coats and rubbers and remained nearly an hour. Mrs. Tallon rose to the occasion as though she were hostess, but the children's cool stares and the ladies' one-sided conversation was too much even for the callers. They soon began putting on their rubbers, evidently terminating the visit, and much more quickly than had been anticipated.

Laura and Helen were too young to understand what this could mean, but felt the lack of warmth on the part of their sisters, concluding they must make up for the deficiency. Laura decided to step into the breach. Smiling, she asked simply, "What is your name?"

The woman turned to her and replied patronizingly, "Little folks like you call me Aunt Minnie.

"Do you work when you're home?" the child continued her innocent questioning.

"Yes," she answered flatly.

"What do you work at?"

Aunt Minnie, very red of face, was bending forward concentrating on adjusting her overshoes. "I teach," she said shortly.

Laura was quick to go on, "Oh, and what do you teach?"

The woman stamped her foot and the overshoe went into place. She arose to make a hasty retreat as she answered, "Fancy work."

Without further comment, the Neely sisters went sadly to their separate places where work must be done. There were no words known to them in the English vocabulary that would express the cruel bitterness of this blow. They did not try to fool themselves with hope and doubt of the pending future. They must meet this calamity calmly as possible.

Aunt Minnie went back to Saginaw. She was gone two weeks and the Neely children almost had begun to hope when their father announced that he would be gone a few days.

The hour was late when he arrived home. Minnie was with him. Bill expressed the sentiment of the family, "She is here all right, every ungainly inch of her." Their only brother had his own approach to life happenings, but patience and dignity had no part with his method.

Leone's natural instinct prompted her to agree with him. However, she knew there was nothing to be gained but heartache in open resistance. She was grateful to her mother for the character she bequeathed through careful training to her daughters. While they would meet this tragedy bravely and discreetly, that would not be so for their mischievous young brother. He would be the main issue in conflicts ahead.

Chapter 16
FATHER'S NEW WIFE

The Neely children with their background of industry, knew nothing whatsoever about such a person as their father's new wife. She would not even take care of washing her own face or caring for her hair. The good-natured Laura was picked to perform these services for Minnie.

Minnie brought one piece of furniture with her, a huge, comfortable rocking chair. She could be found occupying this chair, smoking an evil-smelling pipe most of the daylight hours. "She could think of more ways of causing a disturbance than any other hateful person on earth," Bill declared. And for once, all of the other members of the family agreed with him.

Norman Curl became quite anxious about the oldest Neely sister, Margaret. Norman was in love with her and was eager for their marriage to take place. He wanted to be in a position to take her to a happier environment when the time came. Robert Neely surprised the couple by approving of their marriage but required that Norman remain with him and help run the farm as his son.

The young couple made a tentative agreement to this in fear of Robert's displeasure and the consequent interruption of their wedding plans. The marriage was quietly solemnized at the residence of their Aunt Rita in Standish, and the young couple returned home with Robert that evening. They would be obliged to remain in this troubled household until the logs were sold in the spring and Norman received the salary for his work of the winter months.

Minnie continued to antagonize everyone, including Robert. The children remained out of doors as much as possible. They managed with a combined attitude of patience and endurance to exist in the intolerable atmosphere. The only one who braved the woman's wrath and the possibility of punishment was the irrepressible Bill. When his sisters pleaded with him to avoid anything that could be construed as argumentative, he assured them there would be no fun in that.

On one occasion, old Minnie reached out with her whip in hand, but lost her balance from her seat in the heavy rocking chair. Minnie had fallen to her knees, and the back of the chair forced her forward. The unsavory pipe in her mouth was being forced down her throat! The girls were obliged to dash to the rescue.

"That's where you were foolish," Bill later offered with a grin. "It was an accident that could have met with disaster, and she brought it upon herself."

Leone advised him earnestly, "You are placing yourself on a level with her, and the implication in your remarks are most unbecoming."

"I'll do better next time, Leone," he promised, his eyes beaming with mirth and mischief.

In the early spring when the logs were sold, Norman's two brothers arrived. They had driven down from Gladwin. Robert objected strenuously to the couple's wishes to leave. He declared that Margaret would never be welcome home again if they left at this time. Privately, Leone urged the young couple not to permit their father's dramatic conduct to disturb any plans. The two brothers stayed two days while the talking continued. Finally, Margaret and Norman did take the brave step and left with his brothers. When they were gone, the Neely girls found that a real void was left behind. This was but one more trial in their young lives that was somewhat compensated for by the knowledge that Margaret was happy.

During that spring and summer Leone struggled mentally with the problem of how she was to come into possession of even the small amount of money necessary to make her escape. Each round of thought brought her right back to the point she started from, which was zero!

As the situation they had to contend with grew more intolerable daily, it was impressed deeply on Leone that she must not fail at her plans. She became determined to go before the weather became too frosty in the event it would be too cold if she were obliged to hide out a night or two. She felt finally forced to the conclusion that she must make up a plausible story of having found work in Bay City and needed then to borrow only two dollars necessary for the train fare. If she admitted requiring a larger sum, it would be an admission that she would have to find work with her youth and inexperience. The friends from whom she could ask this favor would not consent to see her taking the risk. She could not censure them for this. Leone was not deceiving herself. Nobody knew her shortcomings better than Leone. However, this was a risk she felt forced to take. Nothing but time and experience could remedy this. Meanwhile, she must remain alert and trust to her faith.

Leone prevailed upon her father to drive her to Standish to spend a week with Aunt Rita. There she went about the business of borrowing the necessary two dollars. She applied first to Vicky, a young woman whom she had known as a friend for some years. Vicky was also employed, and Leone was sure she would not be refused. But Vicky failed her by offering a number of lame excuses. Leone then appealed to her Aunt Rita, but that, too, was a mistake. Leone realized from the discouraging remarks that Aunt Rita would not be of any assistance. Further, on the first opportunity, she would betray the situation to Robert, thus putting Leone's plan in jeopardy. Leone felt desperate. She even tried to whittle the money from two of her cousins, Eileen and Young. These moves were fruitless. They both declared that they would not take such a chance of incurring Robert's unreasonable anger. She then made one final try. There was a young man, Pat, a former schoolmate who was employed at the Photograph Gallery. Here at least she received encouragement. However, Pat confided that he was serving as an apprentice and received no salary.

"If I did have it," he assured her, "I would be happy to give it to you. There is no future for you at AuGres."

Leone told Pat of her disheartening experience of trying to borrow such a meager sum of money.

"Do not be discouraged. Go back home with Robert and try Lea Peary; he is a good scout. If he fails, keep going. You will succeed some place."

As Leone retraced her steps on the wood sidewalk, the cheer of his firm handclasp lingered. "Pat is a good scout himself," she thought warmly.

It was with a sense of keen disappointment that Leone greeted her father. Her hope that she would not see him again for about three years was sadly shattered. She had taken the precaution of remaining near her Aunt Rita during Robert's short visit in order to forestall any betrayal of her plan. With a smile on her face, but gloom in her heart, she climbed to the box of the spring wagon. She seated herself on the clean wool of a sheepskin cushion that adorned the hard board seat in the back. Minnie now was the one who occupied the spring seat at her father's side.

Henrietta and Marie were quite embittered when they learned of the crushing disappointment. The fact that their relatives were so completely out of sympathy was perturbing to say the least.

Leone had more time for reflection and was inclined to be less drastic in her judgment. "Girls, I thought a lot on the way home. The best way to leave may be from here."

She was met with the responses, "How could it be? You would not dare leave from Omer. Dad would catch you. And with all the rain!"

"Omer is seven miles away; that is bad enough," Marie said heavily.

"I will have to go by Saganing," answered Leone. "You know what a show Dad can put on when he finds me gone. He will hit the ceiling, and the best place to stage that will be in the seclusion of home."

"Oh, it would not do any harm for a few people to get an eye full of what we have to put up with," Henrietta protested.

"I guess we are both right," Leone agreed with a faint smile. "But it is out of our hands now. Destiny has decreed that I leave from here, and I must do it soon, or someone will tell Dad."

"The day he takes the share hold sheep back to Maple Ridge will be a good chance," suggested Marie.

Lea Peary was first on Leone's list of people to see in AuGres for the needed loan. She knew Lea was kind and generous, but after sharing the story, she could see at once that her youth and inexperience worried him. He did not refuse outright, but made an excuse that he might get the money and give it to her later.

Concluding that her secret was not very safe with him, Leone turned to go. She was driving Mack, hitched to the sulky. Leaving Lea, she mounted to the seat, and waved good-bye as she drove slowly away. As she drove, she thought that the road had never looked quite so bleak before. She wondered to whom would she turn now?

Near the school she overtook Charles Blake, trundling along on a bicycle. He was keeping to the bypath to avoid the mud. Charles had been employed by her father at one time and was in sympathy with his children.

Leone decided to confide her troubles to him. While kind and generous, Charles never had any money; he was the main support of his parents' home. However, here at least she found a normal reaction of youth to adventure. His eager attention was calming after the past week of cool brush-offs she had received.

"And what does your friend, Katherine, think?" he asked.

Leone smiled. "What does she think? I do not know for I have not told her."

"Katherine would just naturally know the solution to this problem," Charles offered. "How soon will your father go to Maple Ridge?" he asked as he was leaving.

"He will go on Tuesday," Leone replied.

"Then I shall not see you again," he said taking her hand at parting. "Your friend will arrange everything, and I am confident that you will achieve success."

Leone drove back along the gray, muddy road. She drew a rein over the horse's back, but Mack seemed to move ever so slow. The day was Sunday. She wondered now, "What if Katherine was not home alone?" Suddenly, she felt zealous, as though she could not wait another day. Then she laughed at her own eagerness.

She found that Katherine was alone, and Leone felt grateful. The kind woman met Leone with her sweet smiling, never failing self. Her gray eyes twinkled as she replied after she heard the plan, "I am glad, child. And of course, I know where you can get the money. Mrs. Sandy will give it to you."

Leone quickly drove back a half mile to see Mrs. Sandy. She came away with the precious two dollars and all the good wishes a kind friend could bestow. (Among the first things Leone did when she became a wage earner was to return this money). Leone stopped to assure Katherine of her good fortune and to say good-bye.

Katherine took her hand and said, "You will find it difficult to get through the woods, child, and especially after all the heavy rains. But I shall not worry. You are very resourceful, and time will tell everything has been for the best."

There were three happy people when Leone arrived home. She cautiously displayed her treasure to both Henrietta and Marie. Their life had revolved around getting these two dollars for so many months. The magic of actual possession seemed to sweep aside the anxiety of the past weeks and give them the moral strength to look bravely to the troubled future.

Part II

The Break

Bay City, Saginaw, and Detroit

1899 to 1903

Chapter 17
LEONE'S ESCAPE AT AGE FOURTEEN

When the eventful day came, the weather was all in favor of their plans. The rain clouds had drifted; the morning was bright with early sunlight.

No time was lost by the busy determined girls. Their father had scarcely driven into the shadows of the woodland, where the highway to Omer lay amid the stately old oak and elm trees, when busy hands were packing a lunch. Meager garments were going into an old diaper bag, better known to them as the little satchel. Worn and shabby, it was all they had, small, but large enough. There was little to put in it. Leone called to the three younger children. In fear of untimely disclosures, they were happily unaware of the important step about to be taken. They came running, laughing and shouting in the freedom from parental restraint. When they were told about the plan, joy soon turned to sorrow for Laura and Baby Helen. Not so for Bill, he was jubilant! He gave Leone what he called a brotherly bear hug and danced around wild with delight.

"Good for you, Sis," he shouted in glee. "You will make it. You always do."

Not so with the two little sisters. Starry eyes filled with tears. Part with their beloved Leone? The baby wept softly in the folds of the older girl's dress.

"Hold me," she whispered, shaken with sobs. Leone seated herself and took the dear little younger sister in her arms.

"Helen, darling, we must be brave," she counseled. Her own vague ideas of the great city were told again. She described a nice little house, where there would be no room for the unwanted stepmother. All this and much more were repeated now.

"And I will not be here to do my work. Make life as pleasant as you can by helping Marie and Henrietta get my work done. It will be very difficult for them."

"We are getting big now. We will help," they promised. "Only don't be long."

"I will try not to be gone very long," she assured them. She had given herself three years, and three years were long with the end remote and far away. (No, she dare not think of that.)

66

"Girls," she called to Marie and Henrietta who came and stood expectantly, their work still clasped in their hands. "Let's resolve one thing today–that not one of us will step into a foolish marriage."

"Hurrah for Leone," called Bill. Then he inquired, "Now, what train you going to take? The eleven forty?"

"The only one," Leone replied.

"How you going to catch it? You would not dare go to Omer. Dad would see you."

"I shall have to go on past to the town of Saganing."

"Hard going," he assured her soberly. "Seven miles through heavy brush. I found the cows over there a few times. About the only way I could get through was to follow a cow."

The girl smiled and said, "I cannot take a cow along very well."

But the anxious boy was not to be lightly set aside. "You don't know what you are up against, Sis. Your clothing will be torn to bits."

"We have thought of that," she answered. "I will go just as I am and when I reach the river past the brush, I shall find a sheltered spot and change my clothing and shoes and try to look the best I can. It is the only way. We have no choice."

Bill was frankly doubtful of this arrangement, but at a loss to make any change in it. He stood there frowning. "The river is high now, and you cannot cross on the old logs. You will find it necessary to go to the Pine River Bridge, I am quite sure. I will take Carlo and go with you until you are safely over the river."

Leone thought rapidly. She knew the cows had never strayed the miles she must go. She also was well aware of the treacherous brush. Her brother was nine years old, too young to be of help. He was a sturdy, determined little chap. Once started, there would be no turning him back until she had reached her goal. Then she would be obliged to leave him alone in the woods. So far from home, this would fill her mind with anxiety.

"Marie is going with me," she assured him.

He protested this, but the girls insisted Marie was the oldest. After a few faint smiles, warm kisses, choking sobs and high tension little laughs, the two girls waved good-bye and went swinging down the lane with its few stumps, frog ponds, and cow trail. When they arrived at the corner, they took the western path at the end of the familiar old lane that would lead them into deep woods. Leone, worried, was trying to think of some way to prevail upon the beloved

Marie to go back to the protection of the farm and leave her to face the situation alone. Walking briskly, they were soon trying to penetrate the tangled old logging roadway scarcely to be distinguished now. The rapid growth of brush and vines included a predominance of nettles, tall as young trees. The travelers found it impossible to avoid the unwieldy, contaminating presence of the nettles; they had a discomfort all their own. They worked along together almost in silence as the various sorts of lush vines clung tenaciously to their sturdy young bodies. The air was fresh and sweet after the many days of deluges of fall rains. The sun was warm and growing warmer. The girls perspired as they pushed aside the brush. They sometimes paused a moment for the comfort of the soft breeze and to note if they were correctly following the outline of what had been the logging road. Places that proved a little easier and allowed them to move on a little only served to alarm the older girl. Leone did not wish to leave Marie so deep in the woods. Fear of wild animals oppressed her.

She tried persuading, "It will be just as difficult for you to go back alone." She pleaded, "I shall be anxious with no way of knowing if you arrive safe."

"What about you?" asked Marie.

"Oh, me," Leone smiled reassuringly. "I have been in the woods before, you know. I am a regular old bush ranger. I was expecting a battle, and I must go on and take the risk, but it would be safest and best for us for you to turn back now."

Marie took a branch from a weed known to be soothing to the bite of nettles, and sitting on a low stump, she started vigorously applying the juicy leaves on afflicted parts of her tortured skin. Taking a handful of the leaves, Leone followed her sister's example. They worked in silence for a time. Then Marie raised tear-dimmed eyes.

"Suppose I sit here and wait awhile. The river cannot be very far. The going will not be so hard when you get across. You call back 'Ho hoo', and I will answer and can go back satisfied you made it safely."

Leone arose quickly. "The very thing," she agreed taking the worn old bag Marie had insisted on carrying. The two girls clung fondly to one another for a moment. Then Leone plunged into the brush, tears stinging her eyes. No time must be lost. It was a long way to the river; she knew Marie did not round up the cows and did not realize the distance. She must trick her sister into believing the river had been reached and safely crossed. The young adventurer could then go on without further anxiety on that score.

The brush and vines continued to be heavy and difficult, but the girl's strong, young body and brave spirit kept faith. She did not falter when she felt the distance she had come should look convincing. She called out the family signal to the waiting Marie–a loud, clear "Ho hoo."

"Ho hoo" came a voice choking on a sob in the distance. Then Leone's last agreed upon return call came and was exchanged, and the courageous girl was on her way alone.

She looked up at the sun. Time was passing. She must catch the eleven forty and the going was plenty rough. She continued to fight the clinging vines and work her way vigorously through the tangle of brush.

Suddenly she stopped. A familiar sound, faint now and far away came through on the morning air. It was a last good-bye from the devoted Marie. Leone sent back the answering call, but did not pause. Progress was now not as slow as she had reached a place where the undergrowth was not quite so dense.

Having finally reached a point in her calculations, she listened for the distant sound of the river; it was at such a moment she discovered she was not alone. She stood silent and listened, her eager gaze following the point of commotion where some four-footed creature was advancing at a fair rate. Thrashing through the brush, it appeared to be coming directly to where she waited. "It is not a bear," thought Leone. "They are not hungry enough to attack this time of year." She was not kept long in wondering silence. A strong, medium-sized animal coated with yellow-brown hair hurled its way through the vines to her side. The girl's sunny head bent forward. "Carlo, you old dear," she cried. "Come to see me off and you should not."

The dog's ears drooped. He understood her reprimand. She rested a flushed face against his neck and patted him fondly "You are indeed the last link. Now look around for bears, while I struggle some more." He bounded ahead and made the going a little easier, but progress was slow at best.

The sun rose higher, and the day became warmer. It appeared to be near noonday when the traveler stopped and stood silently amid the shadowy green boughs from where a glimpse of the river could be seen. This was not a peaceful, shimmering river of soft murmurs, but a turbulent one with floating debris and dark angry eddies. Leone could hear it easily now above the rustle of the leaves. She felt the October breeze, soft and cool as it played with the tangled hair about her flushed face. "I am not far from the bridge!" she excitedly exclaimed aloud. She quickly brushed aside the hair over her face, scrambled over some intervening fallen logs and vigorously thrust aside the brush. She was soon standing by the rushing river, looking anxiously for the bridge. She hurried along the rough pathway on the riverbank with Carlo but a few paces ahead.

She stopped suddenly, the color draining from her flushed face. The unmistakable chug, chug of a railway train could be heard in the distance. Leone looked again at the sun. It could be nothing else but the eleven forty. She had started out at seven o'clock that morning and tried so relentlessly to be at Saganing when it arrived. She looked about bewildered. What would she do now?

Then her gaze came to rest on a part of an old bridge built of heavy well-worn planking, lying in the river's muddy depths. She looked earnestly at what had been the heavy timbers once supporting the familiar old span known as the Pine River Bridge, lying lengthwise in the river! Other parts of the worn planking had floated but a short distance from their former moorings. The dirt road bed dropped off at the water's edge on each side, indicating where the bridge should be. Closer inspection showed most of it was lying in two parts, one on either side, a short distance from the quite useless framework, immersed in the dark waters.

She drew closer, coming very slowly. "I must ford it," she thought. "It has a tricky bottom, and it will be difficult and dangerous. I must send Carlo home first." She sat down on a log and put her arms about the faithful dog. "Rest with me a moment, Carlo. The train is gone now. We can take the time. Then you must go home and help the girls. They need you, boy, and I do not." She petted him a moment, then pointed back, "Go now, boy, go home." His ears drooped, and he put out his paw. She gravely gave the extended paw a gentle little shake. He arose and trotted away slowly in the direction they had come. Leone sat sadly watching his departure. He stopped once and looked back giving a plaintive little bark. "Go home, Carlo. Go home," she commanded. He turned obediently and resumed his way, soon disappearing in the brush. She knew the well-trained animal would go home.

She arose but knew this fresh disaster could not weaken her resolve. No use lamenting frustrated plans. The thing to be done now was to get across that mean body of water safely.

She thought "nothing to salvage here," as she looked down at her torn clothing and what was left of her well-worn shoes. "It seems to be the only chance. I may as well plunge in." Long and carefully she looked at the threatening river, trying to select a point not too deep. She knew well the danger lurking in those restless depths.

With a firm grip on her meager belongings, she stepped cautiously into the water. The first step brought the murky water to her knees. "Dear Blessed Lord, I need your kind help," she prayed softly. She cautiously advanced, facing up stream to protect herself from floating debris. With each step, the water grew deeper, and, her dripping garments clung to her slim form. She gamely put forth a most valiant effort to keep a safe foothold in the heavily charging current, more than waist deep and growing deeper with each step.

Near mid-stream, she realized she must relinquish this hazardous method of fording the river. The ice-cold water was fast exhausting her strength. She did not become panic stricken. The least misstep could be fatal. Exercising the same degree of caution, she turned slowly and made her way back to a seat on the riverbank.

In the warm sunshine at a point near where she had undertaken the adventure, she remained seated awhile, squeezing water from her dripping garments. It was also noon, and she should be becoming hungry. Leone did not feel like eating, not knowing how long the lunch would have to last. She reminded herself she would have but four cents left of her money when her fare was paid.

She arose and wandered on more slowly along the riverbank. Several wild plans came to her only to be dismissed. The way was getting woodsy again with a heavy growth of slender black ash poles, wood that was the principal source of supply for the hoop makers, an industry common in the community. Familiar signs appeared that suggested some such work was in progress here. Great piles of shavings had been dumped in places where the young growth had been cut away.

Leone followed a road of sorts marked by the iron rim of wagon wheels. She had gone but a short distance when she saw the rough shop of a hoop maker. It was a welcome sight to the anxious girl. If it only afforded someone to speak to, it would be some help.

She timidly went to the door. A man in rough work clothes arose from his bench and spoke to her. "Good morning, Miss. Did you fall in that dangerous river?" he asked anxiously, looking at the bedraggled youngster in alarm.

Leone hastily explained her vain efforts to ford the river.

"Why were you so determined to cross?" questioned the stranger, in a frankly dubious manner.

"My grandmother is very sick and sent for me to come and help care for her. I was trying to catch the eleven forty. My mother was her daughter, and she passed away some years ago." He seemed to believe her rather doubtful story.

"You would need to go home for a change, would you not?" he asked evidently thinking she must be near her home.

"I have a change right here. Do you know any way to get across?" she eagerly inquired.

"Yes," he said slowly, looking at her closely. "I could hitch my team. They can make it at a point a little farther up stream."

Leone felt ready to cry out with relief. "Oh sir, will you be so kind?" she asked eagerly. "I have no money to pay you, but maybe someone will help you when you need it very much sometime."

"I do not want any pay." He laughed good-naturedly and went out to hitch the horses. In a short time he was back, the team hooked to just the skeleton of the wagon. He wore rubber boots and would stand while the girl, he advised, would sit on a long plank that served as a reach between the front and back wheels. "You are all wet anyway, and you might fall, as it is a pretty rough way to cross."

Leone accepted his advice gratefully, holding aloft the precious lunch and satchel with one hand while with the other she clung to the rough plank. The clumsy vehicle creaked, and to the anxious passenger seemed to be spreading out on the verge of collapse as it settled into the depths of the muddy river. Twice the driver stopped a few moments to permit a floating timber to pass them safely. However, in a surprisingly short time, the ordeal was over, and she was climbing down from her precarious perch, profusely thanking her benefactor. The nasty crossing, which had loomed so mountainous a short half hour before was now accomplished. The stranger smiled, waved a hand, and turned his team; he went back the way he had come.

Leone stood watching his broad back retreating in the distance, hands moving rapidly at times, skillfully guiding the horses. They soon climbed the opposite bank and disappeared from view. She turned dim eyes to the blue heavens, "Thank you, Blessed Lord," she whispered reverently. "I am having quite a lot of trouble, but I know now you are on my side."

She looked around to see what her situation offered in the way of a dressing room. Then she spotted a house, vacant undoubtedly for years with all the windows and doors missing. Cautiously she moved forward to take a good look. Inside she saw plenty of cobwebs and dirt. An inspection of a battered old woodshed did not prove any more encouraging.

With a feeling of revolt in her young body, she went out to the small, partly cleared field on the riverbank and sought refuge amid a group of rain-drenched old stumps. There was even a clean little pool of water from recent rains. Leone went promptly to work on her sorry looking young person. She soon emerged with blood from the scratches washed away and her young body scrubbed clean. She did not look so beat up now. She intentionally combed her hair smoothly in an unattractive manner to add somewhat to her years. She was adorned in an old cashmere skirt sporting a ruffle and a shirtwaist. The uncompromising little sailor's hat that had been rescued so many times during her battle with the brush sat stiffly upon her knot of fair hair.

She looked at her reflection from the little piece of broken mirror she carried and gave a little sigh. "Maybe someday I will be more like a city girl," she thought.

Looking around the improvised dressing room, she hastily gathered the discarded garments and old shoes, wrapped them tight and placed them out of sight beneath some pieces of charred timbers. All signs cleared away, she tried to put the package of lunch in the now almost flat little bag and found the opening too small. Rather than repack the lunch, she decided to wait until she felt hungry.

She started out in the direction of what should be Pine River Junction. A freight train came through sometimes and might stop for water. She must be there in a short time.

Not much later, Leone entered the small store combined with the Post Office that served the community. The lady in charge critically scanned the tired looking girl with the flushed face.

"Yes, there would be a freight through at five o'clock, but it took on no passengers." She pushed forward a chair, "Will you sit and rest? You look exhausted."

73

Leone gratefully accepted and was pleased to see a customer entering at that moment. The girl welcomed the opportunity to somewhat regain her poise. She had no desire to betray that she was trying to escape parental control. Secure in a pocket of the bag was a blank postcard and the stub of a lead pencil. Cautious inspection also assured her the precious two dollars was safe. She then brought forth this meager equipment and preceded to write home saying she had safely met the lady who employed her and was on her way. This she addressed to Marie and then went over to place the card in the mail shoot. Leone returned to the chair at the same time that the postmistress finished with her customer. Just at that moment the customer's large dog darted away with a sack in his mouth. The woman turned an anxious face. "What was in the package?" she asked.

"My lunch," came Leone's dismayed reply.

"Well, you shall have a good hot dinner with me." The warmth of the stranger unnerved the girl a little. "It was not your fault," she offered.

Her hostess glanced at the clock. "It is four now. I'm in the habit of an early dinner. I am busy in the store between five and six o'clock. You be the watch guard, and if someone comes in, call me. In the meantime, I'll hasten the dinner." The familiar sounds and appetizing aroma coming from the bright little kitchen proved most comforting to the weary traveler.

Over the nice little dinner, the girl, in answer to questions, told the story once more of her sick grandmother. Afterwards Leone remembered how easily the lady could read the postcard she had sent.

At five o'clock when the freight pulled in, Leone was waiting on the platform by the train shed. She approached the brakeman. "Are you the conductor?" she asked.

"No, Miss, this type of train does not have a conductor. The person in charge is the engineer."

"Can I see him, or will you ask him, please, if I can ride to Bay City?" She wistfully held the two dollars where he could see them.

The man approached the engineer and talked a few moments. "He tells me he could not sell you a ticket to ride on the caboose. It is crowded with a group of noisy fellows."

But he hastened to assure her, "You can ride on the engine."

Her eyes glowed as she turned to look at the puffing black monster. The engineer raised a hand to beckon her forward. Her lean, brown hands grasped the engine rod, and she climbed easily aboard. Gratefully, she seated herself on the little bench as indicated to her by her newest friend while she turned to wave an adieu to the kindly one she was leaving.

The freight soon started puffing and blowing on its noisy way.

They had passed the little station at Saganing when the brakeman to whom Leone had first spoken seated himself by her side on the little bench. After a few opening remarks, he asked pointedly, "Where are you going, young lady?"

"Bay City," she replied.

"And why Bay City? You are rather young to be out alone."

For the third time she told the story of her grandmother.

Jim Abbot looked at her with sympathy in the skeptical glance of his kindly blue eyes.

"You are running away from home," he said frankly, "from your father."

"Yes, I am. That is right," in an equally frank reply.

"That is better," he laughed. "Now we can get along together. Tell me about what you are leaving. It must be bad."

She explained about the five children, all younger than herself, the cruel stepmother, harsh father, the narrow life, and how she hoped to make a new home for them.

Chapter 18
THE ABBOTS

Brakeman Jim Abbot turned to Leone and replied, "Your ambitions are worthy a Queen. If you can look out for yourself, you will be doing wonderfully. You're coming home with me tonight. My wife, Lizzie, understands problems, and she can help you." He picked up his lantern as daylight was waning. "I will be back after a round," he said cheerfully. He chatted with the engineer a few moments and then went about his duties.

"He is a fine fellow," the engineer remarked as his glance followed the retreating brakeman. He seated himself on the bench beside Leone.

"Is he a married man?" Leone tried to make the inquiry sound casual.

"Oh, yes. He has a lovely wife and two fine sons. One is married."

"One is married?" the girl's reply did not conceal her surprise and doubt. "He is very young to have a son who is married."

"Jim was forty-four last birthday. His son is past twenty-one. That is plenty old enough to be married a lot of people think."

Leone lapsed into a meditative silence. She had learned one thing from her stepmother and her friends and that was to first distrust people. When Jim Abbot returned, Leone looked at him earnestly, trying to fathom in her own way just how far he might be trusted. Most of the men she had known wore a full beard like her father. She knew her father could look much younger shaved. She decided to herself that she would accompany this strange man, but stay on the alert.

An accommodation freight serving small towns in the early days of railroading was not very fast. The engine snorted and puffed. The fireman piled more coal on the fire, keeping it with a ruddy glow. The trainman then pronounced to the earnest, bright-eyed girl sitting in a smoky corner on the crew bench that the long trip was over.

Jim had refused to take her money for the railway fare. She still possessed the two dollars, but she knew it could not last long unless she found work at once.

A great thankfulness filled her heart in response to the brakeman's fatherly request, "Come on, kid." With the agility of a boy, Leone dropped to the ground and instantly felt the coolness of the still night air after being in the hot steaming engine.

"You will need a coat, " remarked the engineer noting she had none. "All we can furnish is one of these little denim jackets. Not much warmth in them," he added as he took the jacket and held it for Leone to slip into. "It will act as a windbreaker," he said, as he led the way through the switching yards to a pile of lumber.

The engineer gave Leone a lantern and some matches. He asked her, "Can you climb up there to wait for us to get through switching? You will be safer up there." Leone was sitting on top of the lumber when he ceased speaking. Jim raised his head and smiled. "Just sit still there," and he added, "don't light your lantern unless something happens. Then light up and swing it, and I will come at your signal.

76

It will be a long wait." Leone nodded her understanding, and the man hurried away to his work.

It did indeed prove to be a long wait as the girl shivered in the cold night. She was grateful for the meager folds of the jacket that she wrapped tightly about her. Soon after his departure, she could hear the big freight cars strike the couplings and see the flashing lanterns as the crew gave the necessary signals. Occasionally she would hear the sound of a man's voice and the rumble of the engine. She remained alert and watchful until she heard Jim Abbot's footfall returning.

"Are you up there, kid?" he called.

The girl grinned in his lantern glow as she looked from the top of the great pile of lumber. "Shall I come down?" she answered.

"Sure, come on down," was the response.

Leone swung herself easily to the ground. Taking her lantern, Jim lighted it and then returned it to her hand. "Walk behind me," he advised. "You will find the path narrow and dark."

Jim Abbot proceeded ahead chuckling. He had thoughts to himself about how surprised his wife would be. We have two sons of our own and an adopted son. I have often told her I would bring home a girl, and now here I am doing it at last.

Presently he said, "Do you see the cottage with the open door and the light shining across the lawn?"

"Yes, I see it," Leone responded.

"That is my home," he informed her proudly. "You will see Lizzie in the doorway very soon. But she will be puzzled by the two lanterns."

As they approached the house, a lovely, smiling woman appeared and greeted him warmly with, "Jim, who have you here?"

Jim said, "I finally brought home that girl I promised. She is my girl. You have all them boys."

Lizzie Abbot came and put a warm, comforting arm around Leone. "You made a good selection," she laughed back at him, as she led the unexpected guest to the warm fire. "She is half frozen. Where did you find her anyway?" and she was looking at her new charge as though expecting a reply.

"Pine River Junction. I was hoboing," the girl admitted smiling.

"And did you ride the freight that far? No wonder you are so near perished."

Jim quipped cheerfully, "Nothing some of your good cooking cannot cure. Give her a nice supper and some sleep and she will be like new in the morning."

A little later between bites of the steaming hot dinner his wife had placed before them to enjoy, Jim said, "I want you to know something, Lizzie dear. My girl is not a real hobo. Wait until you hear all about her tomorrow. You will agree with me, she is a queen incognito!"

His wife smiled indulgently. "She is a pretty good hobo, traveling such a distance in one day. That is probably a record."

Trying to assume a wise look, Jim stated, "Oh that just increases her prestige and makes her Queen of the Hobos also."

Lizzie observed, "The poor child is going to establish another record very soon now. I see she has finished her dinner and she is going to show us how fast she can retire and rest."

The weary traveler gratefully received this news. In record time she had donned a beautiful white gown that was furnished her and said an earnest prayer of thanksgiving. She was sliding her tired body between the dainty sheets of the neat little guest room bed when her hostess apologetically opened the door.

"Can we come in?" she asked gently. She motioned to her husband who came and stood on the threshold while she approached the bed. "Jim thought you might be lonesome and we should come and say goodnight."

The girl's warm, slim hands reached out impulsively. The older woman bowed her head and tender arms were clasped around her neck drawing her close to catch Leone's whisper, "Isn't he the lovely man?" lifting humorous eyes toward Mr. Abbot as he stood silhouetted in the doorway.

"I guess perhaps he is a lovely man," she responded tenderly as she smiled an affectionate reminiscent smile in agreement. There was a glisten of unshed tears as she tucked in blankets to guard against the cool night. "We want you to rest well and sleep as late as you wish in the morning."

Leone awoke when the bright sunlight of the new day flooded the dainty little room. It took a moment for the happenings of the preceding one to clarify in her thoughts. She was half expecting the disturbing sound of her father's heavy boots and his harsh, stern voice to break the delightful feelings of rest and security that pervaded here. She closed her eyes in silent thanksgiving to a kindly

78

Providence that directed her to this haven and then permitted herself a few moments of restful calm.

Leone dressed quickly, eager to greet the new friends and go about the task of starting her life's work. Baby Helen's plaintiff little words came to mind, "You can go; only don't be long." These words would come back frequently to remind Leone of her promise.

Lizzie Abbot greeted her new charge warmly and seated her at breakfast with the rest of the family. Jim Abbot had already gone on his run for the day. But there seated at the table with her hostess, she met the two sons who ate hastily and then hurried away. After breakfast, Lizzie listened to the girl narrate in her own simple way a story that revealed not only the complications involving her own future, but also the lives of the little sisters. Lizzie Abbot was all sympathy and understanding. "What an incongruous man your father must be. I did not expect to entirely approve of the drastic step you had taken. It seemed ill advised. However, I see now that there was no other choice. You were wonderful to get away as well as you did with all the difficulties you encountered."

Then Lizzie concluded, "When each one of your sisters becomes old enough, they too can follow your example."

"I am not going to wait that long," Leone replied staunchly. "I'm going to make a home for them and have them all away from there in three years."

Lizzie looked at the young child in amazement. "Are you under the impression that you could accomplish this by yourself?"

Leone emphatically answered, "Hope so. I'm sure going to make a good try at it."

With concern Lizzie said, "While it is a wonderful ambition you have to wish to make a home for such a large family, I think it is impossible. You are only about a year older than my young son. I shudder to think what a child like him could accomplish for himself a year from now. I do not wish to crush your hopes and smother your ambition, but I think it best that you keep your plans temperate. You do not want the bottom to slide out of your life when you begin to realize what a mammoth task you have undertaken with your youth and experience."

Lizzie Abbot's charming, motherly face wore a look of earnest compassion. Her blue eyes gazed intently upon Leone's eager, young countenance as she sat in respectful silence listening to every word spoken by this extraordinary new friend.

The older woman paused a moment as no reply came. She continued, "Do not misunderstand me, my dear. You're like a beginner learning to walk a tight rope. You are accustomed to the ground, something firm and strong beneath your feet. It is something you understand and could successfully cope with, gain your living from and help others. It is now gone, and you are left suspended. You must take the right step now," she affirmed as she put out a hand to Leone, who moved to sit on a low hassock by her side. The motherly hand found a resting place on the girl's silky hair. "You do understand me?" she pleaded, "Do you not?"

Leone answered, "Yes, I understand. I'm overwhelmed by your kindness and interest in my future. I realize only too well how helpless I am."

Mrs. Abbot offered, "Then that is all that is necessary. You will permit me to guide you a little, and you will learn some useful occupation. It is difficult to say what it will be. The only thing I can see from your past experience that could be useful to you is practical nursing. You cared for your mother and the other children. But a place at this kind of work may be hard to find for one so young."

Leone said, "In the meantime I will take any kind of honest work I can get and then be on the watch for a nursing job."

Her benefactor smiled indulgently, "You are a brave girl and surely deserve success. We will go now and see what we can purchase suitable to work in with your two dollars."

Leone hastened to the little room that had been assigned to her. There she paused a moment in her simple preparations for the errand. Leone's dewy eyes moved to a window and gleamed as they rested on two butterflies playing in the golden sunbeams of the warm fall day. The neat little garden with its border of perennials with occasional blooms was somewhat lost upon the girl. Her thoughts were far away with that little group of neglected children nearest and dearest to her heart. Slowly her fingers clinched until the pink nails pressed tightly against the palms. Unconsciously her hands came up to press against each temple in a futile gesture. The tears overflowed, but she bravely blinked them away. "Mrs. Abbot is a grand person," she whispered in prayer. "She knows so much more about life than I do. I cannot help but see that she is right. I will not say anything more about it, she communed, but my resolution stands. I will continue to hope and pray that I can fulfill my promise. It seems impossible, I admit, but I will cling to my illusions. It will strengthen my purpose."

Leone was soothed by this quiet outburst of temperament. It was then she recalled her father's despicable name for her, Stubborn Sal. "And I shall have need of all my stubbornness," she smiled to herself.

As Leone rejoined her, Lizzie Abbot experienced a little thrill of motherly tenderness for this sweet, confident, young, unspoiled child of nature. Together she and the girl went out to stroll leisurely the inviting streets of the little city.

Finding the shops with their attractive displays of merchandise was an interesting experience for Leone, who exclaimed enthusiastic approval of all she saw. They were successful in selecting the plain, little dress Leone needed. Then they called to a newsboy and bought a paper. The few advertisements in the help-wanted column took but a moment to glance through. There was but one that would interest Leone. A young woman was needed for a few days to clean and the address was not too far away.

Lizzie strolled along with her charge and waited at the gate while the girl went in for the interview. Leone reappeared in a few moments, flushed with pleasure in having secured the job. The lady was a Mrs. Lidar.

Leone's companion recognized the name. "Don't be too enthusiastic, dear. This woman has the reputation of being a hard boss."

The girl smiled slowly, "I'm accustomed to a hard boss, and it is only a few days of work."

"I don't like to see you get into difficult circumstances the first thing. Of course, you can quit anytime. Our home is open to welcome you. We would like to have you stay and go on to further studies."

Leone looked at her and said, "I am grateful for the fullness of your great big heart, you and your most kind husband." Leone felt down deep that a watchful Providence had controlled her destiny.

Chapter 19

BAD WORK EXPERIENCE

The following morning found Leone at work under Mrs. Lidar's ever-watchful eye. The woman seemed sympathetic but anxious to get her work done.

The inexperienced girl saw nothing crafty about this and went all out, eager to please. In this first opportunity of her new life she answered frankly the questions as to where she had come from and who she was. The circumstance of her leaving home was soon well known to Mrs. Lidar.

"The police would be looking for you right now to return you to your father," explained the woman. This startling circumstance had not occurred to Leone, but she admitted it was well within the range of possibilities.

Following up on the information advantage, Mrs. Lidar advised that the windows be washed on the outside in the forenoon as most of the patrolmen came on duty at noon, thus minimizing the danger of being seen by them. The woman used other little suggestions of this character during the day, ostensibly to be helpful, but in reality to create a nervous tension. She succeeded fairly well. While she seemed cheerful and showed apparent kindness, she continued to pile on the work and urged its completion. When Leone was finally permitted to seek the seclusion of the drab little room that would be hers for the brief duration of her stay, her strong, young body ached in every limb. Wearily she sank on the hard little bed, scarcely aware of its ungainly features.

The following days passed in the same manner. Accustomed to hard work, she was forced to admit that this was an endurance test of no easy order. She was to have been retained only three or four days, but many unexpected tasks were easily found to keep the girl engaged a week.

In the meantime a little incident occurred to add somewhat to Leone's alarm. One evening she accompanied Mrs. Lidar as a result of her persuasion to a political meeting. The two arrived early and were seated well up front. The huge, drafty hall where the meeting was held proved to be a gloomy place. It was lighted only by a few open gas jets, served by lead pipe at intervals reaching across the large barn-like structure. When the seats were filled, the crowd became restless waiting for some great one to appear and speak.

About then it became apparent that a group of boys began manifesting a desire for activity. They climbed one of the rough columns that helped support the huge building and to which the lead gas pipes were attached. Upon reaching the pipe, some of the venturesome lads climbed out on the soft metal pipes that promptly began to sag to an alarming degree. The sputtering gas jets moved down closer to the heads of an excited audience. One little fellow dropped to a grip with his hands on the pipe swinging his body. After several vain efforts he failed to regain his position on the pipeline. To the consternation of the crowd, as well as his own, the mischievous lad found he had reached his limit. Unless someone would come to his assistance soon, he would have to continue his drop to the hard floor. In the interval, some thoughtful citizen had telephoned the fire department and rushed in a ladder. Upon mounting to the height of the ladder, it was found to be too short to take him down. However, a tall man did grasp his feet, thus easing the weight of his hands until the fire department arrived and completed the rescue.

During this interval the crowd grew very restless, with many of them leaving their seats. The foremost among the latter was Mrs. Lidar. She looked hastily about until she spied a seat that looked like it could be depended upon to stand heavy duty. Calling on Leone's assistance, she succeeded in mounting her short, but heavy bulk to a standing position on this seat, and from that point, she set up a torrent of outcries. Chief among this volley was the repeated name of some police officer, Hawkins, which she happened to know. Leone tried vainly to reassure and soothe the frightened woman, but she remained screaming on her improvised pedestal, until the arrival of police and firemen. This all proved to be a confused ordeal to the country-bred girl. She was relieved when they were again seated.

A few moments later a nice appearing young woman left her seat and came over to Leone. "I think we have met before. You are Leone Neely of AuGres." Here was Myrtle David, divorced wife of Captain David's son, William! She was looking to Leone to be recognized in turn.

Mrs. Lidar gave the girl no opportunity to recover from her surprise. She looked balefully at the young woman and said, "You're mistaken. This girl has lived in Bay City all her life. She's a cousin of mine."

Myrtle David looked unconvinced. "I was quite sure," she began.

Mrs. Lidar interrupted rudely, "You don't need to be. Mistaken identity. That's all."

At that moment there was a stir on the platform, and Myrtle went back to her seat. Leone sat there too embarrassed for words. She would have enjoyed a brief chat with the young woman whom she had lived neighbor to for many months and admired very much as well. The lie as to her own identity so hastily concocted by the dictatorial woman would not deceive Myrtle in the least. It would be much better to be truthful. Leone concluded to herself with this incident that she should not have made a confidant of Mrs. Lidar.

Leone tried to dismiss the incident from her troubled thoughts and turn attention to the speaker. When the meeting was over and they were finding their way to her home along the dimly lighted streets, Mrs. Lidar amused herself by recounting what she called the clever manner in which she had squelched the intruder, thus doing the girl a favor.

Leone's hope that she might be through the next day proved in vain. Mrs. Lidar decided that the woodshed was next in line. The girl brushed and scraped on and washed windows until it seemed the day would never end. The broken rest of the previous night added its own weight against her. It was a welcome moment when the week was over and she was told she might go. Hastily, and almost gleefully, Leone made the necessary preparations for her departure. She sat by the door awaiting Mrs. Lidar to pay her the well-earned wages. Mrs. Lidar was not long in coming.

Looking at the girl coldly, she retorted, "I thought you had left."

"I am prepared to go," Leone answered cheerfully. "I am just waiting for my money."

"Your money! You're not going to get any money."

"Not going to get any money?" as the girl's face blanched pale. "Why, Madam, you agreed to pay me one dollar per day."

"That was before I learned you were wanted by the police. And if you attempt to collect it, I will write to your father myself and pay your expenses back with the money and an escort to see that you get there."

Leone knew the hard woman by this time, only too well. She knew the threats would be made good. Arising without further word, she departed.

84

Strolling slowly on the quiet street, she noted that it depicted the peaceful family life of the little city. It actually had a soothing effect on her aching muscles and throbbing nerves.

Leone reviewed the past week, and realized that her own trusting of others had brought about most of the disaster. If she had not confided in her employer, had not worked so hard, and been so eager to make good, the work engagement would have terminated in three or four days and Mrs. Lidar would have been obliged to pay.

Resorting to her faith, Leone resolved to profit by this mistake. She was thankful she had somewhere to go penniless. Lizzie Abbot hurried down the walk and put a friendly arm about her girl. "My dear, you look all beat out." She exclaimed, "They worked you too hard! Tell me all about it."

Leone sobbed out the whole miserable story.

Lizzie was angry at the cold, heartless creature. She couldn't believe that a woman could be guilty of such conduct. While this was balm to the wounds Leone had suffered, she continued to explain the mistakes she had made to place herself in the power of such an unscrupulous creature.

Amused by such earnestness in one so young and pleased too, Lizzie gave her an encouraging pat, "You are right. It was a blunder that will be valuable to you, if you keep it in mind, and I think you will."

Leone smiled through her tears, "I think I will also," she agreed.

Lizzie took her to the dear little room where a gentle breeze disturbed the snowy curtains. A small bouquet of late-blooming flowers greeted them from the dressing table. Leone exclaimed, "How charming." Her gloomy feeling was rapidly departing in this homelike atmosphere. She turned a cheerful face to her generous hostess.

"There, that is better," Lizzie proclaimed. "Jim will be home early tonight. He will be furious when he hears the shameful way you were treated. I would not want him to see you looking dejected or he would go over there and take somebody apart."

The generous and kindly man was indeed furious when he learned what had taken place. He would go himself to the woman's husband at his place of business and see that the promised wages were paid. But Leone pleaded with him not to do it. She told him of the cold, calculating woman and her own foolish confidence, thus placing herself in the power of such treachery.

"Your innocence does not give her the privilege of keeping your money," was Mr. Abbot's declaration.

Leone nodded, but shared again the lesson she had learned from the misfortune.

Chapter 20
CAPTAIN GILBERT'S WIFE

Leone's dear AuGres neighbor, Katherine, saw the Bay City postmark on Leone's first letters. The postmark made her smile a smug little smile.

When Robert and the girls stopped by to check the mail, Katherine said, "I have a letter from Malcolm's cousin in Bay City, she must have found a postage stamp. She is that stingy." Katherine had a peculiar little way of her own for her jokes. She used a highly keyed whisper knowing sharp ears were alert in the back seat of the high spring wagon, and the coded message would bring swift little feet flying happily at the first available opportunity, eager to hear news of their beloved Leone.

The cows were slow in coming home that evening as Marie accompanied Bill, and they gleefully took time out for the hasty trip through the Half Mile Woods to secure the precious letter. An answer to Leone so she would not have to wait so long had already been written and was left with their trusty neighbor friend.

Knowing ahead of time how difficult communication would be, the girls had agreed that they would write but once a month. After reading the letter frequently enough to practically commit the missive to memory, the conspirators carefully burned it. When the letter bearing the AuGres postmark arrived at the home of the Abbots, Lizzie promptly placed it in Leone's hands. The girl tore it open with grateful interest. Marie had written at length of their father's dramatic behavior upon learning Leone was gone. He had arrived home late from Maple Ridge the day Leone left. He was tired and hungry. Marie and Bill appeared, lantern in hand. Their father angrily demanded that Leone come out. Marie had replied, "It's only Bill and I; Leone is not here."

"Where is she?" he demanded.

Marie hesitated. Bill chimed in, "She left here at seven o'clock this morning. She is gone. Flew the coop. She will not be back." Robert Neely stood dumbfounded for a long moment.

"Where did she go?" he asked harshly.

Bill continued to unhitch the team. He answered cheerfully, "She didn't say."

His father's face grew dark with passion. He turned to Marie, "Do you mean to say she has run away from home to work among strangers? Speak up child."

"Yes sir, that is the circumstance."

Marie went on, "Right then the lid seemed to blow off of everything. He was like a tragedy staging a show. MacBeth himself would have done no more, although it is safe to say he might have done better. He did manage to convey to us that you were no longer a child of his. You must never darken his door again. He may have succeeded in fooling himself, but he did not fool us. This will not change our attitude in the least. We will still know nothing and say less."

Henrietta had written a part of the letter, adding everything she could recall about Baby Helen and Laura. Bill was a good boy and helping well with the work. Her favorite horse Mack was mentioned. Fleet and Fly and other animal pets also came into their writing for a little share of attention.

After the home story, the thoughtful girls covered relatives, neighbors and friends, to Leone's delight. She was not unaware of the under current of secrecy or the time it would take for such a long letter. She knew they had probably worked in the garden on a favorable choice of land well away from the farmhouse. Pencils and paper would have been carefully hidden in the willows that grew rank by the old drainage ditch, where they would be conveniently at hand when opportunity offered. There seated on the warm stand, under pretense of weeding with the rays of a hot sun bearing down on them, one would write while the other worked and watched. Their sister's whereabouts must remain a secret on which their hope to make a better life depended. The only reference to this was, "We are working in the garden."

To Leone this revealed the entire story. The rebellion in her heart and her resolution both grew stronger. Leone was not deeply impressed by her father's dramatic outburst, concluding he had been motivated more by his own selfish interest rather than anxiety for her welfare. She did regret his display of unbridled passion. She knew so well what an unpleasant experience this could be for members of the family. She dismissed as trivial his denunciation of herself, knowing this would last just as long as he deemed it suited his convenience. She knew if she returned successful, he would be at the head of the line to greet her with open arms.

Lizzie Abbot perused the letter with deep interest as Leone handed each page to her. She could visualize this large and interesting family more clearly after reading it. There crept into her generous heart a warm impulse to aid and encourage Leone. If it is within the range of possibility for such an inexperienced child to assist them, she is definitely the one to accomplish this. Leone was quick to learn, strong, and has the fortitude, no matter what the outcome. Her life will be spent in an attempt to make them a better life. She thought, "Yes, I will help her plan."

In the discussion that followed, it was decided the neighboring city of Saginaw would in all probability afford a better opportunity to secure employment as a practical nurse. Saginaw had a larger population than Bay City. The inhabitants also represented more wealth, and a short railway carrying commuters linked the two cities. Lizzie was frank in admitting it was with regret she proposed this change. She asked Leone to continue to make her home with them. Having been denied a daughter of her own, she was reluctant to see this charming girl who had come to them so strangely go out of their life. She added, "I am sure Jim will not approve of your going to Saginaw." Leone looked at her eyes glistening wet and went to her side in silence.

The following morning was one to stir the pulse of the horticulturist. There had been a brisk downpour of rain during the hours of darkness and then a few light showers in the early morning. Then a beautiful sapphire sky with a bright warm sun shone forth. Leone stepped out into the golden rays. Little earthy smells greeted her. The jaded fall flowers had put on a new radiance, holding their heads proudly. The girl's practical eye for gardening swept the scene, breathing its fragrance. A wave of nostalgia crept over her. She went to the little shed, took out the garden tools and was soon absorbed in trimming back the perennials for the winter just ahead. She had heard Jim Abbot say he must get this done very soon. His daylight hours at home were almost nonexistent, except Sunday when he needed rest and relaxation. She worked on contentedly for some hours. When she heard Lizzie's voice calling her, she hastily answered.

Looking critically at the girl's soiled hands, she asked pointedly, "Now, how am I going to make a lady of you? Look at your pretty little hands."

For a brief moment Leone was aghast. Had she done something wrong? Then noting a twinkle in her friend's eyes, which belied the words, she breathed freely again.

Lizzie pushed her way through the screen door and came out to see what Leone had been doing. "Child, you have done wonderful. Jim will bless you for this. I never was a gardener." She continued, "I don't like the feel of the earth on my fingers."

Leone looked down at her grubby hands. "I do not mind. There is something soulful about going down into the earth. I feel sometimes that I would not have quite lived without the contact I have had with Mother Earth. When you see the pale, tiny embryo shoots that you have planted take on a little new life each day, you know there is something in nature that is closely akin to us. They are so grateful for moisture or a stirring of the soil around them."

"When you are interested, it makes the work easier," Lizzie laughed. "And you are the little sentimentalist. You are right, too. But I still do not like the grit on my hands. Come on in and rest while I fix a lunch."

"I will join you in a moment," Leone answered, turning back to her interrupted task. She also resumed her interest and did not think to go in until she heard a call to lunch.

When the Abbots' son Noel came home from school, he brought out the lawn mower. It was soon humming noisily as his sturdy young arms pushed it briskly about. Leone was just finishing her end of the task. Between them they raked and swept off every loose blade of grass. They had a merry time about it, too. Later, Noel confided to his mother, "I have never felt any regret that I did not have a sister. The fellows who have them do not seem so happy about it. I changed my mind today. A sister like Leone would be all right. We had a lot of fun this afternoon," he chuckled. "I even called her 'Old Socks' and she didn't get peeved!"

Lizzie smoothed back the fair hair, kissed his forehead and sighed a little. Smiling, she answered gently, "I understand dear. That is the way life is."

Jim noted the change by the light of his lantern as he arrived home that evening. He went about the attractive little grounds, inspecting everything. Then he took both young people in his arms at one time and told them they made him happy. He added, "I did not think you knew how to fix the garden for winter."

Noel answered, "Dad, you forget. 'Old Socks' is a product of the farm."

Jim did not fancy the "Old Socks" part of his comment, but thought it wise to let this pass. The young folks were getting along. He brought them each a small box of fancy bonbons the following evening, much to their delight. Then he announced, "Tomorrow I will be home early. We will all go down to the coach and see the show."

This was greeted with smiles of approval. Some person in town with enterprise and forethought had refurbished a discarded railroad coach in such a way that it provided a makeshift theater. It was here that the great motion picture industry in its beginning stages was making an initial bid for popularity. Most cities and towns could boast such an innovation.

Leone went to Saginaw the following Monday. Clara Abbot, daughter-in-law of the Abbots, who had lived in that city for most of her young life and could place the girl with friends, accompanied her.

To Lizzie and Leone there was an air of finality prevailing about the move that could not be shaken off, although both tried vainly to ignore it. Jim did not approve. While admitting to himself the young girl might have better prospects in Saginaw, he could not be happy about it. She was still a child with much to learn of the cold blasts in a wintry world. Clara went directly to the home of a woman who made a hobby of taking a friendly interest in young people. They found the esteemed lady at home alone. Her husband, Captain Gilbert, sailed the Great Lakes in command of a ship. She welcomed the charming little country girl as a pleasant diversion for some monotonous hours just ahead. Having accomplished all that could be expected of her, Clara promptly took her leave.

Leone found herself welcomed in the most elaborate home she had ever seen. The appointments reflected artistic selection coupled with good housekeeping rather than a heavy outlay of cash, with the result nonetheless pleasing. When shown to the exclusive guest rooms, she experienced a slight qualm about disturbing its quiet perfection.

Her hostess smilingly reassured her, "The room will take on warmth and beauty with a lovely girl making it useful. Homes, my dear, are built to be lived in, to contribute to our comfort and pleasure, not purposely to be looked at."

"But this one is so grand," ventured the awe-inspired Leone.

"I have put in a lot of time on this house, and I have never overlooked the fact that this is our home where we wish to be comfortable. Everything you see here is practical. You are embarking upon a new life, one where you will from force of circumstance find yourself frequently among strangers. And what to you will be new surroundings, you will from force of necessity have to cast aside natural modesty, which is a very attractive feature for a young girl. You will find yourself too often left out, unless you push forward and take what is yours. You do not need to be bold. There is a happy medium, but you will find you cannot be retiring. Make yourself at home. We will visit again later," she added hastily, hurrying away in response to a soft tone chiming bell.

Leone smiled. Even the sound of a doorbell blended harmoniously. This was indeed art. A doorbell was an unheard of thing in the old farmhouse, and secretly she was not impressed with the shrill, demanding, raucous notes in the peal of the average bell. Left alone, she surveyed the room in all its beauty, mentally comparing Lizzie Abbot's white Swiss curtains, daintily crisp in the little room that had been hers. With the beautiful silken hangings of this elegant guest chamber, Leone concluded she preferred the former. Standing by the great bed, she let one foot glide aimlessly over the carpet's soft pile. She sighed softly, alas for the peace and security of that little room and the good people who made such a sanctuary possible. Already her thoughts reverted to them in a past tense as the girl realized she must go on alone. Investigation in Saginaw had disclosed a meager wage was earned by the average sales lady or factory worker in the very early 1900s in our country's history. Many other avenues had been considered and discarded as hopeless. The search must go on; she must find employment that would pay. Often the thought came, "If I only were a man."

Mrs. Gilbert was abrupt in her approach. "No need for shilly shallying," she said in a cheerful way. "I am anxious to impart any useful information I may have, and I believe you are eager to try and make use of it. Why dally around?"

Leone liked this. The two women lingered long over a substantial lunch: Leone, the younger one so old for her years, and Mrs. Gilbert, the older woman so young for the years that had passed her by so lightly. Both were interested in the same topics. It did not require so much to bridge the distance between them.

"Tell me first," began Mrs. Gilbert, "how you induced your parents to consent to this experiment you have undertaken when you ought to be in school?"

Leone explained briefly.

"You are courageous to say the least. Did you have much money?"

The girl smiled, "a very small amount." She told this new friend the little history of the money.

"You poor child. After you discovered you could not get any more than the railway fare from your friends, it is startling that you could persist with the plans. Your mind must have been filled with fear."

"On the contrary. I did not give it a thought. I knew from the first that all I could borrow would be the railway fare. The friends I could get it from had no money. I did not try to get more. I trusted the Blessed Lord. If I had any fear, I would not have faith. But I was not certain He approved until he aided me to ford the river."

The woman inquired, "And why not approve?"

He also says to, "Honor your father."

"Supposing you had not met the Abbots? You would have probably gone to the police, and they would have promptly returned you to your father."

"I would know better than to go to the police, and I also knew that the occasion would not arise. My faith in He who clothed the lilies was too deep for that."

"And you think your faith brought you through the hazardous crossing of the river?"

"Unquestionably, my faith directed me to a point where such a crossing was to be found as well as necessary assistance."

"And supposing you had fallen among the enemy?"

"He has not promised that we will not meet one of them. I try to be on the alert." In smiling embarrassment she added, "I'm equipped with good pedal extremities."

92

Mrs. Gilbert looked wonderingly at the girl. "Does your faith encourage you to hope you can return triumphantly to your sisters in three years?"

"Even after encountering some of the difficulties, this will depend largely upon my own ability."

"Where did you learn such faith?"

"My mother taught me. She charged me to carry her message on to the younger members of the family. This faith not only gives me hope; it gives me promise. The work is here. I will find it, and then it will be my turn to prove my faith in myself."

The good-hearted woman replied, "Few persons hearing your story could fail to sympathize."

"And very few persons will hear it." Leone said firmly. She then explained the experience she had been through with Mrs. Lidar.

"I believe you are right, my dear. You will accomplish more on merit than you will on sympathy. That is to say, it will be a firmer foundation. Knowledge of your background might influence an employer in such a way that your real worth would become obscure. As for the education, when other young people are out fooling around town searching for amusement, you will be burning the midnight oil, striving to make up for some of the things you missed. You are familiar with many worthwhile things that the average schoolgirl knows very little about. You are strong and a good thinker. You will make up the rest." Continuing, she said, "You have a nice complexion and very lovely hair. I will help you this afternoon. We will try to arrange it in a more becoming style and possibly make you appear older."

That evening Leone had a new coiffure. Her meager wardrobe had been diligently gone over and necessary adjustments made.

The Saginaw afternoon paper carried an advertisement offering a situation for a practical nurse, with no objections to travel. Leone had been the successful applicant and would take this place in the morning. When finally nestled in the luxurious bed that night, she felt it had indeed been a day long to be remembered. Stretching out her bare feet on the cool sheets, she grinned to herself in the darkness.

Leone thought, "I must endeavor to feel at home because I will be in a different bed tomorrow night, just like Mrs. Gilbert said. I must learn new ways." She felt strangely grown up as she tried to fix all that had transpired in a sleepy head. Yawning, she was soon in dreamland.

Chapter 21
TRAVELS WITH MRS. JACOBUS

Mrs. Jacobus, Leone's new employer, proved to be a very charming woman. She was young and beautiful, frail, but making a valiant effort toward recovery. There was a lovely wee daughter still in her first year that Leone found irresistible. Saginaw had been the home city of Mrs. Jacobus before her marriage. They were visiting at present the homes of numerous relatives. One of these sojourns took them to the capitol city of Lansing for ten days. After several weeks spent in this manner, Mrs. Jacobus had begun to feel an urge to travel. She wished to know if Leone would like to first visit her sister Margaret in Gladwin before leaving. The thoughtful employer said it could be arranged. This rather unexpected turn of events surprised Leone. However, as she thought what an unexpected pleasure it would be to visit her sister at her home, she quickly answered that she would gladly accept the generous offer.

In the course of a few days, arrangements were complete to leave her duties in competent hands. That evening found Leone on a train bound for Gladwin. She had written Margaret but could not expect too much of the letter. Mail did not go flying about the country in these times. Thus, when Leone arrived at her destination, there was no one to meet the traveler. Margaret and her husband lived four miles out in the country. Picking her way carefully on the darkened street, she soon located a livery stable. On inquiry there was a team but no driver on duty at the time. Leone was advised to wait at the hotel until a driver could be located and told that it might require some time finding one.

"A passenger at night must be an event," thought Leone as she listened to the ominous tone of voice used by the man in charge.

"The safest thing for you to do, young lady, would be to put up at the hotel tonight and drive out in the daytime."

The night was cold with a threat of storm. Leone found this refreshing. She hastened to assure him she had very little time and did not care to spend any of it in a hotel. She urged him to try earnestly to find a driver. This proved to be more successful than she had hoped. She had waited at the hotel but a half hour when a smart-looking team drove up. They were well-matched, slender, dappled-gray high steppers hitched to an open carriage. Leone was a true horsewoman. Her heart beat a little faster as she looked at the natural arched necks that held their proud heads high. The glossy coats of the horses were shining like satin in the dim light. She climbed to a seat beside the driver. Restraining an impulse to reach and take the reins, she settled down to enjoy the short ride. The spirited creatures did not require a word to start. A slight release on the reins and they were off in no uncertain manner. As Leone and the driver left, the livery stable man again reiterated his advice.

By way of starting small talk, Leone remarked, "He should take this team out himself and leave you at the stable. When he returns, he would know how it should be done."

The driver laughed derisively, "He was afraid of them."

His passenger considered this for a long moment. "Afraid of these beauties?" she asked doubtfully.

"These beauties are killers," he replied.

"Have they ever actually killed anyone?"

"Sure did, only two weeks ago. Killed the driver."

"Are they vicious or just runaways?" she inquired further.

"That's right. Just runaways. Too much life. That's why we are using this surrey. He would have hitched to the hack for a young lady from the city. But you may have to jump for your life."

What unfortunate news! The late rains of fall had left plenty of mud about, and an impromptu landing in a mud hole in her new fall coat had no appeal for Leone. But she also felt confident nothing like that was going to occur. The reins were long and fastened together at the end. She searched about in the darkness by means of her foot until she located the extra length and gratefully noted that it was secure. If the man made good his threat and jumped, the reins would not be hard to find. She had no desire to be at the mercy of the horses flying hoofs.

As they continued, the driver had the team make a turn. Leone peered into the roadside shadows and then retorted, "We should not have made that turn," she said hastily. "This is not the right road."

"Oh, yes, it is. I know your brother-in-law real well. I saw him in the past week. He was standing in the doorway of a house on this road."

"Standing in a doorway would not necessarily indicate he was at home. He could stand in a neighbor's doorway. They were not living in this vicinity. If they moved, I think they would have written me."

"He was at home all right. He had no hat on his head."

Leone smiled in the darkness and made no reply. There was no point in continuing an argument with such an egotistical chap. The surrey was bouncing along over a mud surface road with many ruts and getting worse with every revolution of the wheels.

"You better slow up that team," advised the girl. "There is a nasty creek with a one-way bridge somewhere pretty close."

"I think, by Jove, you're right. It is a poor excuse of a bridge. It goes out every year with the high water, and I recall hearing someone say it is due to be out now."

Again, Leone grinned under cover of the darkness. He had no quarrel this time with unsolicited advice as he promptly starting erratic jerking and pulling on the reins over the high-strung horses. However, instead of slowing their speed, the driver's actions served as a stimulus. The team dropped their heads suddenly in a united effort, took the bits in their powerful teeth, and also took command of the situation. At that moment they also arrived at the creek, and the horses plunged into the water! The makeshift bridge was gone, and so was the driver. At the first splash he had shouted, "Jump for your life." He had also lost no time acting on his own advice.

The water was not up to the floor of the surrey. Leone could see the outline of the team through the gloom. The water did not appear to be very deep. It seemed to reach about to the hub, but it was cold in the frosty night as it swirled about the legs of the surprised horses. They had pranced a little and succeeded in swinging out of the traces and stood facing each other. "Now, how did they accomplish that?" she silently asked herself. "Only half hooked up no doubt," she concluded cheerfully taking the reins.

By this time the fellow who jumped had picked himself up from the creek's muddy bank and was shouting orders on how to reach safety.

The girl turned to him and replied quietly, "Please do not shout. I can hear your natural voice easily. I have no intentions of jumping or leaving this team and equipment unless forced to do so. They are behaving all right. Shouting may further alarm them. I am accustomed to handling horses. Just wait a little, and I will be back and pick you up."

"You don't know what you're up against. Young woman, you will be killed."

Tightening the reins, she spoke gently to the horses. After a little of this persuasion, they stepped cautiously into their places. A pale moon peeped out from behind a cloudbank just at this opportune moment. The moon cast a faint light on the weird scene, but enough to enable the girl to direct the team up the roadbed. Little difficulty was encountered hauling the surrey up on the bank. With a thrill of pleasure, Leone drew the reins in a firm grip over the two beauties. She was pleased to see them tossing their proud heads, champing the bit, displaying a happy indifference to the elements.

Driving along, she turned in at the first gate that appeared. There with the team headed against the gate she stepped down and examined the harness as best she could. In the half-light, unhooking one trace she made plenty of room between them to work. "Even your pretty hair must not get on my new coat," she told them as she hooked up the trace straps inside. "Now we will go find that funny man."

Turning back the horses, they took the ford casually, as did the young girl, without further incident. Leone stopped when across the stream for the driver shivering in the gloom. He showed a chastened spirit and said nothing, and made no move to take the reins. She drove out to the main road and then to where she thought her sister lived. This proved to be the correct place. She silently relinquished the reins to the quaint little man, pausing for a moment with a friendly pat for the beautiful gazelle-like creatures that had contributed a fair share to safety and convenience. A faint whinny rewarded this advance, as two silky heads nuzzled close. "You old pet," she whispered warmly, "somebody loves you." Leone knew that gesture had not been just learned tonight.

There were two members now in Margaret's little family to greet Leone. A chubby baby son had joined the group. With awe Leone gazed upon this wee first member of a coming generation. Tiny as he was, he gave promise of looking like his handsome father, except for having his mother's lovely eyes of Irish blue and her saucy curls.

There was recent news from their little sisters in AuGres. Margaret, Norman, and Leone sat and just talked far into the night. The young people did not attempt any amusement. The weather was prohibitive, and the hours for visiting so precious. Leone was given the privilege of selecting the first coat to be worn by the new little nephew and experienced a hectic hour. On this important mission she never forgot the event, but wondered sometimes in later years when she considered all the uncertainties, if she had succeeded in selecting the correct thing. The hours for the visit were all together too short, and the week together passed all too quickly.

Mrs. Jacobus was delighted to see Leone back in Saginaw so promptly. She planned to be home in St. Paul for the Christmas holidays, and stops were to be made at several points of interest; not the least of these would be the great metropolitan city of Chicago. The little farm girl was thrilled speechless for the moment when this was made known to her. She moved slowly in a detached fashion and paused in a small hallway. Some of the color draining from her face, she stood pensive with clasped hands, breathing thanks to a kindly Providence. Mrs. Jacobus found her there.

"Are you disappointed I am going so far?" Mrs. Jacobus asked anxiously.

"No, no, on the contrary. I am happy about it."

"You look so quiet and grave."

Leone smiled weakly. "Suppressed excitement perhaps. I was thinking how wonderful it would be to see Chicago."

"Good. We can start packing our luggage. Pack the least important things first. We will be here a few days yet. I have a small number of important calls to make." They proceeded to the storage room to sort out the luggage pieces. Travelers in that period did not go forth carrying a one and only neat handgrip with a safety pin under the flap for emergencies. Such a procedure would not make a sufficiently impressive appearance. Leone was aware of this, but was scarcely prepared for the huge pile, eleven in all counting trunks, grips, bags and hat boxes that were stacked neatly by the wall, all initialed alike in gold leaf. "I will telephone Myra to help you with this. She has done it before," continued Mrs. Jacobus, briskly referring to a young woman who had been the housekeeper in her home since her marriage.

Leone in the meantime procured pencil and paper and proceeded to catalogue the traveling cases in the manner in which they were to be packed. Mrs. Jacobus then checked the list, making a few minor changes. That afternoon the girls pinned the order to the curtain and began the task of carrying them out. Meanwhile, with the baby sleeping nearby, they were alone in the big house. The two girls giggled as they hurried with great armloads, shaking the sheets of crackling tissue that every garment must be filled with as they packed. Leone was happy. She enjoyed Myra, who was older, more experienced, small, blonde, pretty, and congenial. Her presence was credited to the same kindly Providence that was making it possible for Leone to go on this long journey. And Leone was looking, always looking, for the work that she could learn to do that would bring a new life to her little sisters. She was in agreement that this was not going to be attained in Saginaw.

True, there were women in Saginaw occupying important positions who undoubtedly earned a high salary. Leone had made it her business on days when at liberty to go where she could see some of these important ladies. All indications led to the same conclusion. In each instance many years had been spent by each arriving at her present important status. This did not coincide with providing hope for her five sisters. No, she was only too happy in having this opportunity to look further. True, working your way through the years, slowly to the top, was not without many points to be recommended, but quite obviously a course to be followed by one with unmeasured time. Wise enough now to keep her own counsel, Leone hoped this position would serve the dual purpose of providing a livelihood and also aid in reaching the objective to which her young life was dedicated.

Leone spent one evening with Mrs. Gilbert. The kindly lady manifested a deep interest in what she called "the way the sands were drifting." She added quickly, "And in such a short time too, my dear. From this vantage point I feel I can safely predict it will serve your best interest to go with the tide. I'm sorry to say my course of direction has not proven infallible in the past, and I have no reason to believe my ability as a foreteller of the future has improved. Nonetheless, I have no misgivings. I am confident you are right in following the path your faith maps out for you."

The blue gray eyes of the listening girl shone with excitement. Her reply, however, was diffident. "I am very grateful to you for the frank encouragement. It helps tone up my ego. For when all is said and done, I'm a very inexperienced person watching for a chance to help direct my destiny by trying to look into the future."

Mrs. Gilbert laughed her delightfully merry little laugh then graciously arose, placing a friendly arm about the girl. "My dear," she said, "I am amused, but not in the way you might think. When you mentioned trying to see into the future, your voice was so dismal, and you spoke so earnestly, it occurred to me you surely were not looking for a soft place to land. It is a good man-sized job you are taking on."

"It is not as bad as it seems," Leone answered earnestly. "It could be that two of my sisters would earn something, however small. We would live simply and perhaps not make out too bad."

"It is easy to minimize our problems by soft peddling into favorable reflection when in reality they have not diminished. You would find there were five coats to purchase, five pairs of shoes, five persons to take on nourishment three times daily. This list, however you compromise, is a long one. When you send for your sisters, take it from me; be ready. Don't fool yourself. When you take them out of their present security, be sure you know where the money is coming from."

"Do you think the day will come?" the young girl queried.

"Oh yes, it will come all right. I'm only advising you to be prepared for it, and I mean prepared."

Chapter 22
LIVING WITH THE MINNERS

Visiting the Abbots on that last Sunday, Leone gratefully placed her hand in Jim's warm, firm clasp. She had hoped he might be at home on this day seated in his easy chair with his paper and his pipe. He looked the embodiment of peace. Amiable, generous Jim, he had been the answer to a prayer when he came into her life. She regretted having to drift beyond the security these good people afforded her. Friendship could be maintained through correspondence, but not the confidence their sheltering roof gave. Their ready sympathy and understanding would also be denied her.

She had written of her prospects to travel with Mrs. Jacobus. This was expected to be a swing of a few weeks around the state. Now she was filled with the startling news that they would go to Chicago and St. Paul. Lizzie greeted her affectionately, "Jim," she said impulsively as her voice fell slightly, "I'll venture you did not see Leone standing here like a mannequin all pink and lovely, showing her new fall outfit."

"You ladies don't give a fellow sufficient credit," he said impressively. "That was the first thing I noticed. I was just holding my admiration in reserve for a moment."

They laughed merrily at his evident embarrassment. "You would think of a good excuse to squirm out on," his wife chided.

"Sure is pretty," he agreed warmly, "and such good taste."

"Did you select everything yourself?" asked Lizzie.

The girl's face flushed with pleasure and modest pride. "Yes, I shopped for them all myself."

"It surely reflects credit to you. Good style, conservative in color, something that will last and give you your money's worth. How are you coming with the new job?"

This was the cue. Leone was eagerly waiting to disclose her top news of the day and lost no time in making known to them all there was to tell of what she fondly hoped would develop into a successful search for that well paid occupation she was looking for so eagerly.

Jim smiled, "You sure are going places, my girl, whether you are going in the right direction or not."

"Have you thought of any objection in following such a course?" inquired Lizzie.

"Yes, I have. Foremost among them is going so far away from the Abbots. Then there is the possibility of becoming ill such a long distance from home ties."

Then Leone went on from there, explaining that her employer was a philanthropist in her own little way. She offered her evaluation that the woman was very thoughtful. If anything should occur to prompt Leone a wish to come home, she was promised return transportation through the cooperation of her husband, a railroad executive.

Jim laughed loudly this time. "My girl, you are a good old lady. Caution herself could do no better. That's right; check all the angles. Never burn your bridges. You have an old head on young shoulders, and don't forget to make use of it." Jim had definite ideas on most subjects, but either through inability or indifference, he rarely expressed them. He looked around now as though the sound of his own voice surprised him. His wife gave him an encouraging smile.

Leone again placed her two hands in Jim's, and he held them tight. "I only hope I don't get too clever and spoil everything," she said demurely.

"Tut, tut, kid. Never say die. If things don't go to suit you in one place, bob up serenely in some other place and carry your banner. I'm betting on you." He reached for his pipe. The amused look did not leave his face, yet there was something decisive about the action. He had spoken.

There was plenty of talk that day. Some of it was inconsequential, but most of it was important, and the ladies did the talking from then on. Jim resumed his role of interested listener.

Noel came in when he saw Leone. He remained to spend the afternoon with them amid the confusion of voices, witticisms, fun, laughter, and, in the end, tears. They had learned to love the poor little farm girl who had come to them so strangely but a few short weeks before.

The Monday following that memorable Sunday was the day the travelers embarked on their journey. For a brief period, the two employed girls felt starting time would find them still swamped with final packing and other interminable disruptions on time. But they underestimated the engineering ability of Mrs. Jacobus. Calmly and sweetly, but with determination, Mrs. Jacobus thought of all the details and encouraged the weary girls.

Eleven packing cases were finally filled and standing in the hall flanked now by Myrna's modest trunk and grip and Leone's humble, but new grip. Leone was to call a drayman to send for a dray to take the luggage to the depot. A dray, as known to the people of AuGres, was a sort of little sleigh with short, but fat runners that slid around easily enough on the snow, but dragged heavy in the sand. This was a very familiar object to Leone all the years of her young life. What puzzled her now was what possible use the dray could be in getting that pile of mostly fancy luggage to the depot. She fervently wished someone else would assume the responsibility of ordering the dray. Finally, when this important matter could be sidestepped no longer, she bravely took the receiver off the hook. But when it came to saying dray, she said conveyance.

"What kind of conveyance?" came the inquiry.

About this time, her ever-alert employer took the receiver out of her hand and said, "Send a dray."

Leone made a mental note of this and also gave the dray her particular attention when it put in an appearance. She gazed in puzzled silence at the heavy-duty wagon drawn by two horses. "Well, it must be known as a dray," she concluded. Mrs. Jacobus had certainly ordered a dray. At long last this and many other more or less important details had been attended to. Many good-byes were said. Finally, at the appointed hour of seven o'clock in the evening, they formed a very correct looking group of young people as they smilingly emerged from a cab. Then the group moved along the platform to the waiting train, which was heading for important Midwestern points. Leone long remembered this event. True, she had been a passenger on a few other occasions, when her own timid little person would be about the only one to board the coach. But she had seen nothing like this thrill-packed event, with its lights, crowd, and hustling crewmen. Her own group was easily the center attraction as they moved leisurely along. It was evident by special attention of the staff that Mr. Jacobus was an important man of the railway company. They took their places in the parlor car as quickly as possible, but not before Leone heard the call of "All aboard" and a singsong voice droned off the names of the train's many stops.

The railroad held a warm fascination for Leone. It was only in the late 1880s that the weird sound of the locomotive whistle broke the stillness at Point AuGres. The whistle was muted by distance with a sound like the call of a lonesome animal for its mate. And now she would enjoy following a natural childlike inclination to stop and stare, but she felt obliged to keep a tight rein on her conduct and not betray her ignorance unnecessarily.

Final good-byes were said through an open window to a small group of relatives who had followed them to the depot. As Leone raised the infant to afford them a farewell look, she felt there could be relief mingled with regret depicted on the smiling faces back of the fluttering hands.

Whiling away the long hours of the journey, the girls giggled about incidents that had not seemed amusing when they took place. They agreed that in all probability, Mrs. Jacobus was not aware of them.

Leone spent her first night in a sleeping coach. It was all so new and strange. She tried to maintain a calmness she did not feel and wondered if she was fooling anyone except herself. However, she did not seem to attract undue attention. She was not trying to appear like a seasoned traveler, only one who could act calmly. As they drew near to Chicago, this became increasingly difficult. The great city loomed in her active imagination as the city of destiny. From the swiftly moving window, she could see the vast number of homes and flat buildings known then as apartment houses.

The one thing that motivated her life promptly manifested itself. Leone prayed hopefully, "Lord, if it might be here, grant me your help in finding the business or profession that could become the coveted job." As the long train ground to a noisy stop, Leone found herself in another new world. The railway station at Saginaw that had impressed her with its importance could set in one corner of the vast building that welcomed the traveling public to Chicago! The crowd was like the county fair! She silently resolved to look sharp and not commit the unpardonable blunder of becoming separated from the other members of the party with her infant charge.

When the luggage was attended to and they were in a cab on the way to a hotel, Myra was anxious to show Leone the large buildings in the Loop District. Leone thought they were wonderful. However, there were other objects she found just as noteworthy, mainly horses, many of them heavy draft teams with fat sleek bodies that hauled the city freight. Equally beautiful were the lighter cab horses. She sighed a little for what might have been, as the lush green acres of the old farm passed in mental review. Here she thought to herself was that market for their AuGres horses.

Their concierge at the hotel proved very pleasant, but did not yield any assistance to Leone's plans. The girls agreed to stand guard over Baby Jacobus on their turn, a plan harmoniously carried out. This gave Leone the time she required to learn what salaries were being paid to the beautiful salesgirls behind counters in the great department stores. The routine to be followed in securing this desired information was much the same in various places. She asked questions at employment offices or at the information desks. While she was becoming more adept at this, she was also becoming more disappointed every day. One person might live on such a wage, but not five. Although she was impatient, her confidence never wavered. Failure was so remote. It was nonexistent in her world.

When Mrs. Jacobus announced she was terminating her visit, Leone accepted the news philosophically. Although Chicago had been the Mecca of her dreams, she concluded that she had done everything within the range of possibilities to locate the phantom job. Leone knew she must be patient.

A light snow was falling. It was accompanied with a sharp wind to remind them as they boarded the train for St. Paul that Chicago was the "Windy City." Soon after they were seated, Leone watched out her window at the swiftly passing landscape being turned into a fairy wonderland. The softly falling snow outside would be a part of the approaching Christmas season. The snow provided a strong reminder of home and the little sisters anxiously awaiting reports of her progress. She had written from Chicago boldly addressing her letter directly to Marie. She would write again from St. Paul, but this time under cover to her dear friend Katherine to learn the effect of the direct letter. The trembling little words of Baby Helen came back to her now: "You can go; only don't be long." It was inevitable that the last pleading command of her youngest sister should be filled with such meaning for Leone. She felt the sting of approaching tears but quickly blinked them away. She dare not yield to such weakness. The stakes were too high.

In St. Paul Mr. Jacobus met them to joyfully greet his lovely young wife. He looked long and fondly upon their baby daughter, taking her from Leone. He gingerly lifted the tiny form. Then as though not quite trusting himself, he smiled and tenderly replaced the precious bundle in Leone's waiting arms.

St. Paul was a beautiful city all covered with snow. It seemed to Leone that sleigh bells were jingling everywhere. Her spirit thrilled to the dancing sound. She was going to like St. Paul.

Home for the Jacobus family proved to be a very large, lavishly furnished apartment in a first class hotel. It was set to rights in a few days and then preparations were made to welcome the approach of the Christmas holidays. They were so busy throughout this season that Leone did not have time to become very lonesome on her first Christmas away from home. The holidays came and went and with it an influenza epidemic, The Grippe, hit the City. Mrs. Jacobus was among the first to be stricken and she remained very ill for some time. Myra was next, then Mr. Jacobus. Leone worked long hours. Everyone was hoping Leone and the infant daughter would escape the illness. Several days went by when the other members of the group were mostly recovered when Leone fell ill. The doctor was hastily summoned, and she was cared for carefully. Days passed. She improved somewhat, but remained very ill. The doctor finally gave out his diagnosis, "She now has what is called an abscess of the antrum, which could have been caused by an accident in her childhood."

Leone knew that the iron bar thrown from the AuGres neighbor's burning house and striking her in the face was the culprit. The doctor recommended the only solution would be surgery. Further, he added the surgery could be dangerous since there was physical weakness from the aftermath of The Grippe. Finally, it was determined that she would have to go to a hospital for very careful attention. With that, the doctor succeeded in talking himself out of a job. Leone decided if she was dangerously ill, she would prefer to be back in Detroit, Michigan, where she would be nearer her aunt and not so far from her sisters and friends.

In a few days she was on the train, very ill and very much alone on the way back. Nothing thrilled her on this trip. She just lay pale and quiet, taking this latest adventure as a matter of course. Perhaps she was really too ill to do otherwise. Leone was met in Detroit by an ambulance and hurried to a hospital. Here smiling gently, white-capped nurses took over. Leone was soon sleeping quietly, dreaming of beautiful girls in uniform who waited on her every wish.

In the days that followed, she watched the nurses' pitter-patter with their light footfall about the white beds and learned they were in various periods of training. They gave their time in exchange for this training and in two years completed the average course. She closed her eyes to think and whisper a prayer. Here was to be found the end of the search, that all-important work. A sense of security pervaded her entire being. She felt convinced the series of events that led up to this moment were all fate. The hand of her kindly Providence could be seen leading the way. All fears of the surgery vanished. Leone had no doubt a place would be found for her in a training class for nurses. Her mother had indeed left her a priceless heritage in teaching her faith. And now she must test that faith in herself. She must make good when her turn was called.

That very afternoon Dr. Minner, a surgeon grown old in his profession, talked with Leone. He advised her there was something unusual about her case. He told her she should improve under the present treatment. However, he wished to move her to another hospital to be under his direct supervision for further treatment of a more complicated nature.

The girl readily agreed and was moved that afternoon. Everyone was so thoughtful of her comfort. She liked this hospital even better than the first one and secretly hoped she might succeed in joining a training class here.

Later, when they resorted to surgery in her case, there was a complication due to her previously broken nose. Dr. Minner's skill was successful, and there was no more trouble from that source. When she grew strong enough, the good doctor took her to his own home. Leone had become acquainted with Mrs. Minner at the hospital where she was a frequent visitor. It was through Mrs. Minner's insistence that her move to the Minners' home was made.

Leone found the doctor's wife to be a delightful hostess. While not a woman who took to her position in society, she was young of spirit, and the years had set lightly upon her. The doctor spent so much time with his profession that Mrs. Minner had leisure time for charity work. Quite often in passing her favors, she chose someone who could contribute a little companionship or perhaps provide music, literature, or art for her pleasure. She kept her contacts, and her friends were legend. When she mentioned in her clear, charming voice that she was somewhat selfish in her interests, Leone returned her glance with a rueful smile. "You came up on fallow ground this time. I have nothing to contribute."

Mrs. Minner laughed, but quickly noted, "I cannot agree with you there. You have youth, the most valuable contribution of all. We are a childless couple. I would love it if we had a crowd of grandchildren like you, even if they were fighting demons."

Time had slipped around; the snow was not so deep now and a few favored spots showed bare ground. Occasional Indian summer days put in an appearance, and then there were hints of spring.

Dr. Minner maintained his own stables. The stableman stopped at the side door for Leone. Mrs. Minner took the reins from the man's hand as she smilingly snuggled her companion warmly with a luxurious white fur robe as they were off behind the flying hoofs. The silvery-toned bells that girthed the graceful team seemed to add a note of perfection to the beautiful turnout and a delightful sunny day as they glided swiftly over the snow. This was not much like the old sleigh at home as it sped along behind her horses, but the bells sounded the same, and so was the thrill. Leone felt an impulse to sing one of the old songs that drifted over the ice of Saginaw Bay in her own brief past as the sleigh with its accompanying bells jingled along on the way to a party at the Rifle River Boom House. She drifted back from her thoughts. Leone's eyes shined as she mentally appraised the skill with which Mrs. Minner managed the high-spirited team. Here was the common ground for the two to meet as kindred souls. They were soon deep in a discussion of the relative merits of horses in general.

Mrs. Minner admired in turn the knowledge and frankness of her youthful guest. Truth to tell, she was a little curious about the dual personalities of this girl. She noted that Leone had the simplicity and inexperience of the average adolescent, but she appeared at will in a different role of maturity well beyond her years, and in the most unpredictable fields.

Leone placed a wise sense of value in friendship. When she decided to confide a little in Mrs. Minner, she prayed for guidance in this venture, hoping to win the influence of her new friend. She sensed that on this friendship could depend the momentous decision of admission for herself to the nurses training class, even though handicapped by her youth.

Leone gave a candid reply to a few questions, but did not volunteer any information about herself beyond a brief outline of her recent trip with Mrs. Jacobus when casual reference was made to her absence from her native state.

She would be under Dr. Minner's care for sometime yet. This would make allowance for a realistic approach to the problem that meant so much to the five Neely sisters. Time went flying past as time long since has a habit of doing.

While the cordial relations of the two strangely assorted friends thrived, Mrs. Minner came into Leone's life when and where there was a definite vacancy. She was welcomed into this void aside from her potentialities. The motherless girl was becoming fond of the little woman with the big heart.

The saddled horses were taken around to the carriage entrance. Leone, her nose packed with cotton and an extra muffler around her throat, cantered along the bridle path aglow with the zest of living.

Leone entered the nurses training that spring at the suggestion of Dr. and Mrs. Minner. This was not brought about by strategy on the girl's part. She had shown diplomacy in hesitating to make a request. In truth, she lacked the courage to request that a stringent rule be set aside in her behalf, especially when she felt indebted to the Minners now for so many generous favors. They had listened to her simple little story fraught with faith and devotion. The doctor looked at her thoughtfully, "You should have training that would fit you for a higher class of work and enable you to earn more money. Our nurses training class would do that." His words were slow and meditative. His appraising glance was fixed on Leone, and she wondered if he could see the rapid beating of her heart. "Your age is the stumbling block," he continued. "You are scarcely sixteen, are you?"

"I'm not quite fifteen," she steadily answered.

"Your way of life has made you an old-fashioned child, trained you to take up work better than some at eighteen years. If we have to bend the rules to conform to us, a year should not make so much difference."

"There is another stumbling block," the girl said bravely. "All the income I will have is the few dollars a month the hospital pays."

"Oh that," the doctor said indifferently. "Mrs. Minner will fix you up with a nurse's clock and one of my thermometers. There are extra uniforms around, so don't worry. Later, you can take special duty to earn a little extra sometimes. You will have to burn the midnight oil to keep up with your studies. You're prepared for that no doubt?"

"Yes," she replied, "I am." Then she attempted to express her gratitude but went in tears instead to the waiting arms of the doctor's wife. The good doctor left the room; suspicious moisture was in his own eyes.

Chapter 23
SUCCESSFUL NURSES TRAINING

The new girl from AuGres entered the nurses training class very quietly, entrusted at first with that part of the work requiring the most labor and the least skill. Leone got off to a good start. There was nothing too humble or laborious for her to do. She brought with her to this new life the things her early training had the power to bestow: stamina, patience, a complexion glowing with health, and a cheerful spirit evidenced by a ready smile. The patients loved her.

Being known by her classmates as a protégée of the famous Dr. Minner and his philanthropic wife did not afford a great amount of popularity for the new student. If she was aware of this, she gave no sign, applying herself to her studies and duties with an earnestness that slowly won the acclaim of the other members of her class. This was brought into prominence when Leone received some expensive gifts from grateful patients chief among them--a watch. She accepted these honors humbly enough, but in spirit, she was exuberant! A watch was the one thing she had most hoped to be able to have someday.

A nursing career she knew was truly going to be a means to an end for her. That Christmas season some thoughtless individual in the nurses' parlor wound up the big phonograph and put on a "Home Sweet Home" album, and Leone's thoughts immediately went back to the old farm. Among other things, she knew that fast horses roaming succulent meadows, untrained, were just one of the many problems her brother and sisters were facing

Expressing her hopes and achievements, she wrote letters to the girls boldly now. The sisters were not surprised that Leone had already located an occupation that gave promise of fulfilling their requirements. Not that they had such absolute confidence in their sister's superior ability, they simply had faith that did not doubt.

As months passed, many suffering patients had reason to be thankful for the endurance of the generous young country girl who would come back frequently at night for special duty. Occasionally she received regular fees for the work, but more often only gratitude. The floor nurses teased her about this. They dubbed her patients, "Neely's rag babies." Leone did not mind, as the money she received was sufficient for her simple needs.

There were also embarrassing moments. A small group, including two doctors, were meeting one day over a cup of coffee in the cafeteria lounge. Leone, on an urgent invitation, reluctantly joined them. The inclination to remain aloof from such gatherings was a normal one. The other girls were always up to the minute on current offerings at the local theaters and other pleasant ways of spending time and money. In Leone's carefully mapped course, there was no allowance for such indulgences, and she did not fancy the out-of-date feeling it gave her to be a member of an amusing group in which she could take no part.

A Dr. Holcomb welcomed her to a seat on a small stool by his side. Leone, slightly embarrassed, seated herself somewhat gingerly. This provoked a laugh at the girl's expense, and someone said she was timid because of her youth. This brought up the subject of ages, and they merrily started guessing one another's age. Leone busied herself with the refreshments, dreading the moment when all eyes would be turned on her. Dr. Holcomb did the guessing when it came her turn, and he said sixteen. Leone always thanked the Irish side of her parentage when she pulled out of a dilemma like this. Glancing up now with just the right amount of twinkle in her eyes, she calmly said, "Thanks, Doctor, but I expect I would appreciate the compliment more ten years from now." He looked at her in a speculative way. "I will not be around then," he replied.

Leone's friendship with Mrs. Minner proved firm and enduring. The woman had come into the girl's life just when her dependable friend Katherine was swept so far away and seemed now but a memory. The doctor's wife was gratefully welcomed in her place.

The good woman enjoyed watching Leone's rapid development. When the girl was free from hospital duties, the two ladies could be seen often enough on the bridle path, cantering along and enjoying the doctor's beautiful horses.

Occasionally the student nurse would get to go home with the doctor to spend the evening with the Minners. A driver with a handsome turnout would call for Dr. Minner, who took the reins himself on the return trip, driving along the tree-flanked street at a fast gait. There was a thrill in every hoof beat for the country-bred girl.

The Minners maintained a summer home at Grosse Point. Many happy hours were spent here: boating and sunning as the little swells splashed gently on the warm, white sands of the beautiful Lake St. Claire. Frequently there were other guests of different ages. Leone enjoyed them all. Sometimes they saw the better shows and all of the best musical offerings.

When Leone graduated at only seventeen, it was a proud day in her life. She had entered upon her duties on a spring day nearly two years ago. The other members of the class had begun their work. The graduates formed in a crisp, softly starched line to receive their diplomas. Leone not only carried the highest mark of her class, but she also had to her credit the greatest number of hours on floor duty. With these hard earned honors went the offer of a good position in a private sanitarium in the City of Chicago. Leone lost no time accepting the wonderful career opportunity. The goal she set for her future was to earn enough money to go home on a visit. She planned to take Margaret and her two babies and try to persuade Robert to sell the farm and move the family. Leone truly believed that the Neely family's future loomed the clearest in Chicago.

Some months later Leone arrived in Gladwin. Good-byes had been said to the dear friends in Detroit, and the fruitful ties that launched her on a nursing career were now severed, perhaps for all time. This had not been lightly done. She had lingered in the sheltering arms of Mrs. Minner. Even the good doctor bestowed a light kiss upon her brow. But in the end, duty won. She must not deviate from the course she had mapped out, though its lines were cruel and sometimes hard to follow. The prospects of going home had become much brighter in the past few months. Letters from home reported that Robert and Minnie were not only separated; they had secured a decree of divorce. Minnie had sued Robert for all and more than he was worth. Marie had been selected to appear as a witness. The children had what they called a "get-together" the evening before the trial. Marie raised somber eyes and gazed with a troubled look on the little group, consisting of her three sisters and brother. "Perhaps it was wrong for them to part," she said gloomily.

"Why should it be wrong?" asked Henrietta.

Marie answered, "Well, after all, it's breaking the bonds of matrimony."

"Are you thinking of that marriage as regular? Don't fool yourself," Bill offered scornfully. "The Lord never tied that pair; that was strictly the Devil's work."

"I guess you're right at that, Bill," Marie responded, more cheerfully.

"Of course, I'm right, and don't let that wobbly conscience of yours spoil everything."

Robert was overtaken by the result of his own folly and had become quite humbled. This coupled with the relief experienced by the children through his wife's removal from the household could not be measured by expression in words. The memories of Minnie's galling presence spurred Marie's valor.

Bill declared that Minnie was like a brooding hen, taking a peck here and a peck there. Marie looked at Bill quietly. He met her glance with his mischievous grin. "It's true, Marie. Don't bottle up anything in court tomorrow," Bill advised. "Give em the facts."

Marie thought of this wise counsel as she walked bravely into the Standish courtroom at her father's side the following day. For the most part, they were anxious moments as she listened to the sound of her own voice in the presence of an immobile judge. Marie spoke in defense of Julia's children and did not falter. However, when Marie learned that Minnie was allowed the flock of sheep started by her mother, she became somewhat dubious of her own

ability as a witness.   But her father was jubilant since he had been
afraid of harsher treatment.

Neely Family in 1898

Back Row: Leone, Henrietta, Marie, and Robert's sister Rita
Front Row: Bill, Margaret, Helen, Robert Neely, and Laura

Leone Employed as Nanny in St. Paul, Minnesota in December 1899

Leone as a Nurse with Marie in 1903

Henrietta and Marie in Front of Their Chicago Tailor Shop in 1905

Henrietta in a Suit She Made as a Seamstress

Neely Girls and Friends in Front of Chicago Drexel Avenue
Apartment in 1907

Neely Girls with Friends in Chicago Park in the Summer of 1907

St. James Hotel in Edmonton, Alberta in 1907

Temperance Hotel in Edmonton, Alberta in 1907

(Photo Credits to the City of Edmonton Archives)

Henrietta

Mike Courting Helen

Marie and Her Husband Fred Hastings with Children
Ronald and Ruth

Bill Mayouck Shoeing Horses in 1910

Bill Mayouck with Early Seattle Fire Department Equipment

Part III

A New Life

Chicago

1903 to 1907

Chapter 24
LEONE'S OFFER TO RELOCATE

When the train drew up on the scheduled hour, all the Neely family members were standing on the platform of the neat little railway station awaiting the arrival of Leone and Margaret with her three young children. Their beloved faces turned with anxiously watching eyes as the powerful, puffing locomotive swept to a standstill.

All the impressive railway depots viewed by Leone in her travels were dwarfed in memory now as this familiar scene arose before her. Blinking away the happy tears, she stood humble in her moment of triumph, her generous heart filled with gratitude. She stepped down from the coach into her father's waiting arms. Robert greeted Margaret warmly also. Looking upon his beautiful grandchildren for the first time, he forgot all his harsh words. He led the way back to Aunt Rita's home, proudly carrying Baby Mary in his arms.

The little town of Standish was celebrating. The following day would be the anniversary of Independence. The girls yielded to the pleadings of relatives and friends to remain until late the next day. Leone danced that night in the town hall to the gay strains of music rendered by the orchestra of which her cousin Young had long been a member. Many friends came from the different towns, both that evening and on the following day, as news of the Neely's presence was spread. Friends came trooping in, and among them was Bob Garner, the friend who had purchased Fleet and Fly, Robert's fast colts. He had but recently become their proud owner. They were still untrained when purchased. He made a carriage team of them, and a handsome team of high steppers they proved to be.

Leone eagerly expressed a desire to see them. Approaching, she remained out of sight, calling Fleet in a voice once familiar to the sensitive creature. Fleet made a prompt reply, a repeated low caressing whinny she had reserved as a colt for Leone alone. On coming closer to the team, Fleet reached forth a proud head, eloquent as words. This convinced and deeply moved Leone. She must go home at once. Baby Helen's plaintiff little voice summoned her, "You can go; only don't be long." Nostalgia so valiantly resisted in past months swayed her now.

Robert agreed to her request to go and left for the livery stable to get the horses. When Robert drew the horses up at the home of his sister, Leone, Margaret and her family were all eagerly awaiting him. However, Leone took the time to greet Mack. He recognized her at once, snorting and pawing the ground urgently with a fore hoof, and was eager to attract her attention.

The ride home seemed like it was taking forever as Leone sat by her father's side. The horses moved slowly along the dusty road. When at last she was clasped in the arms of her sisters, her pent-up emotions gave way. She wept and laughed in the same breath. Each with a tight grip on Leone's hands, the two little ones escorted her around to see all the familiar things.

It was in many respects a very different experience than she had anticipated. All the familiar old objects did not look the same. After being used to the high ceilings of the hospital, the rooms of the old farmhouse seemed so close overhead. They ate supper seated about the handcrafted table that their father had built. Leone was so excited she could scarcely swallow! After supper she rushed forth hand in hand with her little sisters to see everything out of doors before darkness fell. They stopped at the horse barn, the cow barn, the garden, and even the farthest away fields and got back in the fragrant twilight with the fireflies softly fluttering back and forth. Leone had seen nothing that seemed as it was in relation to herself. She wondered if she could ever become adjusted to this life, if obliged to again. Later that evening, as they were seated in the old living room with the oppressive ceiling overhead, Robert was easily approached on the subject of selling out. "Money must grow on trees where you come from," he responded.

"Oh no, it must be honestly earned there as well as here. The difference lies in the fact there is money to pay you after you have earned it, and there is none here," Leone replied. "What would you think of selling out, Dad, and moving to Chicago?" she asked.

He smiled as he sat in his old easy chair puffing on his pipe. Leone noted that in her absence life had just lightly touched him. He had not a gray hair in sight. His strong features had the same healthful glow, and there was still that same air of self-satisfaction about him.

His daughter studied him as she spoke her thoughts back with a tired mother who had gone on. Leone swallowed the painful lump

126

that arose in her throat as she turned what she hoped was a cheerful expression to her father, "I think it is the best thing we can do."

Robert offered a surprising agreement. He offered, "The cattle are gone, and so are the horses. Now the sheep are gone, too. The potatoes have not paid for the planting in the past three years. I guess we might as well go before we starve out."

A note of resignation and appeal he attempted to put in his tone was not lost on his daughter's keen perception. She promptly placed it in the category of exaltation where it belonged. She knew how good he was at passing his responsibilities on to someone else, then feeling free to believe they had not existed. "Well," thought Leone, "if he could see hope glimmering afar that he might succeed in unloading his large family, she was not only ready, but anxious to assume this responsibility."

The next day was packed full of thrills for Leone. She had slept well in her old room, the victory of youth over nerves. The tangled garden was still wet with dew when she seated herself on a big flat weed bed that would protect her uniform from contact with the earth. She cautiously pulled weeds, shaking the soft soil that clung to the roots, mindful of the tender young vegetables.

The familiar little golden birds with jet wings flew forth and back through the branches of willows that stood as they did in former days along one side where the drainage ran and the sweet alluring fragrance of honeysuckle pervaded the fresh morning air. A golden sun was rising to join forces with the blue of a perfect day.

Bill came into the garden carefully picking his way. Cheerfully whistling, he grinned as his sister pursed her lips and lifted a provocative face for his kiss. "I guess my face is clean enough yet." He agreed, "I just washed," as he bent his head for her caress. Then gingerly seating himself, he followed her example and started pulling weeds. "Gosh, you're up to your old tricks; aren't you, Sis? I thought you would be too high-toned for that."

"Indeed," she answered blandly. "There is no higher labor than this. It is the Lord's work feeding the human family."

"I had never thought of it in just that way before. That's about right. Still, it's not a fancy job. How did you come out with Dad? I went to bed and did not hear."

"He agreed it would be a good plan to sell out and go to Chicago."

Bill looked at her calmly, the grin gone from his face. "And is it such a good plan after all the years we have put in here clearing this land?"

"I get your point of view, but there is nothing we can do to save the situation. Even if we had stock, Dad would not give us a free hand to run the farm, and you see what his methods do. Our mother was the marvel at management who made a successful farming venture here."

"I am forced to agree with you, Leone, although I know I will not like the city. I could not think of remaining there. However, it may be one way to get a little help from Dad." He continued, "He would be forced to pay moving expenses."

"You think he will not stay with the family?"

"Not him. He will just take the money and fly the coop."

Leone was silent a moment. Then she said thoughtfully, "You are probably right."

"That's the way I figure it at any rate. I could be wrong. Do you think he holds his years well?"

"Absolutely. He doesn't appear a day older than when I saw him last. Has his disposition improved?"

"No. He is just as quick on the trigger as he ever was. He is just one of those things that time does not change."

"I thought he acted more calmly."

"As for that, he is running out of victims. Kids are growing up. Stock is about gone. It is not worth his while to go on a rampage. There is nothing to vent his wrath on."

His sister looked at him, a glint of amusement in her eyes. "Are you serious, Bill?"

"Oh yes. Never was more serious in my life than right now." He arose extending a hand to Leone, "I think we best go into breakfast. The dew is about gone, and I plan to rake that hay."

The girl laughed, "I have my eye on that job."

"You can have it. I will hitch up the rake as soon as we finish breakfast."

They moved off down the path. "Looks like we have company from Gladwin," Bill remarked. Margaret and Henrietta were coming toward the garden with the little ones. Bill gave them a comprehensive look. "Them two are the beauties in this family," he said indifferently. "But that doesn't go for so much. Beauty is only skin deep."

128

Leone smiled. "Henrietta holds the baton as the family wit also, and both girls have the family characteristics of being useful members of society. They are both good workers."

"There is the weakness," he scoffed. "Smart people don't work." He raised his voice for the benefit of his other sisters, "What are you girls dragging those unsuspecting infants through the briars for?" He took little Mary, lifting her in his strong arms as he spoke, looking with mingled admiration and affection at the pretty child.

Margaret's warm, happy laugh answered him, "You forget they are ancestral briars and look good after you have been gone for so long a time."

Leone liked to remember that breakfast as one of the highlights of her visit. Afterwards, still wearing her smart uniform, she mounted the hay rake. Bill placed the reins in her hands, the humorous grin back on his face. Taking a hand fork, he started pitching the hay. Leone thrilled once more to the click of the hay rake and the song of the birds and the locusts. It gratified her to find Mack had not forgotten the fine points a clever rake horse was expected to know. When Leone turned in at noon, the field was all raked.

After feeding Mack, he was hitched for the road and a delightful visit with Katherine followed. The years were taking their toll, and Leone saw that Katherine's strength was failing. The woman placed a gentle hand on each side of Leone's face, looking long and lovingly upon her. "You are still my own dear girl," she whispered brokenly. "You have not changed." Leone did not remain long, fearing for Katherine's feeble strength.

There were great plans for the following day. They would go huckleberry picking to McDonald's Prairie where this fruit grew wild in sweet abundance on lush bushes. Robert had the wagon ready at an early hour, loaded with feed for the horses, and Leone declared that she had never seen so many buckets in one place before.

Margaret would remain with the babies and Henrietta. It was agreed all the others should go. With buoyant spirits they climbed to a place on the wagon. The distance was only about four miles. The horses jogged along lifting clouds of dust that was flying high. Marie declared the huckleberry marsh would probably be at its best because there had been a brisk rain just two days ago. Her prediction proved to be true.

Leone enjoyed the day. The shrubs and grasses were all washed clean, and the fragrance of huckleberries filled the soft air. Pretty mosses warm and dry-like were like deep carpet pile beneath their feet. She wore her nurse's uniform and jaunty cap with its band of distinction. She found this gratifying, for she met several of her former classmates and was not adverse to a little pardonable display of what she had done for herself during her absence.

At noon time they sought the shade of some tall shrubs and even found logs shrouded in dry and varied colored mosses. Here they took seats to enjoy the dainty lunch. Their tea, made of water from the deep well according to their own method, was still somewhat cool. Leone took her cup as she sipped with a deep satisfaction and stretched out two feet that were beginning to tire. She watched Robert who was always at his best as host serving the lunch with a genial decorum so becoming to him when he chose. Friends joined them while they lingered over the refreshments, some of them unknown to Leone. Robert proudly presented, "My second daughter from Chicago."

Leone recalled the years that were past, dating back to her early childhood, with her heart bleak in the shadows of his unkindness. She had looked forward to the time when her father would take pride in her reflected honors. Now the time had come. However, she found herself quite indifferent to this change of attitude now.

On the way home they were still laughing and singing, defying the dust. All ran in to see Katherine a few moments, leaving a small amount of the choice berries. Their visit brought a flush of happiness to her faded cheeks.

When the sisters with Margaret's three babies went aboard the train at Standish for the return trip at the conclusion of their visit, two grand and wonderful weeks had passed into oblivion. Good-byes had been rather a cheerful affair for the Neelys, knowing they would meet again as soon as the arrangements could be completed. Margaret was happy to go home to the waiting arms of her young husband.

Leone's thoughts of her old friends were of a very different character. She realized she had said to them a final farewell and that they were aware of this as well. Leone had also spent a day with Jennea MacKeen, her mother's friend and confidant. She was still her queenly self, but time had a way of taking its toll. Leone would be in no position to permit herself the luxury of another trip to AuGres.

The two sisters said a fond good-bye when Margaret changed cars for Gladwin.

James Abbot, Lizzie, and their son Noel were at Bay City. When she stepped down to the platform, Lizzie greeted her with affection, while Jim just stood there and looked almost doubtfully. Leone ran to him.

"Is this my little girl?" he asked taking her hand.

"Yes, the very same tramp you brought home to your unsuspecting wife."

"You have changed. I would not know you."

Leone reached her other hand to the boy. "Do you think I have changed, Noel?"

"You have surely grown up." He gave her a quizzical look. "You have taken on height," he told her.

"And grace and maturity," added Jim with emphasis.

Lizzie laughed her warm, friendly laugh. "Jim has been counting all day on greeting his little girl with a proper hug. Now he finds you all grown up."

Leone turned to him and put two arms around his neck.

Looking slightly embarrassed, he kissed her gently and then lapsed into customary silence, his eyes beaming a welcome.

They talked until far into the night. Then Leone slept soundly in the little room that had been assigned to her many months before. Noel had gone to bed the previous evening, so when Leone appeared in the morning, he was curious to hear more details of her experience. "It was a wonderful victory for you over your Dad," he said with boyish enthusiasm.

Leone looked thoughtful. "I never considered it in just that light," she answered.

"What else could you make of it?" he asked scoffing.

"Perhaps I did not try to make anything of it. I would not think of victory for to the victor belong the spoils."

"Sounds too warlike for me. You will think you have the spoils of the other type when you have all them kids on your hands," he added.

Lizzie sat quietly listening. She gave Leone an encouraging smile. "Noel is weighing your problems from his own standpoint. I don't think you need worry. You are making a better salary than the average man more than twice your age. Your success so far has been an event of unique significance, phenomenal in fact. Your sisters have been trained as you were. It will not be all smooth sailing, but you will ride out the storms. I was very skeptical at first, but I believe now in your faith."

Chapter 25
NEELYS IN CHICAGO

A week passed when a letter came. Leone tore it open in feverish haste and read it in silence. Then she stood weakly reminiscent. When Baby Helen had given her childish command, "You can go; only don't be long," Leone realized it was a big order. She allowed herself three years, but the culmination of the time or what it would bring forth was very indefinite.

Standing now in the glow from a window, a little breeze from an open sash lifted the limp strands of stray hair from her damp forehead. The years were about passed. The date now was late August. The 5th of September would come up in the following month. Leone gazed and let her thoughts drift to the time they would be reunited. They were to arrive in Chicago at eight o'clock on the first Tuesday evening of the coming month. The girl's eyes filled with tears of joy and thanksgiving to a generous Providence that helped her over the many obstacles that impeded her progress, and now the great day was soon at hand.

Come evening, Leone hurried out after her day's work was done in search of a small flat. It must be cheap; shabby was not important. They could paper and fix it a little, but it must be rent she could afford to pay. She could not expect her father to remain with them. Whatever he did, she could not in the light of past experience count on him as an asset.

When the place was finally located, it was less rent than even she had anticipated. A rear entrance was sadly in need of repair. The rooms had not been repapered in years. It was a sight, a painful one, thought the girl. But it could be improved by plenty of work and a little expense. The location was good, near a small, but important business center. She promptly paid the rent and secured a key. This was the first concrete evidence of the realization of her dream.

Leone was filled with excitement and anxious to share the news with her friend, Cleo Ramsdale. Cleo was a generous young woman with whom she made her home for many months, and a warm friendship now existed between them. She hastened at once to inspect the flat and saw an opportunity to aid Leone. Cleo was long an open admirer of the devoted girl. This was an answer to her oft-expressed wish that she might be of some assistance.

Cleo was a dynamic force at the friendly art of homemaking. She had much experience and made a study of this important work. She found the flat roomy with good windows, shelving, and closets. It was, however, in such a sorry state that a shovel would be an important tool to remove ashes, soot, bits of linoleum, and trash of all sorts including small boards. Cleo looked in at the rubbish then picked her way around the debris in search of a clean spot to hang her coat.

Leone looked at her in dismay. "You're shocked. You would not have taken it."

"Oh, yes, I would at seven dollars a month. We can do wonders with this joint. Give us a little time. It was good that you forewarned me. We have plenty of cleaning equipment."

The two young women proceeded to work with a heartiness required by the discouraging task. Their efforts soon gave a promise of success. The next evening Leone bought a stove, a bed, and window shades, which meant she could then occupy the flat. Cleo loaned her pet dog, Pete, for a bodyguard. The flat was on the ground floor, and a family lived upstairs. Yet, it seemed a lonesome sort of place, so Pete was very welcome. He was small, black, and a sturdy fellow. He just bristled with canine desire to sink his fangs into an intruder every time a board creaked or an unusual thump aroused his zealous and over critical suspicions. This conduct on Pete's part, while not conducive to hospitality, met with Leone's complete approval. They became fast friends. After leaving in the morning, he had two blocks to go to reach home. Leone could watch him one block before he turned the corner. Cleo said this was a perfectly safe procedure. The little fellow trotted off home according to expectations and proved dogs could be trusted. She smiled a knowing little smile. Pete was educating her. Cleo gave her a piece of old carpet as a bed for Pete in place of his own nice soft cushion for use during his enforced absence from home. Leone had been somewhat dubious about this arrangement. She placed the improvised bed in what she considered the most favored spot when she retired.

The nights were cold, and a sharp draft was blowing through an opening in a cracked window glass. It seemed to proceed along the floor directly on the dog. Leone rolled up a small piece of rag and stuffed it tightly in this opening. "That may help temporarily," she thought.

It was daylight when she woke from a night of undisturbed sleep. A quick glance revealed that Pete was missing from his carpet. She sat up quickly. There lay Pete stretching himself lazily on the most remote corner of her large bed! Leone laughed aloud, "Pete, you villain. Is that what you settled for? If Cleo were eyewitness to this, she would declare I was spoiling you. I will admit I humor you, but your character has been formed for a long time."

For the balance of Pete's stay, the carpet was on the floor, but Pete was on the bed. Leone placed a worn cotton blanket on his corner every night, and he did not make the mistake of moving off its limits.

The girl was startled one evening. Cleo was involved in some community work that prevented her lending a helping hand. After dinner with Pete close at heel, Leone hurried back to the task that each day was looking a little brighter. She had undertaken the task of papering the kitchen and was well past the halfway mark. She hoped that tonight's efforts would make a distinct showing. Working around a window, she removed a shade and was carefully placing the final pieces that constituted a perfect fit about the frame when Pete suddenly took on a most belligerent air. Leone, well aware that something was amiss, had no time to take any action before the intruder put in an appearance. Placing his hands on each side of his face, he pressed his eyes close to the windowpane and shouted. Leone found this disconcerting, to say the least. This was not the word to describe Pete's reaction. Every hair on the little warrior's body was standing upright. He was seething inside and shouting threats of mayhem to any and all contenders. The girl took him in her arms, and together they approached the enemy. After the confusion quieted down to a point where anyone could understand anything that was said, it was learned that the stranger was a man trying to deliver some things Leone had ordered. She kept Pete in her arms while the man was present, advising him to put in his

134

appearance at the door in the future. After his departure, she carefully replaced the shade, deciding the window should remain covered.

A welcomed letter arrived in the following day's mail. The farm had been sold on a cash basis, and all that remained to be done was dispose of the personal effects. All the livestock had previously been removed.

Leone's Chicago flat was putting on quite a decent air, showing to a marked degree all the hard work the two young women put into it, especially the kitchen. Leone was most anxious that this room be spotless. Buying the furnishings, she found herself hard pressed for money. Her father had sent nothing. Disposing of her treasured watch and some other jewel trinkets brought in a tidy sum. She was happy to receive the money, although she deeply regretted that she was forced to dispose of the jewels in this way. It was the only jewelry she had ever owned, and all had been gifts from grateful patients and were connected with tender little memories. It seemed ruthless to dispose of them, but there seemed no other alternative. Cleo and Leone now worked longer hours. Leone moved about as though her feet were responding to music. There was joy in her heart and a song on her lips. Cleo felt her own pulses quicken in response to this delightful mood. Even Pete seemed to strut as though cognizant that something important was about to transpire.

Leone, deeply grateful to Cleo for her moral and physical assistance, expressed her gratitude and also feared that Cleo was doing too much. She worried her health might be adversely affected. This warning amused Cleo. "Never fear. I shall cling to the ship. The show must go on," she insisted.

Leone deeply appreciated the fact that Cleo had such a kindly interest in the coming of her sisters. However, she realized their arrival would be something in the nature of relief to her generous friend. Leone could scarcely await the time, but it came eventually. Leone found herself stepping off the old Cottage Grove cable car on winged feet to the Twelfth Street Station to meet the incoming Michigan Central train.

She could still conjure the thrill of years past of that moment in her life. Dashing through the iron gate, the girl approached a man that appeared to be the conductor. She had seen him step off the train that was grinding to a slow stop. "I'm here to meet my father and sisters," she said breathlessly. "I hope they have come."

The man in uniform turned an appraising look her way, "Are you the girl from Michigan?" he asked.

Leone nodded.

"I guess they are aboard all right, a backwoods man behind a mattress."

"If you mean that my father wears a beard, he does," she answered simply.

He looked at her critically. "No wise man should be carrying a bird cage tied up in a red bandanna with two canaries, one completely nude except for a single tail feather."

She looked eagerly at the train. It showed signs of stopping as she spoke, "They had two birds in the early summer, but they were both properly feathered."

"One is not properly feathered now," he informed her. "I am surprised to see you," he continued. "The old man gave me a line on your history. I expected to see a woman of twenty-five at least. What will you do with that crowd? Take my advice and ship them all back to Michigan on the next train."

She gave him a brief summary of the flat and her plans. He put out his hand and grasped hers warmly. "You are the right kind of stuff, girl, and you have my best wishes and my sympathy as well," he assured her. "God bless you, and I predict your success."

The train pulled to a stop at that moment. Her hand touched the rail as she bounded up the steps. Down about the center of the car were the Neelys, preparing to make a leisurely exit. They looked so forlorn, or was it a lost look? Leone's heart was full as she greeted them.

Always quick of wit, Henrietta seemed to be the only one who shared her thoughts. She put an arm about her sister, "Courage, darling," she whispered.

Leone's curiosity prompted her to take a peek behind the bandanna. The bird stood there and then cheerfully hopped around on the perches. The little creature seemed to be enjoying its unique featherless status. Her father patiently explained that he did not expect it to re-feather.

"But," asked Leone aghast, "why bring it?"

"Oh, the baby would not part with that," he said flatly.

She put an arm fondly about Helen as they moved along from the car. The porters were coming in to clean up. This was the end of a designated run.

The Neely family rode on a streetcar for the first time that evening. Robert paid the fare with pomp worthy of the occasion.

The family members were delighted with Leone's flat. It proved more comfortable than they had hoped, accustomed as they were to the large rooms of the old home. Her sisters could scarcely wait until morning for their busy hands to begin work on the wallpapering job. When Leone arrived home from work on the evening of that first day after their arrival, she was most happily impressed by what had been accomplished.

Leone had noted that the girls had very little to wear and winter was not far away. Henrietta had secured a job to learn dressmaking. She would receive two dollars per week. "Not a very heavy salary," she remarked in her amusing way. "But it will more than pay the rent, and it is within walking distance."

As time went on, their father said nothing about contributing any money to the cause. Occasionally, he did carry in a few groceries, but that was all. The girls held a little meeting on the subject and decided some strategy would not be amiss. They would decoy their father down to the shopping center. It was decided that Leone and Marie would arrive first at the department store. Laura and Helen would be accompanying their father. Arriving at the appointed place, Leone went in search of a personnel service, a saleswoman who could move from one department to another and make sales. In the meantime Marie attracted Robert's attention. The experienced sales woman who had promised Leone that Robert would be eating out of her hand within ten minutes magically appeared. She turned her undivided attention to their father. Robert was still a good-looking man, and he was well aware of it. He was tall, well dressed, had plenty of hair, and egotism, to no end. He was like wax in the hands of the shrewd girl. He was soon led to believe it was his party and that his beautiful daughters were in need of clothing for both warmth and appearance. The windy city could have some very cold weather. Autumn was slipping away.

Leone took enough apparent interest to sanction the purchases when her father showed signs of terminating the buying. The girls promptly agreed, thus saving him embarrassment before he could put his wishes into words. The bill was eighty dollars, not much to divide for the four girls. It would be better than nothing. Matter of fact, it was much more than Leone had hoped for. It was mostly yard goods. The sisters would make it into clothing. The four older

137

girls could wear the same size. Leone was fairly well dressed. They all cheerfully shared with one another.

A warning came from Henrietta, "It will speed us up a bit to be short of clothing. Whoever is dressed first will be wearing the smartest costume."

There were many exciting subjects to keep the talk about the dinner table interesting over the dinner that evening. Even Robert acted like a man enjoying his children.

The girls were thrilled with the beautiful new materials. Plans were made for the styling of each piece. Bill secured a job that afternoon according to his plans. "A decent job, too," he declared. "I will be farming in the city parks."

This sounded good to Robert. He decided he would try to get on at Bill's place of work, which he succeeded in doing the following day. Marie at the same time secured a place learning millinery. She would be paid one dollar the first week, two the second with an increase of a dollar each week until she was receiving a salary. Helen and Laura both started to school.

On her way home Leone stopped in a shop to rent a sewing machine. A salesman promptly reminded her, "You should buy one on your good salary."

"There is more than enough places for the dollars I earn," she replied. "But you have given me an idea." She proceeded to tell him about her father. The salesman promptly agreed to put the sewing machine in her home on trial and make an attempt to sell it to her father.

When the girls were preparing the evening meal after their day's work, each one was blithely contributing some bit of news from the day's experience to a spirited conversation when the door opened cautiously and their father entered, followed by three persons. A shower of rain had blown up, and they were all dripping. Robert made way for them through the crowded kitchen to the living room where the bird was on exhibition in all her naked splendor, the single tail feather cleaned and preened to perfection.

"What is he up to now?" asked Laura in an undertone as she softly followed them. She was back in a moment. "Showing the bird," she reported.

Helen was indignant. "That makes poor little Cheapy nervous. I'm going to tell Dad not to do that to the bird."

"I hope your remarks have the desired effect," Henrietta added. "The bird is going to be a nervous wreck if he continues escorting people through here."

Just at that moment the interlopers departed.

Helen went in to note the effect on poor Cheapy.

The girls turned to Leone. "How long are we going to tolerate that pitiful little freak of a bird around here?"

"We cannot be very prompt about removing it. Helen might suspect we did it," the thoughtful older sister reminded them.

"That big boy who lives upstairs said he would ring its neck anytime we wanted him to," Marie told her.

"We could not have that. Cheapy's neck would show bruises," Leone insisted. "I have some chloroform I was using to remove spots that will do the unpleasant job."

Again the door opened, this time admitting a larger group of inquisitors. They followed Robert at a brisk pace, shaking water from damp clothing about on the new rug.

The girls were furious. When the group departed, Leone took the broom to whisk up the worst of their damp tracks; Helen read the riot act to her father. She insisted that he "not have Cheapy made ridiculous."

"Cheapy was that way already," Robert responded. "That's why people want to see her."

"They would know nothing about her if you did not go out and tell them," she sobbed in anger. When Helen got through talking to Robert, he realized his reign in the old style was over for all times. Whatever influence he might yield in the future with his family would not be automatically guaranteed. Only truth and kindness would merit their respect.

Their father worked in the park a few days with Bill and liked it. He had other plans, however. They were somewhat vague, but taking shape. It was about time for him to get into some kind of mischief again when the sewing machine salesman showed up. This encounter proved a useful and valuable method of directing his restless tendencies. A nice new sewing machine was successfully added to the family possessions.

About this time the freight arrived that had been sent from the old family home, a huge box. There were also huge charges that could not be avoided. But finally Leone had the lid off and was peering curiously at the lot. She had not counted upon finding anything very useful, and, therefore, was not too disappointed. The contents were principally family pictures with wide wood frames that even in that remote day were no longer popular and were almost worthless. The girls used the frames for kindling wood. Leone would have welcomed some few things of intrinsic value. One was a figurine, cast from bronze by her uncle, one of her mother's few valued possessions. It had stood a silent sentinel as a doorstop during their childhood. Inquiry of her sisters revealed their father had decided they would have no further use for that and had thrown it away. However, there was one thing in the familiar contents of the box, her mother's shawl, that Leone lifted from its folds reverently, but with mingled feelings of sorrow. "I thought old Minnie got off with this," she said.

"She did," Laura answered, "but Aunt Rita took it off her on the street one day in Standish and returned it to us."

"Bravo, Aunt Rita, " Leone said in grateful tones.

Chapter 26
NEELY MEN'S DEPARTURE

Their father had made the acquaintance of and was frequently seeing a man who was engaged in advertising Canada's great Northwest, principally the Alberta country. The gullible Robert listened eagerly for every word. It finally dawned on Leone that he was already convinced of the wealth to be found in this land of the shining sun. It was their brother, Bill, who was skeptical of this move. And Robert evidently wished to take his son with him. This cast a shadow on the happiness of the Neely girls.

The children all loved their father, and Leone especially recalled the lonely years she had spent away from her family. She could not reconcile herself with a thought of their one remaining parent drifting off to such a great distance alone, much less the consideration of separation from Bill. However, she knew that Bill did not like the big city. He would really be happier in the wide-open spaces. Bill had declared, "I like both horses and the range."

So, there really was no argument. The girls had what they wanted, and there was always the hope that Robert might make some sound investment that would insure a comfortable living for him and his son. But there was also the fear that some smooth vendor of charms or a strong arm might relieve him of the mental strain he considered sufficient to guard his pocketbook.

The Neely girls had tried in vain to persuade Robert to remain with his children. They reminded him of the good job both he and Bill were leaving and how useful this income was to the family. They also pleaded that it was a comforting assurance to have the family united. Arguments of this nature were all useless. Their father was refusing all responsibility. He told Leone, "You wanted the girls; you have them." He told her he could not see how they would make out and he "did not care." It was a frank statement. Further persuasion was useless, so, Leone chose to remain silent. Robert Neely was adamant in his determination to go.

When they were ready to go, it was with just two-days' notice to take advantage of some special rates that were being offered by Canadian Railroad. Robert was as excited as a small boy going to a circus. He bought the two tickets and quickly packed a small trunk that he had used in his youth and then telephoned the drayman to take the baggage to the railway station.

Robert had been so excited though that he forgot there were several railway stations in Chicago. The train was to leave at six o'clock in the evening, but he had no idea where his trunk had been taken. Robert Neely decided to depart for the city center in the early afternoon to institute a search for the trunk. However, he inadvertently took Bill's ticket with him. He also neglected to leave any instructions as to which station they were to go to catch their train.

Leone came home in mid-afternoon to allow ample time to see her father and brother off on their long journey. The Neely offspring waited for a time and then decided to go down to the Union Station where they figured it would be where most likely they would find the train bound for Canada.

This did not prove to be correct. First, there was no train leaving at six o'clock, and secondly, there was no sign of their father. Leone decided to go downstairs to the baggage room to see if the trunk had been there. The logbook showed that the trunk had been removed and taken to the Twelfth Street Station that afternoon. The young family members hurried off to that station. However, when they arrived they learned the train had already pulled out, just seventeen minutes earlier.

141

Six of Robert Neely's children stood looking at the clock in wondering amazement. An attendant then approached them and inquired whether they were the Neelys. When he learned that they were the Neelys, he said he had a message for them. Their father had put Bill's ticket in the mail, which should reach them on the morning delivery. Robert would wait for his son at Portal, North Dakota. The children stood again in disbelief of what they had just heard. When they inquired why hadn't their father delayed starting the trip for a day, the man had no reply to the moot question.

That afternoon Bill purchased necessary clothing with the money he had earned. And now to quote his own words, he was "dead broke."

The time was near Leone's payday, so all that remained from last payday was a small amount of change. They had all hoped their father, who was well aware of this, would enclose some money with the ticket, but he had not.

What was to be done now? Bill was a big boy, but only a child in age. He could not be permitted to leave on such a big journey without money. There was only one thing to do, and that was to get a small loan.

Leone proceeded without delay to call upon a family for whom she had done many favors. Mr. Hall, a teacher, had been out of employment for a year with a very serious illness that had darkened their home. On several occasions Leone had nursed and aided them in a number of ways. Their son was through school now and employed. Mr. Hall, too, had been back at his teaching profession for many months. The Halls' son, who worked at night, was home when Leone stopped by their home. When she asked for the favor of a small loan, he refused her without hesitation. Leone was bitterly disappointed in him for his quick refusal, but was not to be discouraged in her mission. She had no difficulty securing the loan from a neighbor upstairs whose character was built on a more generous caliber.

Only Leone and Marie went to the railway station to see Bill off. The other three sisters said good-bye at home. When the trip had claimed enough time to reap its cruel harvest, the sisters thought sadly of their beloved brother. He had stood tall and boyish with bare head and fine features shadowed now by the familiar little grin as he vainly tried to be humorous. The girls felt if they had tried to prevail upon him to remain with them, he might have done so, but they did not. Thus, they blindly cast aside an opportunity given them by an ever-watching Providence. When the train went huffing and puffing and clanging into the distance, it bore their brother from them, leaving a gloom that was hard to put aside.

Upon arriving home, they found Mr. Hall waiting for them humble and apologetic. He had brought the five-dollar loan for Leone. It was too late. Bill was far upon his way.

Chapter 27
LIFE IN CHICAGO

The sisters soon settled into a practical routine of living. Every dollar they earned went into a fund. When the bills were paid, the balance was used by the one in the most pressing need for her personal comfort or adornment.

The girls were very busy. There was sewing to be done, and they were all working on furthering their education. Even Leone, after all the special courses she had taken at evening school, was still very interested in a course of study.

Helen was doing very good work in her studies, so good that her teachers were making a point of bringing her excellent grades to the attention of her sisters.

The girls grew happier each day in their home life and enjoyed going to church every Sunday. There was a nice young man who paid court to Leone. There had been others. However, if their attention showed signs of becoming serious, they were slowly and graciously avoided until they became discouraged. There could be no marriage for Leone at this time.

Helen came home from school on a cheerful day in mid-winter and approached the birdcage. Lying on the bottom of the cage, pale and still, was the lifeless little Cheapy. The older girls sincerely hoped they appeared innocent of the deed when they gathered about in sympathy and noted the effects of what was one of childhood's tragedies for their baby sister.

It had been a cold, nasty Midwestern winter. However, some cheerful spring days followed that gave promise of better times to come. Everyone had been content to remain in warm office buildings all winter however stuffy; they furnished protection against the sharp wind. The first warm days brought everybody out who could furnish an excuse for the purpose.

The landlord of their flat had such an excuse. At least he so informed Marie, who later regretted she happened to be at home. He did not appear in a very charming mood and brought up the subject that was troubling him without delay. He had received notice from his agent, Mr. Smith, that some of his tenants demanded a spring-cleaning. He had come around in person to inform them that such hopes were futile. He was renting his flats at such a low rate that he could not afford improvements anywhere. Marie could see that from his viewpoint at the moment. With the hope of putting him in a happier frame of mind, she pushed the door back on its hinges. She invited him in and showed him around all the rooms, and related, "You can see we were not the tenants who put in the request. We did the papering ourselves and are quite proud of it."

"You have good reason to be," he assured her. "This is a good-looking flat. It was a dark, grubby looking place the last time I was here. Bright and cheerful now," he chuckled. "Looks a lot better." He was moving to the door on his way out, jovial now in comparison to the gloom of his first appearance. "In fact, it has improved so much it will just mean a raise in rates to fourteen dollars a month for you young ladies, beginning next month."

Marie was amazed at his audacity and told him so. "When you have decent tenants that respect your property, you do not appreciate them."

His chuckle became a loud guffaw. "That's all right, young lady. I can take it. Just have the right check ready, and don't expect me to change my mind."

The frugal Marie found this turn of events very disturbing to her peace of mind. She felt this to be a grave injustice. Henrietta tried to cheer her. However amusing her remarks, they fell far short of the requirements necessary to lift the spirits of her sister to a customary level.

Presently Marie thought of what she considered a clever idea, to report the matter to the police. Leone had been away from AuGres long enough to know the police had no jurisdiction over problems of this nature. After a few moments of consideration, she concluded it would be best to remain silent. This could be a first hand experience for her sisters that could do no harm and might possibly be useful. At least Marie would be doing something to exhaust her pent-up angry emotions.   This might require a little stretch of the imagination, for Leone did not expect it to have any effect on their landlord.

Laura accompanied Marie as they went out in search of a police officer.   The girls watched from a window a few moments.   They were all laughing at the serious manner in which Marie was engineering a plot to even the score with their greedy landlord.   The officer who accompanied them on their return was a gentleman of the old school.   He was listening kindly, intent upon being of some assistance to the girls in their dilemma.   Marie showed him the outside hall, worn and soiled.   Then she invited him in to inspect their nice, clean flat with its bright new paper.   "And you did this all yourselves?"

Marie assured him they did, even furnishing the paper.

"Now, ain't ye young ladies the shining example for all tenants. I wouldn't want to be doin' such a big job meself and not even a thank ye.   I'm a worker when there's work to be done.   This man don't know when he's well off.   There is no law coverin' this style of knavery.   I can be of no help to ye with this kind of a skunk.   But I can advise ye where to move, out near Washington Park.   Ye can have a nice flat out there all steam heated, no wood coal and ashes to spile your pretty hands, mind ye.   And near the Park where ye young ladies should be, and the rent will be but fourteen dollars a month, possibly less."

They thanked him and listened to more of his paternal advice. "One item in renting was to have a lease by both parties that states what ye do and what ye don't do.   If ye young ladies had a lease now you could live here a year with no raise in rent."   His quaint Irish accent struck a responsive cord with the Neely sisters.   After all in their own blue veins ran a bit of the same strain.

When he had gone, they found Helen was not happy with the thought of moving out near the Park.   She had been behind in her grades, but with the cooperation of her present teachers she was making progress and would overtake her class this year and with perfect grades.   She preferred to remain with her present teachers for the balance of the school year.   All her sisters promptly agreed. There was also carfare to consider for Henrietta and Marie.   This would offset the difference in rent that existed between the two districts.

They went flat hunting right in their own neighborhood. There was no difficulty in finding a nice light, clean, steam-heated flat for nineteen dollars per month. Counting the cost of coal and wood they had been using in their flat, this turned out to be less expensive than their present abode. Their stove could be sold because a nice gas range had been installed in the new flat.

A few days later a billing for twenty-five dollars from the Smith Realty Company was received in the mail. Henrietta went to their files and taking the rent receipt covering their occupancy, she put them in Leone's purse, and asserted, "You have to go to their office and set them straight. We don't owe them a cent."

"I'll set them right, sure enough," laughed Leone. "But I'm glad we do not owe them. We would not find it very easy to pay."

The following evening after work, Leone hurried to Smith's Realty office before closing time and showed the man at the window her receipt. She advised him, "I received this letter from your firm. You will see by my receipts that there is some mistake. I do not owe your firm anything."

The gentleman took the papers from her hand and looked them over carefully. Then he responded, "The receipt date is for a different month."

Leone was quick to reply, "But we were not occupying this house during the month covered by this bill."

"No," he answered. "That is for the time the house was idle. You had a lease and placed yourself through this instrument responsible for the rent until we secured another tenant. That time proved to be one month."

Leone was dismayed and attempted further arguments. Finally, the man pointed out the clause in the lease to her. She could see it was quite useless to continue the discussion. She feared his threat was in accordance with state law.

In the weeks following, Leone was the recipient of several more letters from the Smith Realty Company that had begun to take on a threat to hail her to court. The Neely sisters gave this matter some serious consideration. With their changed fortunes they were just nicely able to pay their rent, but they could not afford to also pay rent on a vacant house. There was just no money to pay a lawyer, and they wondered what could he do anyway. Leone recalled that in the city of Detroit they had a Protective Association for Women and Children. She reached for the telephone book, and after a careful survey of its pages she found the address of an office that might help her solve the problem. She then presented herself at this office for an interview, and it was there she received helpful advice. If the prospective tenant was thoughtless enough to sign this type of lease, the matter she was involved in was according to state law. However, he also explained to her that there was protection for people of small means.

She was advised to put up a defense for herself. "If you do not try to defend your cause, it will go by default and will be more difficult later." The case would be heard in Justice Court on the west side of the City, far out and requiring a journey of two hours.

The Neely girls went into a huddle to decide a course of action. Leone, as the senior member of the family, was in the habit of wearing clothes that made her appear older than her years. When she started for Justice Court to put up the defense, she was wearing a jaunty little white suit that fitted her perfectly. A small blue hat with a schoolgirl trim of little white wings adorned her head, and her hair had undergone a slight change. Her striking outfit had been borrowed from fourteen-year-old Henrietta. That was not all the strategy produced by the family huddle. Leone was swinging blissfully along the street hand-in-hand with her little sister, Helen. The girls had rummaged a bit for a dress for Helen that if it did not make her look younger, at least it would not add anything to her years.

Arriving in court the two girls remained quietly seated in the crowded courtroom. While they looked out of place in that weird scene, they did not attract much attention. When Smith versus Neely was called, Leone went forward holding Helen's hand closely. The judge looked right past her and said loudly, "Is the defendant Neely present? Come forward, please."

"I am the defendant," Leone said quietly.

"You, the defendant?" he repeated. "Do you maintain a household?"

"Yes sir, my sisters and I."

He looked at Helen and asked, "Is she your sister?"

"Yes sir, there are five of us. I am the oldest, and she is the youngest. Three work and two go to school."

The judge flopped the papers to a different place on his desk. "Your case has been heard, Miss. No cause."

"I may go?" Leone asked wonderingly.

147

There was a nodded assent. The two girls tripped out of the gloom into the bright sunlight. Leone thought sadly of the long row of stern faces that lined the sacred benches. Each one was intent on their own problems, but some of the feminine ones had shown traces of tears. It would take more than a foxy looking white suit and a juvenile face to smooth out all of the forehead furrows she saw depicted in that courtroom.

The Neely sisters were grateful to have their troubles minimized and thought it would be proper to write Mr. Smith acknowledging this and thank him. They proceeded to do this at once and then began to breathe freely again over the incident.

As it turned out, the girls were reckoning without due consideration for the resourcefulness of the Smith Realty Company. After the expiration of the number of days required by law, Smith took a change of venue to the next nearest Justice, and Leone was again called to court in the same building to face the same charge.

Henrietta had opened the letter and acquainted herself with its contents. "This is dumbfounding," she exclaimed and then read the summons aloud. Her sisters all agreed with her.

"We will have to try some more strategy on them," Marie said firmly.

"I do not have any hope that it will work so smooth this time," Leone confessed. "The case will naturally be brought before a firmer judge."

This time on the designated court date, Leone and Marie appeared in court only to learn that Mr. Smith was unable to put in an appearance. Their case was postponed and a new date set. The girls thought ruefully of the long journey they must take again, but knew they must. The next time the case came up, the procedure was the same. Leone decided to be more sharply alert. She watched intently any man who could by a stretch of the imagination be Mr. Smith. In a short time after listening carefully, she felt confident that she could label Mr. Smith. After hearing a number of cases, some of them going by default, the man she had identified for herself as Mr. Smith chucked his leases in his coat pocket and started for the door. He was evidently aware that he would be running a gauntlet. The man moved fast, but the girls moved faster overtaking him in the hallway. Leone said, "I have a case coming up, Mr. Smith."

"You," he said. "Who are you? I never saw you before."

"Oh yes, you have. You have my lease in your pocket. I am Miss Neely."

Taking the papers from his pocket, he glanced through them, and then looked back to Leone's eager, determined face. He turned and with much reluctance went back to the courtroom. Leone remained by his side where Marie joined her.

"My men were not careful enough," he grumbled. "I had no idea we ever rented a house to such a young person. Who is this child?" he asked pointing to Marie.

"She is my sister. We paid every cent of the rent while we occupied your place, and that is all we can pay," Leone said defensively.

At that moment they were called before the judge. Mr. Smith made the plea. "I would like the case Smith vs. Neely dismissed. There are mitigating circumstances. Had I known of them sooner, the case would not have been brought before the court." The judge dismissed the case. Leone turned and thanked Mr. Smith in person.

A move to the St. Lawrence Building provided them with better sunlight and more room to place their personal effects. The girls were unanimous in proclaiming their former landlord did them a favor. "Quite unintentional, you may be sure of that," Marie said grudgingly, to the amusement of her sisters.

A nasty cold wind was blowing in from the Great Lakes reminding the inhabitants of their city and that winter had not lost its grip. Arriving home to the cozy steam-heated rooms after buffeting the chilling breeze on slippery streets had further cause for the sisters to be grateful.

When the sun returned to power and a welcome thaw was in full swing, Leone came blithely home one evening to find Marie and Laura enjoying what appeared to be the best joke of the season, judging by the laughter they were indulging in. The merriment hushed quickly when Leone appeared. Marie looked somewhat defiant. A deep flush suffused Laura's expressive face as she tried vainly to suppress her hilarity.

Her sister came in smiling, wondering what was so amusing that she could not share. It was evident that they were slightly embarrassed.

"Am I such a killjoy that all the fun must cease when I come on the scene?" Leone asked.

Laura, still trying to restrain her hilarity asserted, "This would not meet with your approval. It is against your ethics to laugh at a fellow when he is down."

Leone gave her a bewildered look. "Who's down?"

"Our former landlord. When we went by there on our way to school this morning, the pipes were thawing in our old flat, and the water was flying in torrents, all over the walls and everywhere, even running down the street. It has been vacant since we left, and the plumbers were just arriving to work."

Leone did look slightly regretful as she exclaimed, "And ruining our nice wallpaper. Wonder why they did not shut the water off outside?"

The girls were very happy and contented in the St. Lawrence flat, until early summer, and then they became ambitious. This worthy quality can be a very disturbing factor, whether it ever arrives at successful fruition or not. Among their acquaintances and friends were several ladies of esteem, who by their industry and tact succeeded in keeping extra rooms rented in their home and in this way made money to pay the rent of their home, plus a tidy little sum besides. The Neely sisters decided to try this method after due consideration. They went about it carefully, first renting a house for twenty-five dollars a month that was suitable for this purpose.

This time there was a lease, properly signed, of which the girls had a copy. They moved into this place with caution, sacrificing their own comforts to furnish the rooms properly. They decided if the renting business were unsuccessful, they would not be left with much unnecessary furniture.

Meanwhile, they came to another major decision to make. Should Leone give up her profession? Marie and Henrietta were both doing very well as seamstresses, their chosen line of work. Leone's salary was not of such vital importance now. The clinic where she was employed was moving far out on the North side, where they would occupy their own new building. It was too far for Leone to hope to commute to work every day. The thought of going to work nursing in private homes was not an appealing one. To be gone at night from her young sisters would not be a good arrangement. But the most compelling argument in this decision was the ambition to take up the study of textiles and learn the business of ladies tailoring. In time the sisters hoped to open their own dress and hat shop. Just at this time an opening of this nature

150

became available through the influence of a friend who was in this line of work. Leone would receive seven dollars per week to start.

Marie did not approve of this move. "Leone has brought such wonderful things into our lives through her profession, and she has been such a marked success. It seems like flying in the face of Providence to give it up," she told Henrietta.

"I don't agree with you," her sister answered.

Marie continued, "Perhaps you have not thought of it. There should be grave consideration before when you throw away anything as wonderful as a nursing career."

Henrietta offered an earnest observation, "Marie, you are too serious. Leone will not be giving up anything. She can go back to her profession at any time she should choose to do so. There is no reason to believe she would not become a success in some other line of endeavor, and in the textile arts we could all be a success together. As a nurse she must go on alone. I feel that for the present, nursing has served its turn. You and I are making money. Leone has this offer, and she should take it. We will make out very well financially, and it may be the steppingstone of some importance to our future."

Marie considered this for a time. "You may be right," she conceded. "When you think of it that way, it doesn't sound so disastrous."

Leone accepted the opportunity offered her with a ladies tailoring firm. After working there for some weeks, everything was going along smoothly. The sisters were all becoming rested in body and spirit. They were living close to church as well as a beautiful park.

Chapter 28
FUN WITH HOUSE GUEST JANE HALL

One cheerful day in midwinter, the Neely sisters were hustling about as usual, occupied with the various tasks that filled their young lives and kept them busy, happy and contented. Just before lunchtime, Mrs. Hall appeared in the shop. She was ushered into their home by the girls as they greeted her. She had a sad story to tell that gave them some concern. Mr. Hall had been suddenly stricken with what appeared to be, and the doctor agreed, was a serious illness affecting the heart. He was taken to a hospital, located on the South side, near the vicinity where the Neelys lived. Mrs. Hall had been a visitor at his bedside that morning and would return there when visiting hours permitted. In the meantime she had stopped by as an old friend of the Neely girls. There was nothing lacking in the hospitality offered. She was seated comfortably near a warm radiator while a nice lunch was being prepared. The girls all listened with sympathetic attention to what she could tell them concerning her sick husband. Mrs. Hall was in a very anxious frame of mind. There was only one son, Cliff, who had finished his education. Only one daughter, Jane, would graduate in June to become a teacher. However, the family could not hope to exist on Cliff's salary for so many months, not to mention hospital bills and funeral expenses. The woman was in such a blue mood that the girls declared even the atmosphere was blue after her departure. She came again the following day, and the girls listened in sympathy, as the grievous tale was unfolded along the same lines.

There was a third visit early one morning when Mrs. Hall was at their door again. The frail woman had remained at her husband's bedside all night. Now scarcely able to speak, she managed to convey the message, "Mr. Hall is gone." He had passed away an hour previous. The girls sympathized and cared for her until she felt stronger and went home to her bereaved family.

They later learned that Mr. Hall's remains would be taken to the homeland in Iowa and that the family would move there when arrangements could be made. But they also learned that the move would be with one exception, their daughter. Jane must stay to finish the school year. How this was to be accomplished, the Halls did not know. But her future depended upon this, and it must be done. After Mrs. Hall left, the Neely sisters sat down to hold a caucus. They went about it with none of their customary resolution. Each one knew what the others were thinking, but they seemed powerless to put thoughts into words. They just sat there pondering. After a time Marie said dismally, "What will we do about a proposition like that? It is bigger than we are."

"I do not know," Leone answered. "One thing we may as well face now is that we are going to be asked to invite Jane here for the six months."

Lifting both hands, Laura spoke with a repelling, decisive attitude. "Let us be positive about one thing. Do not offer to take her until they beg us to do so. They have relatives here better able to do this than we are."

Henrietta agreed, "I think you're right on that point. And we should not forget how those we hoped to depend on for just two dollars when we needed it so badly turned a bleak heart and a deaf ear on us."

Leone turned to Laura with a little smile. "You do not take such a decided stand most of the time. Laura, darling, do you really think it would be so bad?"

It was a quick reply. "Yes, I do, and I do most of the cooking. Of course, I realize that she is practically here already, but it makes me feel anxious now to think of it."

"Laura is right," Marie said firmly. "Should we make such an offer before they put their hopes into plain words and ask us?"

Henrietta looked at her sister sharply, "I do not think that saying no will be difficult. We would feel differently if the Halls had played square with us. When Leone received favors, she did her part fairly."

"But we still must be fair," interjected Marie. "Our mother always insisted on going more than halfway."

"And we have gone more than halfway now," Laura said caustically.

Henrietta smiled, "Maybe we should not allow ourselves to become too decided. Laura is thinking of that extra stack of pots, but Jane is not a child and should be of some assistance."

"Indeed," Laura said scornfully. "She will dust a chair when she sits in it. That will be all the help she will contribute." Leone arose and concluded, "Obviously there is no use in looking for a pink lining in this cloud when it doesn't have one. I think we all agree with Laura that it will not be smart to compromise. If we wait, we will not find it necessary to yield anything on either side."

And in fact, Mrs. Hall did come in person to ask the favor.

Leone was frank, "Our home is crowded now with five girls in a flat. Jane would be obliged to share my room. We are just not prepared for permanent guests." She continued, "I naturally thought she would stay at the home of your nephew, John Hand. They have a commodious home of two floors and only one little child."

Jane's mother had many objections to offer against this suggestion, "The Hands family had made no overture of assistance. If they experienced any sympathy in regard to Jane and her coveted

153

diploma, they carefully concealed such weakness." And she added, another objection looms, "Carfare to their suburban home would be forty cents, while from the Neely's home it would be but ten cents."

This was an argument that weighed heavily as the Halls had no money for carfare. In spite of their intentions to concede the issue from the first, the Neely girls still took three days to respond with their answer.

Henrietta had her joke over this. "It is my guess that we succeeded only in fooling ourselves since Jane arrived on the very next streetcar after a favorable reply in the way of a telephone message was made. Her suitcase was evidently packed!"

The Neely girls felt for Jane not only because of the death of her father but also because of the sad experience of being deprived of the independence of home life and family. However, since the sisters had also experienced this selfish family before, they did not rush in welcoming Jane. Deciding to use the slow approach, the girls never imagined trouble. Their attitude was found to be well taken. However, in just a very few days the guest had usurped a position in the household second to none! One of her favorite pastimes was to leave the dinner table every evening and then take all necessary equipment for her homework and establish herself in the center of the parlor; she considered her spot to be the best point of vantage for lighting. Then she would proceed to unlace and remove her shoes, kick them off in a careless fashion some distance from her chair, spread out her books on other furniture she had moved to accommodate her whims, and then work there until nine o'clock.

The Neely sisters maintained a living room for an entirely different purpose and had no intentions of permitting this unseemly intrusion to continue. However, the next problem was to prevent it without an open break in their relations. Leone tried hints to no avail. She then informed Jane that the girls were expecting company.

Jane looked up contemptuously, "Your guests are not familiar with homework? They should be," she replied and went on with her studies.

"It is not the homework that is so out of place, Jane. It is your bare feet and the furniture dragged about the room. It looks as if we are moving."

"Oh, if the doorbell rings, I will run out. I must have perfect quiet for my homework," she said in an offended tone.

"You have chosen the wrong room for perfect quiet, I assure you," Leone said warmly.

At that moment, the doorbell gave out a warning note. Jane grabbed her books, slid a foot into one shoe and went scrambling out of the room with as much of her paraphernalia as she could reach easily. However, she left one shoe and an unsightly pair of stockings on the floor, as well as other marks of disorder.

When the caller departed, Jane who was wearing one shoe, came limping back and reestablished herself in her stronghold position once more.

Leone went out to the kitchen to find Marie who was explaining something in hush tones to the two little girls. They were all giggling merrily. Leone listened a moment and giggled also. They all knew by now that Jane was such a coward that she was afraid of her own shadow. Their plan was to have Marie go and call on Mrs. Ball, who resided in a flat next door, and borrow an old English uniform. The uniform had been the property of Mr. Ball, who had worn it at an early age. Because it was a smaller size, it was not much too large for Marie. There was also a felt hat with a broad brim to conceal her hair. Next, Marie undid the lock on the French window that opened out to the lawn. She hastened out to complete the scheme. Mrs. Ball even came to the back door within a few moments to await the outcome at closer range.

It came shortly. Uttering a wild shriek, Jane came running, pale and trembling. She was alarmed beyond control. She exclaimed, "A thug was breaking in the window."

The girls closely followed by Mrs. Ball made a grand rush for the front room, with doubtful cries of, "No, no, impossible."

Jane summoned the strength to call out a warning, "You will be shot."

To make their bluff appear further believable, they hurried through the window, looked around and returned by way of the door. Laura replaced the bolt on the window, and they all filed back to see how Jane had survived the ordeal.

Jane was reclining in a chair, shaking and very pale. She had, however, sufficient strength to declare with emphasis that she had seen the brim of a man's hat and his eye as he cautiously pushed open a window. After encountering this danger, Jane took no further chances being in the front of the flat. Locking the rear door

155

carefully, she moved herself into the kitchen where the two little girls did their studying when necessary.

"How did you think of anything so smooth and successful?" Leone asked Marie.

"Well, I knew she would be afraid. I concluded that it was worth trying."

"Well you sure used your head and you seem to have succeeded perfectly. She was so firmly entrenched in that room, I thought she would never move. It was a very clever scheme!"

Chapter 29
SMALLPOX SCARE

The Neely sisters found the business of conducting a rooming house had many disadvantages. Chief among them was the labor involved. They soon learned this could not be regulated to the two little girls, however willing they might be. And the older girls could not do it justice and be gone all day. So they finally availed themselves of the good police officer's advice and moved to Hyde Park, located on Drexel Avenue. It was near Washington Park where in the winter they would enjoy steam heat.

Leone paid every last penny of the rent on the big house to the Smith Realty Company, returning the keys and the lease. When they finally became firmly entrenched in the commodious, cheerful flat on Drexel, the girls heaved a huge sigh of relief, as now their troubles seemed minimized.

Chicago was a city filled with wonders for the Neely sisters. It was overflowing with crowds of people going rapidly in all directions, all bent on the furtherance of their own business. Moving to Hyde Park added to the marvels of the great city. Hyde Park was a beautiful part of the metropolis with its enclosure of parks and amusements. There were many fine homes, representative of wealth and splendors that ornamented Drexel Boulevard. This overflowed to many side streets, and even the shops manifested finesse not to be found at stores in the St. Lawrence District. Moving even this short distance was like taking up residence in a different city. The girls never tired of looking at a skyline where the intricacies of the work of man arose to meet the divine handicraft. Occasionally they strolled down to the water's edge where a great city met a great lake to witness the phenomenon that never grows old, a gorgeous sunrise.

Deeply entrenched in these recollections would always remain the memory of a perfect eclipse. The sun arose on a dew-dipped pink and silver morning looking enormous in size as it came into view across the shimmering waters of Lake Michigan.

They were formalizing plans for some time to open their own dress and hat shop. This latest venture, Henrietta declared, required more brain expansion than anything they had previously undertaken.

"Yes," Marie agreed. "It takes money or wits to get things going. As we have no money, we will have to depend upon our wits."

Leone joined in the laughter that followed and then remarked, "Even wits can be pushed too far."

Henrietta arose. "Let's go downstairs and see what that ground floor flat has to offer. It has been vacant so many months. The rent should be reasonable."

All the sisters followed, maintaining quiet in the hall. There was no difficulty gaining entrance. Closing the door, the Neely girls rambled delightedly through the rooms, seven in number, too large for the average family. The flat would aid them nicely in their ambition. There were two parlors. With the addition of a few pieces of furniture, including a full-length mirror, the business of dressmaking could be conducted here. They would not attempt to carry a stock of goods at this time. Instead, they would fashion the customer's own material. Even the hats could be made to order. They found glass enclosed shelves suited to the carrying of samples for this purpose.

The practical Marie proclaimed, "Moving is mere detail."

"Troubles do minimize when a group of strong, willing hands get together and work for the same purpose," Leone agreed smiling.

"If in company with their heads," Henrietta interjected.

They all agreed that their heads and their hands would be closely allied. With a determination to make this business a success, they must pool all the resources they possessed. This was accomplished, and they were in business in a few days. Their sign, which read "NEELY SISTERS DRESS & HAT SHOP," was hung in the front window. The girls decided that Leone would undertake the work alone at first. The location proved to be an advantageous one and was a fair success from the start. In very short time it was necessary for Henrietta to join forces with Leone to do justice to their own unfolding business.

The cold winds brought about all the customary latent danger with its many little periods of distress as well as the joy that the old city of Chicago was heir to. The winter following proved no exception to the rule. Adding to the inconvenience and discomfort of the people was the appearance of a formidable number of smallpox cases. These patients were removed on observation to what was then known popularly as the "Pest House." Thought of the dread disease did not trouble the five sisters who were blessed with good health. They were quite indifferent to a smallpox scare.

Leone and Henrietta were busy with their dress shop. Marie was going forth and back each day to a style center in the great metropolitan wholesale district. She was eagerly working to gain a foundation that would direct the style along most up-to-the-minute lines for later that season in the Neely sisters' own little hat and dress shop.

February arrived with its frost in the air, light snowfall, and penetrating wind.

Helen came home from school at the close of the first week in that memorable month with slight signs of a little rash erupting on her dainty pink and white skin with no accompanying fever. Leone did not attach much importance to this, especially as Helen informed her nearly everyone at school had experienced this slight malady. Monday morning found the annoyance about gone. Helen insisted upon not breaking a perfect attendance record, and the older girls-- attaching little importance to the matter--did not object. She experienced no further annoyance. However, later that week the sisters were made aware that Helen had brought home the contagion. When Sunday dawned, Marie was the only one in the family showing no signs of this slight nuisance. Later in the day when Sunday callers dropped in and openly admired the warm color the girls had gained by moving near the park, the sisters were much amused and laughed aloud when the visitors had departed.

"If this little rash improves our appearance so much, we should be positively beautiful with the smallpox," Henrietta remarked scornfully.

Marie shuddered, "Don't say such things. It seems like inviting disaster."

158

Monday found them each returning back to normal, and they went their separate ways.

Leone and Henrietta compared notes to decide which one of them showed the least signs of their nasty little affliction. They decided that the better appearing one would meet the customers. It was determined that Henrietta would be the one to greet customers, so Leone headed to the workroom.

The day passed smoothly until about two o'clock when Leone looked up to find Marie coming in the rear entrance, apparently ill with disaster written all over her pathetic little olive face.

Leone went quickly to her sister's side, "Darling, what is it?" she inquired anxiously. "Are you ill? You look as though you had been caught in an earthquake!"

Leone was answered by a burst of tears amidst violent sobbing. Marie could make no reply. The older girl held her close, trying vainly to soothe and comfort her. "Try to tell me what happened?" she pleaded.

"Smallpox" Marie gasped just the one word. Then she stopped in a breathless silence.

"Smallpox?" repeated Leone in awe-stricken tone. "Your skin does look queer, but you are probably just coming into that little rash. What made you think of smallpox? You have been out in the cold wind, and you always did have a sensitive skin."

"I will catch smallpox if I go to the Pest House," she wailed in a fresh outburst of weeping.

"Go to the Pest House? Why should you?" asked Leone in dismay.

Marie managed to whisper between her sobs. She had gone to a doctor's office to satisfy a growing anxiety among her co-workers who were looking upon her with increasing alarm. The physician whom she consulted promptly called in a skin specialist from an adjoining office. They both agreed on the diagnosis. She had overheard them telephone the Health Department and then agree to detain her until the ambulance had arrived. This unexpected turn of events made her blood feel like ice in her veins. It also brought out her natural heritage, the fighting Irish. She was little more than a child alone with all the odds stacked against her. Somewhat daunted, she decided to fight. Rising quietly to leave the room, she found both doctors at the hallway door. They were big fellows and determined. Marie was little, but more determined. She had pushed past the doctors and secured a hold on the door handle. However, Dr. Bern had put a strong shoulder against it and warned her, "You have my deepest sympathy, Miss, but you have nothing to gain by leaving here. We will follow you promptly to your home and remove you from there. If that happens, you will expose everyone that you come in contact with to this dreadful disease."

"I have no smallpox," the girl shouted.

This outburst had the desired effect. Dr. Bern had other patients. He stepped quickly, if reluctantly, aside. Marie speedily opened the door and glided down the hall with a clarity that displayed no weakness. The elevator soon dropped her to the main floor. Once on the ground she stepped onto the first streetcar that appeared. She let it bear her some distance from the point she would have normally boarded the Cottage Grove car. All this precaution was taken even though she had a consuming desire to get home and hopefully to safety. The trip home had been uneventful, and she was evidently quite ahead of her pursuers. And this was not even in the age of fast motors.

While this tragic tale was unfolding, Leone was busy making her sister comfortable. When Marie's warm shawl wrap was removed, Leone folded it about her and advised, "We will hide you in the closet of the vacant apartment. There will be no one around in this kind of weather to look for an apartment."

Marie was aghast, "We would not dare to hide me."

Leone looked at her doubtfully. "With that face, my plan is the best. We will have Laura come out in your place."

Marie smiled for the first time. With Laura's pink and white loveliness, she knew this plan would succeed, and she laughed a fluttering little laugh.

They hastened to the dark closet, in the "To Let" apartment upstairs. Leone closed the door after helping fix a seat and hurried back to carry through her plan.

She had not long to wait. She answered the doorbell. A young man was on the threshold. He gave her a card and announced, "I am Dr. Reynolds from the City Health Department. I have a warrant to take a Miss Marie Neely, a smallpox case, into detention. She did very wrong to come home. Dr. Bern tells me that she is an advanced case."

Leone smiled disarmingly. "At that time my sister had been out in the cold wind. She has a very sensitive skin, so she looked bad, no doubt. She was an hour on the warm streetcar and has been home an hour in the warm rooms and is looking quite normal now, baring a slight rash that we have all had."

"Marie," she called raising her voice. "Dr. Reynolds from the Health Department is here to see you."

In a moment Laura, a vision of pink and white health, entered the room with a complexion so perfect it seemed almost enhanced by what appeared at first glance to be tiny dabs of carelessly placed rouge. Closer inspection revealed that this was the intruding skin eruption.

The doctor was a young man. He lifted his gaze and met a roguish smile in eyes of Irish blue. He was looking slightly embarrassed as he placed a chair for her. "Do you mean to say that Dr. Bern pronounced this case smallpox?" as he leaned toward the patient.

"Let me see your tongue, please."

The same disconcerting and smiling eyes looked at him as a pink tongue came obediently into view.

The doctor looked further embarrassed. "Thank you. I'm sorry to have been obliged to disturb you."

The "make believe" Marie assured him that she did not mind as he humbly bowed himself out.

Following this incident, the Neely girls had no trouble in persuading Marie to remain at home until her skin was quite normal, which proved to be three days.

Chapter 30
SOCIAL TIMES

The Neely sisters were not interested in business and the art of making a living to the exclusion of social life. They were bubbling over with fun and at a moment's notice would join friends for a little adventure.

The great city was all new to them. A trip to the park or amusement pavilion was only the price of a dime. They found it both strange and interesting that on their list of friends could be counted Mr. and Mrs. Frederick Ball, Mr. and Mrs. John Scanlon, and Mr. and Mrs. Thomas Fitzpatrick. A small number of charming girls were also found to be among their intimates, chiefly Katherine Curray and Jackoline O'Donnel.

There were a small number of clever and amusing young men on this list also: Willis Hand, Charles Wheaton, Carl Sundstrom, Ben Smith, and Jimmy Greely. There were many other girls and young men at all events. However, this list comprises the names of persons whose friendships contributed most to the sisters' social life.

Willis Hand was easily the outstanding member of this group. A nephew of Mr. Hall, Willis met Leone when she first came to Chicago. He had been patiently devoted to her during the intervening months. However, Leone had honestly discussed the subject of marriage with him early in their friendship, advising him that marriage was not for her.

"And why not?" he'd asked.

"Duty demands I stay with my sisters until they are old enough to fight their own battles with life. I will not miss these years. I will find them intriguing. I'm young enough for that."

"Yes," Willis had agreed. "I'm in the same boat about the marriage part. I could not think of wedded bliss on my salary."

"You might get a better paying job," she offered honestly.

"I get an average salary now, although it scarcely covers average expenses for a bachelor."

"Then I would find it necessary to look for some nice girl who would have me."

"Sounds too exciting," he said dryly and began turning the pages of a magazine while Leone moved to start brewing a nice little supper. She liked the friendship that had grown between them and was happy to keep it just that.

"Willis came as usual after this clearing of the atmosphere," Leone said, speaking of it afterwards to Cleo. She shared further that their conversation took place before her sisters came to Chicago. Continuing, she added, "Upon the arrival of my sisters, he moved naturally into the position of older brother and advisor. It was quite evident that he is happy with this intangible relationship."

Some days later and early one morning the telephone gave a long shrill peal. Leone stirred on her pillow, trying to arouse herself from a deep sleep. She reached for the light switch, taking note of the time. It was near five o'clock in the morning. "If that was the phone, it would be a wrong number at this hour," she thought. The repeated jingling, compelling sound of the bell and sleepy voices of her sisters again disturbed the customary stillness of the hour. Hastily sitting up, she slid her feet to the floor, then her toes into soft slippers. Rising, she glided quickly across the room. Leone removed the receiver from its hook and answered softly, "Hello."

"That you, Leone?" came the response in a firm masculine voice.

"Yes, this is Leone."

"Cliff calling. I was just about to leave the office after my night's work, and I was going to drop by your place. It's important that I see you. I called to learn if you would be home."

"Where else would I be at this hour?" she asked. "Has your mother fallen ill again?"

"I figured you would be home, but I wanted to be sure. It is out of my way to go to your place. I have to transfer from the Halsted Streetcar at this time in the morning."

"Cliff, tell me what on earth is the matter?" begged Leone.

"I'll be there in a short time and will explain," he said quickly and hung up the receiver.

Helen was awake as she shared the room with Leone. Marie and Henrietta were also sitting up in bed with puzzled interest. Leone repeated every word of the conversation in hopes that they could see if by piecing together anything from the tangle of words that passed between them that would warrant this presumption.

It was near six o'clock when Cliff's strong finger was placed on the Neely sisters' doorbell with sufficient force to resound throughout the building. Leone rushed to the door, opening it quickly with "Come in, Cliff. Tell me what is the trouble? It must be something dreadful to prompt you to come at this time in the morning."

Cliff smiled, "Oh, no. On the contrary. This is the best time for me. I'm on my way home now. It would be necessary for me to break up my sleep if I came later."

"The only thing I could think of was that your mother had taken sick."

"She is quite well now. Matter of fact, they are all going to a picnic and caught me short of change. I want to borrow five dollars. That is all there is to say or explain."

Leone felt limp. Such egotism as this was more than she could hope to question with any degree of success. She reached and took a flower vase in her hands that was standing on the mantle above the

163

fireplace. She removed a five-dollar bill that came in late on Saturday, the previous day. She handed it to Cliff in silence.

"Thank you," he offered putting the money in his vest pocket. "I must be off now." And rising to go, he added, "I like to get my regular rest, and I have spent quite a little time on this already."

Her hair in curl paper and wearing a dressing gown Leone accompanied him to the door. As she stood on the threshold of her apartment, the tall handsome young man turned to say, "Good morning and thanks for your kindness."

And just at that moment, the hall door opened admitting the building janitor.

Closing the door, Leone rejoined her sisters. Laura was awake now. "What did he want?"

"To borrow five dollars," Leone answered.

"Incredible conduct," Marie said tartly.

"But not from him," Leone noted hopelessly.

"Arousing us from our sleep over an hour ago," Henrietta said with a scorn.

"Strange he would not get such a small loan where he works," Marie grumbled.

"Someone should heave a rock at that boy's cranium and let some light into his brain," Henrietta added with a smile.

"Not in that head!" Laura replied with grim emphasis. "It is empty."

However, even Willis could not watch the enthusiasm of the Neely sisters without becoming somewhat imbued with ambition. Cultivating the friendship of some fellows with musical talent, they organized a nice little orchestra, with Willis as manager. Eventually they engaged a hall and conducted a series of dancing parties fortnightly throughout that winter. This provided a pleasing interlude, a social as well as financial asset for the young men engaged in the enterprise.

Sylvia Hand and the Neely sisters were the hostesses assisting them in the arrangements. The closing night came late in March. All the young people resolved to make this finale a special success, inviting everyone whom they thought would fit into the picture. The reward for this zeal was a delightful crowd.

Leone presented to Willis a pretty, vivacious young woman, a customer of the dress shop whom she invited, promising her a pleasant evening. She was a divorcee with a young child. She had enlisted Leone's sympathy when she complained of a drab existence.

Willis seemed kindly toward her, introducing her to other boys, and Leone was pleased. Later, when home-going time arrived, Willis came up in an apologetic mood. "Would the Neely girls excuse him from escorting them home? This was the last night to play for his group and there would be some extra taking down of equipment to be done."

As a small crowd was going their way, he was readily excused. This was the last they saw of Willis. Many days later it was learned he had transferred his interest to the widow. Within a few weeks they were married.

Leone wondered if the feeling she experienced at this unexpected turn of events could possibly be defined as regret. After all, she seemed to have lost a good friend and a good customer, too. Then again, that temporary weak spot in the region of her stomach could come from participation in destiny. She soon gave up the notion of trying to figure it out.

Helen and Laura came rushing home from school one spring day filled with excitement. White City would open to the public within a week as a special attraction for the resumption of their amusement activities for the summer. The management had completed arrangements and would have an airship on display. It was built during the winter months by some enterprising youth in the City of Pittsburgh. It had soared on its own power, making a triumphal landing at moorings in White City. It would be on display for the benefit of the sightseeing public for the small sum of ten cents.

"We must see that," exclaimed Henrietta. "But don't be unmindful of the fact that the small sum of a dime takes on the proportions of a half dollar for the Neelys."

"Oh, I forgot," Helen laughed. "There are so many of us. We can never hope to do anything on a really small scale."

Leone looked up from the work in her hands, "And would you lop off a sister or two for the privilege of seeing this airship?"

Helen giggled some more. Leaning, she placed a kiss on the side of Leone's slender white throat.

"I would not give up one of my honey and gold sisters for a week to see all the airships in the world. But I do want to see this one. I am going to watch the *American* to see if they have any passes. That newspaper carried a lot of them last year."

Laura picked up the paper. Helen helped her unfold and search its many pages for the coveted passes. "No luck this time. I think it is too early in the season for passes," Helen said regretfully.

"And that airship is only going to be there two weeks," Laura added.

Cliff Hall, Mr. Hall's tall, good-looking son, called on Leone in great anxiety one afternoon. His mother was very sick. Erysipelas, her old enemy, had attacked again. Leone had taken such good care of Mrs. Hall on previous occasions such as this, and he feared for his mother's life, unless she again came to their assistance.

Leone answered gently, but firmly that she had her own business financial problems demanding her full time and attention. "Besides," she responded, "any trained nurse whom they called would care skillfully for Mrs. Hall." After repeated further pleas and promises to pay the highest wage, he got nowhere on his request. Cliff was forced to accept Leone's refusal.

However, Cliff came again the next day. Mrs. Hall had become much worse, in spite of all the care they had lavished upon her. The doctor despaired for her life. Her two brothers had been called to her bedside. She did not recognize anyone now. In tears he begged Leone to try to help her, and the girl could no longer refuse.

Three days and three nights had passed when Mrs. Hall weakly opened her eyes to this world once more. The first person she saw was Leone; she gently whispered, "Old Faithful."

Leone stood by, changing the applications. At first the fever dried them quickly, but the fever was smoldering now, and they did not require frequent change. Leone decided to go home for a good sleep.

Just as she was leaving, Cliff's voice called to her, "Do you see that dime on the hall table by the fern?"

"Yes, I see it."

"Do you know whom it belongs to?"

"You, I suppose."

"No, it is yours. I put it there for your carfare."

After a moment's consideration, she reached and picked up the small coin.

Leone came again the next day, finding the patient much improved. Mrs. Hall's hair was pasted down tight to her head as a result of the continued applications of the potent solution that helped save her life. It had now become dry and stiff from contact with the air adding somewhat to her discomfort and nothing to her looks. Leone decided to brush it out. She went to a drugstore to select in person a brush suited to such a complicated task.

Leone was patiently at work trying to restore some slight resemblance to what nature intended in the vanquished locks when Mrs. Hall asked, "Do you know whose five dollars you took to the store just now?"

"Yours, I would think."

"No, it belonged to you. My brother, John, left it for you. He said he wished he had many times that sum. He was so grateful to you for helping save my life. The doctor promised he could save me if you would come to carry out his instructions. This disease is such a bad thing to have in the blood, and nurses are afraid of the contagion. My other brother, Ed, left five dollars for you also. I was obliged to use it because I was short at the time. As soon as I can, I will save out the 10 dollars and take it to you myself. And of course, my son will pay you as he promised."

Mrs. Hall's precarious state of health was prohibitive for Leone to make a candid reply, even if she had chosen to do so. She instinctively glanced on the hall table as she was leaving, but there was no dime.

Helen and Laura were delighted when she arrived home. They were thrilled with the most exciting news. Laura explained to Leone that White City would have an airship of its own. The one on exhibit for the previous week returned to its home base in Pittsburgh.

An afternoon paper carried the news that an airship was under construction for the exclusive use of White City for exhibition purposes.

"We will see one yet," exclaimed Helen. "We will use some of all that money Leone collected from the Halls."

"You may well laugh and look doubtful, but it's the same old story." Leone then gave them a detailed account.

"We may as well laugh," Helen said.

Henrietta was lifting the covers off from various boxes with an enigmatic expression, "The same can be said for a lot of things that have come into our lives through stubborn Leone. I am so excited. I cannot think clearly enough to decide what I should begin on."

"Oh, work on little Tommy's suit," Helen said quickly. "Mrs. Fitz informed me that the picnic is going to be this Sunday."

Henrietta paused, some materials suspended in her hand. "The Hibernians' picnic?" she queried.

"Yes, the Hibernians' picnic," was the reply.

"They would not allow Tommy to wear the little man's suit to a picnic. I'm just making it for fun. We happen to have that short remnant left from the bolt of goods we sold. He is such a cute, upstanding little figure; I could not resist the temptation to see him in a little man's outfit."

"When his parents see that tiny vest with the cunning pockets, it will get very respectful treatment."

"I hope they let him wear it plenty, or it will soon become an antique. Someday, children's clothes will be more like their elders'. I think we should go to the picnic by ourselves. We know so many people, and there will be plenty of boys."

"Good idea," Marie agreed. "It will avoid that little embarrassment about carfare. Leone must be about run out of excuses to account for her paying the carfare."

"I don't think she gives any excuses. There are just so many of us, and we nearly always travel together. The boys are good sports when they have the money, but salaries are so small they simply do not have the money." Marie thought this over a moment: "Then let's just take Jackoline and Katherine with us." The group concurred. Sunday morning gave promise of a perfect day. The girls hurried. They would attend church, and the lunch must be already packed since it was a long streetcar ride to the suburban park where the picnic was to take place.

Laura, dashing through the hall, paused impulsively by the open door of a wardrobe and stood there in an attitude of indecision. "Girls," she called in a shrill voice. "Shall we wear our glad rags?"

"We must try to look our best, but we will have to wear wash rags to a picnic," Marie replied reflectively.

"We will not find washrags very becoming to my tall, graceful shape," Laura answered cryptically.

"Wear your white skirt and jacket," Marie advised through a mouthful of hairpins. "We must hurry."

"Oh that pleated skirt requires so much ironing," Laura grumbled, taking it off the hook, "And I am hurrying. I am two jumps ahead of you girls now."

Jackoline and Katherine appeared just as the Neely sisters completed their preparations.

The group of girls arrived at the picnic grounds in good time. The contests and games were scheduled to begin at two o'clock. There was an orchestra playing at a pavilion. The girls sauntered along slowly, directing their steps in the general direction from whence was coming luring Irish airs. They were an attractive group of girls, mirthful and carefree. Irish eyes, trying to be alluring, sought them out, and they were not of the feminine type. Thomas Fitzpatrick, already on the floor, did the honors for the boys. Soon the older girls were dancing.

Kitty, Laura, and Helen went to find Mrs. Fitzpatrick. Later the girls moved along, planning to witness the contest. Three of them could now boast a charming escort. If there did not seem to be enough young men to go around, Leone would walk alone.

The games were strenuous, the rewards worth striving for, and rivalry was keen. They were a happy, merry crowd. All had their own favorites, some for reasons of kinship or friendship, some chosen at random for their outstanding ability in a hard-fought contest. Leone was not without a hero. He was in the later class, well up in front, tall and attractive. She favored him with a smile when he distinguished himself through the finals. Helen came and joined them, somewhat hurriedly, her face alight with youthful eagerness. "Crowds were rushing to the tables," she announced. She with Katherine and Laura leagued themselves with friends. "We are holding a table, and everything is ready. The coffee is made, and there is plenty of room."

Henrietta interrupted, her blue eyes gleaming, "We have company."

"There is a place for everybody," called Helen, leading the way back to the reserved table.

Leone lingered. She had observed a young man coming her way in company with a woman friend. She recognized her hero of the contest and it was always a delight to meet Mrs. Delaney, quaint and from the "Auld Sod," to quote from her own vocabulary.

"Leone," she said in her shrill high-keyed voice. "You will be meetin Bernie Gile."

"Now, Mr. Gile, this is Miss Neely. Be shakin hands in the good old American fashion."

He gravely extended a hand to Leone; only his eyes betrayed amusement.

"It was at a Hibernian picnic and in a like manner to this, I first met me Johnny." Mrs. Delaney chatted on, "And I've lived a fine life with him since." Scarcely waiting for a reply, she continued. "You will be seein him here today. He is a fine lookin, upstandin man yet. He is a tradesman, me Johnny is. He never was built for no tiller of the soil; tried to grow some cabbage one time. He drowned em with kindness in a few days. Never gave em a chance to grow. No, me Johnny was built for a tradesman. I will be off lookin for him now and leave you young people to your own whims. It is eat en time, and me Johnny will be expecting his supper." She was gone in a moment, as quickly as she had come.

Left so unceremoniously, the two young people turned to one another in some slight embarrassment. To Leone the presence of Bernie Gile was not unexpected, but her usually glib tongue did not seem to move in its customary manner.

"I enjoyed seeing you participate in the contest. You have the ability to win," she said smiling.

"And I am happy to admit I saw you cheering and derived from your cheers and smile the incentive to win."

"Your line is tipped with blarney," she assured him with some hesitance.

"I did not see you in the girls' contests."

"No, I did not enter. Two of my sisters won some prizes. I thought that was enough from the Neelys. You must be hungry?"

"Yes, I would like nothing better than a midday feast right now, but there is nothing for sale here. May I ask you to have dinner with me at a restaurant?"

"Oh, let's just join the picnickers. We girls brought a basket."

"Sounds plenty intriguing. If I may be so bold on short acquaintance?"

"Oh yes, you're quite welcome." Leone led the way.

Bernie hesitated when he saw six girls and three boys already seated at the festive board. Their laughing voices indicated they were having fun. And unless the basket was a somewhat bottomless affair, its contents he was sure could not be expected to go around. However, he was reassured by the happy group themselves. The basket was one of those regular picnic hampers that contained unlimited quantities of goodies.

170

The young men proved to be friends. Leone introduced the girls. There was a place set at the table, apparently awaiting him. He seated himself at their invitation and then viewed the situation with alarm.

"I am intruding. You were expecting someone." They all laughed in the way young people have of doing.

"Indeed, we were expecting you," Henrietta assured him peering into the hamper. "And as hero of the day, we saved you two drumsticks." She placed them unceremoniously on his plate.

He looked embarrassed, "I'm afraid you are too kind. A chicken has only two legs."

"This chicken had four," she said saucily. Again they all laughed.

Larry looked across the table with narrowed eyes, "Better be brave. Faint heart, you know that old one."

Leone turned frankly to Bernie as she poured his coffee. "It just happened your place was set." Then she explained to the others, "He is starving after all the contests he took part in."

"Listen to the music," Jackoline said, her eyes shining. "The dance is resuming, and we will be resuming in a very short time."

"I hope they dance some Irish reels," injected Leone. "I love them."

"Oh they will," Bernie told her. "We will ask for them." He looked around the group, his eyes glad, "I was just trying to think where I have been all my life as I see seven lovely American girls."

"Bernie can be the blarney," Henrietta said as she continued passing more sandwiches. Then she added, "Looks like we may have too much. I hope we do not have to toss it away."

"No, no. Save everything," the boys advised. "We will all have another sandwich after the dance." With this promise, they hurried to the pavilion to dance the Irish dance. The rhythm was a part of their emotions. The Irish reel could be in progress for hours with no break in its rhythmic perfection; no caller, no wild swinging, just a perfect artistry of the dance. Bernie did honor to his ancestry, following the intricate steps with grace and precision. Leone happily listened to his clear tenor voice as he joined softly in the folk songs for her ear alone. He was master of the typical wit and humor of the traditional Irish youth. She learned he was a railroad man with uncertain hours of leisure.

171

It was near ten o'clock when the girls moved in the direction of the streetcar for the slow ride home. It had been a long day filled with many pleasant diversions. All the boys accompanied them and waved good-bye as the car pulled out. But it was Bernie who paid carfare for seven and saw the girls safely on the car.

Bernie Gile was a captivating young man. He had succeeded in winning for himself an enviable place in the friendship of all the girls. There was something special in the character of this young man with the quiet voice and the ready smile. Marie remarked about this phase of his manner, cheerful, but not shrill. Her sisters dubbed Leone's big moment to be very soon.

"Yes," Henrietta answered musingly, "that's it. He is restful and comforting, apparently happy in the prevailing atmosphere. Do you think Leone will come to love him?"

Marie looked thoughtful. "No," she said slowly. "She has schooled herself too well for that. It is easier to keep from falling in love than it is to fall out of love. I think she would refuse to see him if she found her resolve weakening."

"But," Henrietta's tone was terse, "What about Bernie?"

"Without being personal, Leone was very frank in making her intentions clear to him that she could not marry for a number of years. She plans to remain single until Helen is independent. I was present when they discussed the matter."

Henrietta pursued the issue, "And what did Bernie have to say about that?"

"Very little," Marie's responded. "I might say he appeared indifferent."

Henrietta deliberated for a moment before continuing. "He visits us just the same, takes the crowd out for a good time as usual, and Leone is still popular with him." She concluded, "He is an exceptional young man."

That fall the girls decided to plan a Halloween party. Jackoline and Katherine took a personal interest in the planning. There were two large parlors and a dining room in the spacious old flat. Traditional decorations could be used at nominal expense. All seven of the girls were motivated by but one ambition when grouped together. They were totally engrossed in working out the complicated details of the party.

The freedom of their new life would be given expression. This was the first celebration they attempted while they laughed and chatted, cutting and pasting as they talked.

"I have a wonderful disclosure to make," Laura announced, her eyes shining. All the girls looked to her in pleasant anticipation. "It can be summed up in one word, cornstalk," she said, her voice vibrant.

"Oh," Marie remarked in a falling key, "I thought of cornstalk, too. Then I remembered we are not living at AuGres anymore."

"But I have found some," Laura insisted.

"You have? Do not keep us in suspense. Is there some way to acquire them?"

"Sure thing. All it takes is brawn. We will have to carry them three blocks; our acquaintance, Mrs. Tower, has them in her garden. All the good corn has been removed. There are many small ears showing corn-silk, and the stocks have not been frosted."

"It is wonderful that anyone would have the courage to plant a few hills of corn in a city crowded like Chicago," Leone said in a surprised tone.

"Or where they could find a plot of ground to plant it?" Marie added skeptically.

"Singular as it may seem, they found the ground and planted the corn, and we can have the stocks," Laura added merrily. "I promised to go for them this evening. We will be less conspicuous carrying them in the dusk."

All the girls laughed. They would not mind carrying such a treasure right through the crowd on State Street. "I would carry my share on State Street," Leone agreed, "But I am glad we do not have to."

Helen and Leone did not accompany the girls on their errand for the corn. They remained at home to prepare for the rather bulky addition in the way of decorations.

When the girls with their merry tinkling voices had gone, an unusual quiet pervaded. The two girls worked almost in silence, taking their mood from the momentary stillness. Leone trailed back in spirit to the past, and many thoughts flooded her memory. As children they would work long hours on the frosty ground separating the corn from its stocks. A tarp would be spread on the big living room floor and the corn placed there, a huge pile to be husked in the evening hours. This could be a task made lighter by fun and

173

laughter, something that was an unknown quality when work was being done under the supervision of Robert Neely.

She could look back now with tranquil thoughts to those years of tempest and strife. Tender memories were all that lingered. Bitterness had burned itself out.

The Halloween decorations were perfect. The lighting effects were produced with the aid of jack-o-lanterns and trick wiring. A witch served refreshments from an iron pot that was standing on its own legs before the fireplace. A Halloween menu included dead beets. Traditional games were played from diving for apples to "I win, who follows?" The party proved to be everything the girls had hoped it would be.

Chapter 31
FAMILY VISITS

One evening as they were about to sit down to dinner, the doorbell rang. Henrietta hurried through the hall with her thoughts on a good dinner, cooling nearby. On opening the door, she was speechless, but she quickly reached out her arms to a tall young man. Helen gasped from her observation point in the hall, "Bill, I'll bet you." She ran to the door crying, "Girls, it is him."

They were all at the door by this time. Leone and Marie put an arm about him and led him in. He was Bill all right, but such a sadly, different Bill. One entire side of his beloved boyish face remained immobile. Even when he talked, there showed on that side what had been a very bad wound, cut through the ear, scarcely healed as yet. On the other side was what remained of his old habitual grin. He looked forlorn and tired, but they were all excited.

"Let's try to eat our dinner," Leone suggested, making an effort to speak calmly.

Bill answered in a normal voice, "Show me some home cooking, and I will eat."

They hovered around him like mother birds. His hearing had not been harmed, strangely enough. He explained how the accident happened. He was helping in the lumber woods when with his ax he thoughtlessly struck a sapling borne part way to the ground by a falling tree bent in a taunt position. The sapling had thrown the ax back with such force he was fortunate to escape with his life!

"Oh, it will be kind of a nuisance. Folks will have to run around to my other side to see if I am laughing at their jokes."

Helen looked at him with tearful eyes. "I shall make it a point to be on your laughing side all the time. Tell us about Dad. Where is he? We have not seen him for months."

"We took up land adjoining and fixed up a house that was on one side. Then I got the measles and was pretty sick. When I was halfway through that scrape, Dad got discouraged and ran out on me. I have not seen him since."

"Did he leave someone to look out for you?" Marie asked.

"Nope, not Dad. He left me sick and alone on the baldheaded prairie. Dad never did take his family very serious."

Leone looked at Bill, "Did he leave you any money?"

One side of his face smiled. "Did he leave you any?" he asked in turn.

"What did you do?"

"A neighbor drove up and took me home with him. I was given good care. I rode the range that summer for them. They were poor people. I made the debt even, and they paid me a little."

The girls looked sympathetically at their brother while they made a few candid remarks about their father.

Bill lifted a warning hand. "Hold on, girls. Have you forgotten what Mom would say?"

"Even I know that," Helen remarked.

"You don't remember from Mom. You could know it though. You tell it."

Helen responded. She would say, "Remember children, he is your father. No matter what he does, he is your father." Helen's little face was solemn as she spoke almost reverently.

"There definitely is something we are indebted to him for," Bill continued. "And that is our wonderful mother. Father picked her out for her fine qualities, and that surely helped us all over the bumps that we had then. Her influence still guides our lives. We were very young when she left us, and if we live to be old, I think we will continue to follow her wishes. That is conclusive evidence of her exceptional character, and Dad was destiny's link between us and our lovely mother."

Leone gazed at her brother in wondering silence for a long moment. "Destiny's link," she repeated thoughtfully. "That is a good category for dad all right. Are you doing more serious thinking, Bill?"

"I guess not. I don't have much to think with you know. "

"I believe you are more thoughtful than you admit. I am glad you do not harbor a grudge."

"Oh no, I would never keep one of them things around. I have no space for it." Again they saw the uncanny half grin, but not a muscle moved on the immobile side of his face.

Leone arose with a sinking feeling at her heart. "I must fix up that wound. I believe your face will be almost normal with some care and the passage of time," she said in a tone meant to be encouraging.

The girls were happy to have Bill home with them. He would be forced to stay for a time until the wound was entirely healed. There were things he could do to help them in the way of fixing shelves and delivering orders. An important item about this was to get the money when the goods were delivered. Bill proved to be good at this.

Helen came home from school one day with a face slightly swollen. Leone gave here a little taste of pickle.

"Yes, it is the mumps all right," Helen agreed.

The girls heard this with consternation. AuGres was such an isolated place that they were not exposed to contagious diseases. Few such cases came to the hospital. Even Leone had eluded them until now.

Henrietta was next with a light attack on one side only. She was recovered enough to meet the customers when Leone became ill with them. She was very sick, a lingering case of first one side and much later the other side. Bill carried her out on the porch a few times. If she attempted to laugh, she choked with hysteria. There was not much trouble for Laura, but Marie developed a serious condition and was suffering intensely.

Just at that particular time, Robert Neely walked in on his most dejected family. Marie's face was so swollen, even her eyes, that she could not see her father. Robert scarcely waited to greet his family before he quickly hurried out. He returned shortly with a small sack of beans and then proceeded to cook them as quickly as he could. Working all night, he continued filling small bags with them, keeping them hot and applied to the painful faces.

Not afflicted with the disease, Bill retired to sleep. "With such a capable man in charge, there is no need for me," he declared.

The heat or whatever magic the beans contained sufficed to say, "They done the trick." In the morning the mumps had about vanished. The patients were able to laugh and eat a light breakfast.

The girls were eager to learn where their father had been on his travels. He told them many places, but mostly Cobalt, Ontario. He spoke in glowing terms of his journeying.

When he was rested and alone with Leone, Robert withdrew from his pocket a well-worn wallet. He took from his wallet four carefully folded ten-dollar bills. "All the cash I have," he offered, "and this is from wages I earned. All I got from the old place is gone." He gave her three of the pieces of money, putting one back in his billfold.

His daughter marveled anew at his assurance. He also spent some more of his money escorting his two little daughters to White City. They reported a wonderful time but did not see the airship, as it was not on exhibition as yet.

Norman, their oldest sister Margaret's husband, came through Chicago on his way to Memphis, Tennessee. Having sold his place in Gladwin, he was in quest of a new location to make a home for his family. He stopped for a short visit with his wife's people, promising to come with Margaret and the children when they moved to their new home. He thought this would be in Albion, Michigan.

Robert got a job on a farm near Chicago. He would come occasionally to the city to visit his family for a day.

Meanwhile, the scar and its effects were improving on Bill's face. The girls were enjoying his visit. He still called Leone, "Ole Sal," and his greatest pleasure was to tell her some whimsical story, putting himself in an uncouth light.

Just as she would start a little lecture on the proper method of selecting correct friends, he would tell her more of the story. It was so incongruous that Leone would be forced to laugh at herself.

He would say just as he did when a little boy, "It's fun to fool you, Leone. You are so gullible."

Leone thought to herself that Bill was still a boy, but not a little one. "Stay a boy as long as you like. It's nice to be young," Leone advised him.

"You're right, Sis. People take life too serious."

Chapter 32
NEELY MEN'S SECOND DEPARTURE

Bill had secured a job on an area farm. When he left their flat, he had told his sisters that he planned to earn enough money to return to the Alberta country. His words were, "I like that part of the earth."

Robert Neely came home to his daughters for a brief visit once more. He had quit his job on the farm, having accumulated enough savings to satisfy some of his cravings for the wanderlust that loomed greater on his horizon than love for his children or any other obligations that he could be expected to have.

The girls were happy to have him with them, even for a little while. It was an opportune time for Robert's visit, as the girls were looking forward to the pleasure of a visitor, Gael Gremon from AuGres. Gael was studying voice and music in Chicago. Her father was a leading businessman back in AuGres. As a small boy, he was well known to Julia Neely's family, having been placed in Julia's custody by his foster father on numerous occasions.

Gael had talked to the girls and accepted their invitation to dinner on Wednesday evening. Robert's eyes glowed with pleasure when he listened to this good news. "She has a beautiful voice. I must ask her to sing."

"I do not think she will sing without music, Dad," Laura answered, "and we have no piano."

"Oh, just for our pleasure."

"She will not, even for our pleasure," his daughter insisted.

"Gael Gremon is an artist in music. Them kind of people have a musical soul, tuned to perfection," was her father's response.

Leone retorted, "And music that is imperfect jars on them. Do not be disappointed when she refuses your request for a song."

And Gael Gremon did refuse for one very obvious reason, no music. Still, Robert enjoyed every moment of that eventful evening, and the girls did also. They found Gael beautiful and very charming. There were many news items to relate about AuGres. In the hearts of all the Neely family members, it was still back home. They enjoyed all the interesting news update and experienced a little gloom when the evening ended.

The following day their father left the city on his trip. His destination would eventually be Cobalt, Ontario. He did not buy a ticket direct to that point, intending to spend a little time in places that intrigued his fancy as he went his leisurely way.

That afternoon the doorbell sounded on its customary loud jangling note. Henrietta answered the summons and admitted Mr. Hall and his wife, who appeared to have quite recovered from a recent illness. The woman looked lovely in a new suit of excellent design and workmanship. A good-looking hat completed the ensemble, and her nice brown hair was becomingly arranged.

The girls were always pleased to welcome Mr. Hall. They had confidence in his sincerity. He appeared as usual, kind, patient and pale looking. His old black suit was neatly pressed as always. However, Mrs. Hall seemed certainly at her best. Her health appeared to have also taken on a definite glow. Leone sincerely expressed pleasure in seeing her looking so well.

"My health is better now than it has been in years," Mrs. Hall agreed. "And I have not been as well dressed in ten years as I am now. Cliff bought me this nice outfit. It is his selection. I would have taken something cheaper. He says the best in clothing is like buying sterling silver as long as it is in existence."

"It looks nice on you. He surely has good taste." Leone agreed.

"He bought it for me as kind of a celebration for my recovery of the last illness. I have been subject to serious illnesses since Cliff was a little boy, but that last bout was the nearest I'd ever come to passing. I'm convinced if you had not come to my rescue that time, Leone, I would not be here now. And the several previous attacks were not so serious because you took care of me from the start."

Mr. Hall looked on in his kindly genteel way. "By the way, Leone, did Cliff ever pay you as agreed?" he asked.

"No, he did not," she answered abruptly.

He gave her a troubled look. "There is no excuse for such carelessness. He has money in the bank and did have at the time of his mother's illness. I'm ashamed for him," his father said in an abashed tone. "I shall speak to him at once."

"I have not done so well myself," Mrs. Hall said apologetically. "I have only just now succeeded in saving out 10 dollars. The two five-dollar bills my brothers left for you."

Opening her purse, she withdrew the money as she spoke and placed it in Leone's hand. "Don't worry about the salary Cliff promised you," she continued. "He will pay you. He is honest as the sun I'm proud to say."

179

Not sharing Mrs. Hall's opinion of Cliff, Leone made no direct reply. However, she did offer that the sisters needed the money and would appreciate having it. In the months that followed, this well-earned wage was not forthcoming, and no further mention was ever made of it by the Halls.

The cool, fall winds were putting in an appearance of harsher things to come. This was the time that Bill, their only brother, collected his wages and with the money he bought a railway ticket with the Canadian West as its destination. He arrived at the home of his sisters for a brief visit and announced he was very soon going to vamoose for the West. This was not unexpected news for the girls, but nonetheless, disconcerting.

Leone offered, "I'm sorry, Bill, that you cannot be contented in your own country."

"That is too much to expect of a red-blooded man with cowboy tendencies," was Bill's retort.

"There are plenty of cowboys in the land of your birth," Leone answered.

"I suppose there are, Sis, but they are strangers to me. I would not know how to go about horning into membership with them. And I have friends and a bit of reputation to go back to in Alberta."

"But your ticket does not say Alberta, Bill. How is that?"

"Easy guessing, Leone. They paid me such a small wage. I did not have enough money to go any further. It is range country where I will land. I will have a fair chance; don't worry."

"With winter so close at hand, I do not think it is the best thing to do. We have a little money I can give you, enough to take you to a point where you are known."

"Gosh, Leone, that sounds fine. To tell you the truth, I did not like the prospects any too well." He smiled, the immobile side of his face slowly resuming a natural appearance. There was reason to hope the scar would not be as disastrous as they had first feared.

In a few days his sisters regretfully accompanied Bill to the railway depot to say good-bye and stand once more in the cold fall sunshine weighing this problem with tear wet eyes as the train pulled out. They watched their brother standing alone on the observation coach rear platform until it faded away into the distance.

Chapter 33
VISIT FROM CAPTAIN JIM OF AUGRES

The next exciting event in the lives of the Neely sisters was the unheralded appearance of a ship. The Captain was James Makeen of the Great Lakes, better known to the girls as Jim, their former neighbor in AuGres.

Leone answered the doorbell and gave a little cry of delight that summoned her sisters. "Jim is here," she called, greeting him warmly.

"It is great to see you all in Chicago," he said and "making such a good go of life."

"It does not seem at all strange to us now," Marie answered, "but I freely admit that it was a bit odd at first."

"Yes," the genial familiar Makeen smile faded from his countenance for a moment. "Chicago is a far cry from Point AuGres. You did well to get away from that place. I've been trying for years to persuade my folks to move from Bay City."

Leone looked at him in dismay. "But Jim, they are the very heart and soul of that community."

"Yes, but Mother just wears herself out."

"You're probably right, Jim. But the devotion she has for her friends and neighbors in Bay City is most important to her. And while AuGres actually has many redeeming features, I would have preferred to stay, if given a fair choice."

"What do you mean, a fair choice? I understand that Robert almost signed out when you left."

"Dad was quite dramatic for a while. However, he recovered promptly enough when he found I made good. What I regret is that we worked long years to clear and till that rich fertile land to garden fineness and had a good start in horses, too. Our racing stock could have been turned into draft horses, if Dad would have listened to reason. Bill is growing up and could have been an important man instead of the wanderer he is now."

Jim acknowledged, "I weaned myself away from that place so long ago that I would not be able to see its fine points if I tried, and I do not intend to try now."

"I was only speaking for your parents' point of view. There was nothing there for you," she agreed decisively. She knew he was already at the top of his profession.

The girls folded up their work for the balance of that precious day. After a delightful home-cooked dinner, they strolled out to the boulevard, meeting Jim on his way to join them. They all meandered slowly along by way of Washington Park where gems of the rose gardens grew in abundance; the soft night air was heavy with the delicate fragrance. Going on, their young voices gay, they eventually found themselves at San Sousa Amusement Park. The group indulged in some of the wild rides that young people considered fun and then sat awhile continuing the chatter. Jim was frank in saying that the Dipper Ride was dangerous. The girls found this to be a rare bit of intelligence. Jim was famous for his bravery on the angry wind-swept waves of the Great Lakes where profound and terrible danger lurked. He had been the recipient of honor for risks taken in the darkness of night, and Henrietta reminded him of this.

"Those were necessary risks to save lives, and it was not fun," he answered. "The Dipper Ride is an unnecessary risk."

They knew he was justified; yet their mirthful laughter could be heard on a gentle evening breeze.

"It is only riders who stand up when they should sit down who cause accidents," Marie assured him.

"They can all ride on it, but not for my money," he said with finality.

The enchantment of Captain Jim's visit lingered for the girls. When he left them on the corner by the Cottage Grove car, it was with the assurance his ship would dock in a Chicago port on a return trip within two weeks and he would come again. There were sailors in his crew from AuGres, and he said one would accompany him on his next visit. The girls were thrilled.

The breakfast table next morning was the scene of much animated conversation.

"We must make plans for the evening's pleasure," Henrietta declared. "The weather is so warm now, I think out-of-doors is our best bet. The amusement park is such an innovation right now."

"If it was not for the expense, I would think that White City would be best," Marie remarked in reply.

"We will all want to go," Helen said complacently, thus making sure she was included in the plans.

Blue eyes twinkling, Laura sat there with the most smug expression, accompanied by an occasional giggle.

"Laura has thought of the Golden Nugget," Leone said, smiling. "I can tell when she puts on the look of a cat that swallowed the canary and then suddenly starts to giggle. That always means that she has come up with an answer for us."

"That's true," Laura admitted modestly. Then she added, "But this is a little more devious than usual."

"It must be something fiendish this time judged by past record," Henrietta retorted as she looked at her sister intently. Ripples of laughter followed. Everyone knew that anything even remotely akin to destructiveness was an unknown quality with kindly, gentle Laura.

"My reputation is at stake this time," she admitted. "Let us spend the evening at White City and decoy Jim on the roller coaster."

The very thought of such a plan provoked peels of laughter from the girls.

"It would be fun," Leone agreed, "but the scheme is not practical. There would be too large a crowd, with five of us and perhaps three boys. So many tickets run into money too fast."

Laura was still smiling. "I have not played my ace yet." Then she offered her ace, "Our American newspaper is carrying a large number of passes in the advertising columns. We can order ten papers and start clipping." The girls were pleased with the proposal, and Laura agreed to order ten copies of the *Chicago American*.

Chapter 34
BACKYARD AIRSHIP EXPERIENCE

The season drifted along into midsummer before White City showed much success with the airship. It began taking little trips, serving to frighten some of the foreign spoken inhabitants of the great city. They thought the huge contraption floating around overhead was something of a fiendish character. Many of them were terrified.

Meanwhile, the little sisters were deeply interested in seeing the airship. The girls planned going on a Sunday, a day when it made a short flight and they could see it rise.

One afternoon in midweek the paper came out with a story that the airship was drifting around over the west side of Chicago with a dead engine. Built somewhat after the line of a present-day blimp, it was buffeting a rather high wind and refused to come down. Helen and Laura read this news with avid interest. "Too bad we live on the Southside," they remarked.

Leone had worked late that night. She was tired and had gone out on the back porch to relax. In the alley she observed a very large crowd of boys creating quite a disturbance partway down the block. The boys were all looking up in the direction of the heavens. Despite dusk falling, she could plainly see the huge form of the much heralded airship not so high above the housetops. She could hear a man's voice in pleading tones coming from up there, but not a word could be understood in lieu of the racket kept up by the urchins.

Leone felt an urge for action. She went to the boys, begging them to remain silent one moment to enable them to hear what the man was saying. This admonition fell upon deaf ears. The airship was slowly drifting.

Leone ran quickly into the house, all the while thinking rapidly. She knew she needed a harmless weapon. And then a clever idea dawned, the broom! Grabbing it, she dashed back with the business end of it foremost. She swung it about at the noisy young men. This conduct startled the unruly youngsters into a moment's silence, allowing the pilot's words to be understood. "Grab the rope and pull it down," he repeated.

Someone saw the rope trailing across the roof of the neighboring doctor's house as it tore the gingerbread trim from its peak. Some happy man finally got hold of the rope. Fellows that had not slid down a banister in thirty years came down that way now, in various types of disarray. There was manpower enough on that rope in two minutes to overwhelm a giant. Finally, the stubborn airship came to earth, and the only possible place to stake it down was the backyard of the Neely sisters.

True, they had not more right to the backyard than any other tenant who occupied a flat in the Drexel building. However, there were other contingencies. The back door of their apartment was the only door opening directly upon the scene. Entrance from the building was through the gloomy basement. The gate from the alley was promptly put under guard. The Neelys had the only telephone at hand. The monstrous creation was now captured and tied up at the back door. The huge balloon was shaped somewhat similar to an enormous worm. Suspended there in the gathering dusk, it was some forty feet in length. The huge sides glistened from the occasional light rays. It appeared panting, restive and defiant.

Crowds rapidly gathered. A group of police officers appeared, and the pilot was questioned. He was Harry Wilde, eighteen years of age and married. "Yes, the airship was owned by White City." The officers took the pilot home, leaving two patrolmen on guard.

When the confusion subsided, the girls proceeded quietly with a little plan of their own: to telephone all their friends about the startling news. The airship was tied up in their backyard and would fly the next morning at ten o'clock. After preparing refreshments for the officers on guard, the sisters retired at a late hour.

In the morning when the window shades were raised, the girls became suspicious. Within an hour this suspicion was confirmed. All the people living within a radius of many blocks had acted instinctively in conformity with the Neely sisters' little plan and had telephoned everyone on their list of acquaintances. The crowd appeared from everywhere, in small groups and large groups. Each streetcar arrived loaded--not even standing room available--and then left completely empty. Thousands of people lined the streets with little chance to see the takeoff. Friends of those occupying the rear flats of the Drexel building had the better opportunity. They were ushered out to the back porch where the next-to-the-best view was to be had. The girls were in possession of the ringside view and made the most of it. All their friends were on the ground.

The pilot appeared at an early hour. The girls learned he was the entire crew and the manufacturer as well. The balloon was factory-made, but the rest of the crude mechanism was his own, and the heart that beat in his young breast was not that of a coward. He required a daring spirit to seat himself astride that precarious triangle perch and slide his own weight backward if he wished to go up and forward if he wished to go down. The young pilot had only a life belt about his body. The highlight of the morning came with the appearance on the scene of the bigwig gentlemen in command from White City. They arrived in the latest model motorcar. When they saw the vast crowd of people and took into consideration all the free display, it did not meet with their approval. When they finally worked their way to the daring young aviator, their humor was not of the best. It is probably safe to say that Harry Wilde was not experiencing the most peaceful moments of his career either.

185

However, the altercation was of short duration. He listened to their remarks in respectful silence; then he favored them with a cool appraising glance and picked up his gloves.

"You may take it, gentlemen," he said quietly. Turning, he started for the gate.

But the gentlemen did not want to take it and regretted their hasty remarks. Amid their humble apologies, he went back to work. The show must go on. The rudder seemed to be the thing that caused most of the trouble; at least that was the part where the young man concentrated his efforts. If he was seething inside, he did not show it. He calmly worked, and the crowd had patience that matched his own as they waited.

The hour hand was crowding eleven when he announced the magic words that he would try to fly. There was not much preliminary to the take off. The bags of sand he used for ballast were already in place. Taking his seat astride the top rail of the triangular ladder-like affair, he placed his feet on the bottom rails, made fast his safety belt, turned, and bestowed a tender kiss on the teary face of his pretty young wife. Then he shook hands gravely with the police sergeant and the two bigwigs from White City. The gas bag was already straining at its bonds. He gave the order. The contraption rose, wavered an instant; the engine started turning, and then it departed like a bird. It was seen to come down very soon, this time in the park. The crowd hurried after it, but the Neely sisters did not join them. They had seen the airship.

Helen came in the front door with flushed cheeks and announced, "Just think, we would have missed all that if Leone was not the determined person she is!"

"Yes, however, it is a relief to get back to normal," Henrietta remarked. "But I'll also admit that I may miss those charming police officers."

Marie smiled and added, "Too bad we were so busy with such a crowd of clever looking fellows on deck."

"I know two fellows I sure wish were here," Laura said regretfully.

"Would it be two?" Henrietta asked curiously. Her teenage sister had never manifested the slightest interest in boys before.

"Yes, two," answered Laura. "Dad and Bill. It is just too bad they miss all the nice things. I guess they are not interested in the things we do."

"They could get work in the city and live with us if they wished," Marie said earnestly.

Chapter 35
DAY'S BOAT TRIP WITH BERNIE

Leone accepted Bernie's invitation to go on a Sunday excursion across the lake to South Haven, Michigan. "Just you and I for once, Leone," he coaxed. He was always so charming, good-natured and generous. Leone looked at him thoughtfully. Did he have hopes that their nice, platonic friendship would develop into a love affair? She hoped not.

"Wear your new outfit, Leone," her sister Henrietta had advised after Bernie had left.

Again Leone looked thoughtful, "Why my new suit?" she asked. "That trip could be rough on a new dress."

"Why so?" asked Henrietta.

Leone answered, "There is such a mob of people on open decks, and sometimes the crossings are stormy."

"Not much danger of a storm this Sunday, Leone, and I think it would please Bernie," Henrietta urged.

"He might be happier if I did not please him," Leone said soberly.

However, Leone was wearing the striking new costume that was simple but distinctive when Bernie called for her on Sunday morning.

Not given to extravagant speech, he just stood there for a moment with his fine blue eyes alight and extended his hands. He then clasped Leone's hands with unusual warmth. "Leone, you look simply ravishing," he said admiringly. "And so early in the morning, too."

Henrietta quipped with a smile, "She doesn't look like that every morning. It's a new dress. Leone's tall, graceful form makes an enchanting display rack."

Bernie laughed and favored Leone with a joyful little hug as they turned to go.

"I'm delighted to find you in such good spirits," he said. "We will have a long day together. It is nice to start out happily."

187

By mutual consent they stopped at an ancient church near the Loop District to enjoy the early service. Afterwards they were among the first to go aboard the ship as it stood at anchor all white and beautiful. The decks were gleaming in the morning sunlight as they found seats on an aft deck. A soft wind blew in from the great lake and fluttered the ship's awnings. Gentle waves washed against the sides of the great boat. Just then a whistle sounded as the decks became more crowded.

Leone's smart little sailor hat was held cleverly in place by a chic veil that gave promise of withstanding the strength of the day's breeze. Bernie was seated beside Leone with his eyes resting on her bright face. Their little world was quite complete. The rush of merrymakers filing into every available space did not disturb them. Leone's gaze wandered over the restless blue water, and she thought how scenic it all was. She thought there was no need to borrow from the mountains, hills, or valleys to add additional grandeur to the magnificence of a great lake.

As the big boat steamed out of the harbor, they looked at the receding Chicago skyline with a feeling of contentment. The day would be a torrid one in that great city of restless souls.

Bernie lifted his eyes from the moving throng on the deck. "I believe there are not enough seats to accommodate the crowd," he remarked thoughtfully.

Leone looked about with doubt in her eyes. "There are a large number of seats on the inside decks, but they appear to be occupied."

"Yes," he agreed. "We are fortunate in having good seats, but when we leave, they will be promptly taken."

She smiled, and then answered, "This is a nice corner. We can stay here for some time and then try for a more sheltered spot."

Just then a sharp gust of wind ripped around a corner of the deck and caught boldly at their clothing. Bernie reached playfully as though to rescue her from the elements. The breeze forced rising dark clouds to appear from seemingly nowhere. The big steamer made rapid progress and was soon out from the shoreline. The heavens were coming closer, darker and more angry-looking every moment. The great body of water churned violently as it threw huge foam crested waves far into the air. It seemed as though the ship was plowing her way right into the center of a heavy thunderstorm. The passengers became alarmed. A small group waited upon the captain for the purpose of requesting that the ship turn back and return to the harbor. The committee was informed, however, that conditions were not sufficiently alarming for such a drastic course. Instead, all passengers were ordered to the enclosed deck where basically only standing room was to be found. With some of the least fortunate, signs of seasickness were becoming apparent. Friends had become separated from one another, and children were crying. The prospects for one glorious day had become turmoil as the vast throng milled about in a meaningless melodrama.

Bernie viewed the situation with deep concern. "This is a hard turn of events," he said gravely.

"They have cut down the speed a little," Leone replied as a way of saying something.

"Yes, they will arrive about the time we should be leaving," he said bitterly.

Leone turned a smiling, sympathetic face. "Bernie, I know you have so few Sundays off on your line of work. However, it will be easier to take if we try to remain cheerful."

"In this bedlam?" was the answer in a sarcastic tone.

They were silent a few moments while the harsh lines of Bernie's strong face softened. His eyes devoured the trim lines of the girl at his side. His voice was gentle again as he spoke, "I have looked forward so long in hopes of having this one day alone with you. The interference of a storm did not occur to me."

"We are alone," she replied softly. "All those people are strangers."

Bernie nodded, his blue eyes twinkling. "I'm going to leave you to the mercy of the wolves," he said more happily. "I want to try my influence to induce the captain to turn back and also possibly to find a box or something you might use as a seat. Do you think you can withstand the pushing and hauling of the crowds sufficiently for me to find you when I return?"

Leone nodded with a smiling acquiescence as she put an arm around a pillar. The storm was making known its presence with violence.

Bernie returned disappointed, but he had succeeded in finding a wooden bucket, which when turned upside down would serve Leone as a seat. "You will have to permit me this one peeve," he said. "It would have a rim!"

"And in the meantime I shall seat myself inside the rim," she told him gleefully.

They then turned their attention to the window. The giant boat was moving slowly; deep and heavy waves dashed over the outer decks. The great lake swirled and threw its weight far into the air, angrily confronting the worthy heavens. The big ship also tossed at the murky clouds that hung low in a dark and menacing formation. Their grim, threatening depths was like the mouth of a mammoth cavern greedily awaiting a victim.

Ship bells sounded again, and the big boat slowed until it was scarcely moving. Vivid flashes of lighting shot through the gloom and were accompanied by the terrific roar of thunder. Darkening clouds hung lower as the huge boat with its precious cargo bore slowly on. Lights were set aglow and detracted somewhat from the weird scene.

Hours passed throughout the harrowing experience while Leone sat patiently on the bottom end of the little wood bucket near a window. Bernie remained crouched on the floor beside Leone, but not nearly as patient.

The hopeless appearing shadows lifted as the day wore slowly away. The wind continued to howl in fitful gusts. Soon it became less violent, and the passengers were permitted to move about the decks.

Few passengers availed themselves of the privilege. Most of them were exhausted as well as fearful of the possible hazard of the rain or windswept outer deck. They were also afraid to partake of food or drink.

Leone and Bernie welcomed the change. Bernie zealously carried the bucket until he found a shelf in a remote corner to conceal it with the hope that it might be found for the return trip.

The ship's officers continued to increase the speed somewhat as the storm abated. The water remained rough, however, and the regular speed could not be resumed. It was estimated that the boat would arrive at South Haven about the time they should have been leaving for the return trip. When the ship finally docked, the faint and weary passengers were informed that the boat would remain at the pier but one hour. A portly member of the staff was stationed at the turnstile as the would-be merrymakers disembarked. In a groaning voice that Leone felt she would always remember, he called out, "This boat returns at six o'clock. At six o'clock this boat returns." This was repeated over and over in a monotonous singsong voice that continued without variation; not a single inflection changed in his tone.

Bernie and Leone found it a relief to get beyond hearing distance of the monotone voice. All they could hope to acquire in the short time ashore was some refreshment. This they succeeded in accomplishing by maneuvering and winding their way back for the return trip. They both fervently hoped it would be a more agreeable experience. The boat nosed its way around from the moorage as a brighter hue appeared in the heavens. All eyes turned to the eastern sky as a most perfect of rainbows shone forth in its entire splendor.

Bernie and Leone had reached the upper deck by this time. "It is a happy omen," he exclaimed. "Let's go up on the little deck for a short time."

Leone was reluctant, "But that must be the crow's nest. Do you think that passengers are allowed up there?"

Bernie was confident. "Sure. There is such a secure railing and no signs to the contrary." He looked at her appealingly as he spoke. Leone took his hand confidently as they climbed the narrow stairway. But she inquired, "And if the wind lifts and carries us out into the deep blue waters, what then?"

Bernie's smile deepened. "We will be quite safe," he promised.

The breeze quickened at intervals. Leone stood by his side as their gaze wandered across the turbulent waves. The sun was getting low in the west and could now be seen though a rift in the clouds. The sun's golden beams played on the restless foam-crested waves like a gleaming silvery path.

"It is like the path of our life together," Bernie said earnestly. "The Providence offers a beautiful uncertainty. I would like to follow through to what lies beyond with you. We could be happy together, Leone."

So, this was the end of their nice friendship, she thought sadly and a fitting sequence to the harrowing day. Now she believed that she must go out of his life in the most kindly way possible. Sometimes it was kindly to be a little cruel, but that was not the case tonight. Bernie, staunch and true, had experienced enough disappointments for one day. Leone offered, "You are forgetting obligations, Bernie."

"It is not right that you should have such obligations. I will help you with them. The older girls will be finding a husband soon, and we will make a home for the two little ones, you and I, Leone."

191

"It sounds like happiness, Bernie. But would it be with my burdening you with my troubles?"

"Yes, true happiness can be trusted to take the hurdles. It must be of the character that reaches out."

Both Bernie and Leone were glad to go back on the big deck even though it had an overload of humanity. Protection from the piercing wind could be found. As the ship drew further out, the waves grew heavier, and again the speed was cut down. After a time when darkness settled in, the couple was forced to abandon the outer deck and crowd once more within the limited confines of the closed deck. Bernie again secured the little wooden tub he had hidden so carefully. Leone was grateful for this meager accommodation in the way of a seat. The wearisome trip finally dragged to a close as the tired crew made fast the big ship in its own berth at Chicago. The time said 2:00 a.m. when the huge crowd disembarked.

By the time Leone and Bernie reached a streetcar, another hour had passed. With the prospect of another hour on the jangling Cottage Cove car, they wearily seated themselves.

Bernie turned to the girl at his side with a quizzical half-guilty expression, "How did your fine new dress survive the ordeal?" he asked anxiously.

"Very well, I think," was Leone's response.

The look of concern on his face relaxed. "I feel grieved for the manner in which my plans miscarried today. I had looked forward a long time to this trip when we would have a cheerful day all by ourselves."

"It was just one of those things in life over which we have no control," offered Leone sympathetically. "While we cannot brush it easily aside, we must try to do just that."

Bernie's grin was rather weak. "You were wonderful, cheerful and patient while the day did everything outside of physical violence. It was the limit."

"Not quite the limit, Bernie." There was more mirth in her smile. "Now we have one more blow to take."

"One more blow?" he questioned. "What could it be?"

"We are riding on the last car to connect with south Chicago, and you are scheduled to go out on your run tomorrow."

"Of course," he responded in a flat voice. "It has been such a tedious day I did not think of that. What will we do?"

"There is only one thing to do. You must remain on the car. I'll be quite all right going on home alone."

"You are a comforting person, Leone. Most girls would not consider taking such a chance."

Leone was quick to reply, "It is no chance. This is a peaceful community. There is no danger."

"What will your sisters think of a man who would consent to you walking home from the streetcar at four o'clock in the morning without an escort?"

"My sisters are sensible people, Bernie. They will regret such a circumstance was necessary, but they will understand."

"And I am forced to consent. My relief man is on his vacation, and the trains must be kept moving."

When they arrived at the corner where she must leave the car, Bernie assisted Leone to the sidewalk almost in silence. He was bitterly disappointed by the day's events.

She watched his lone figure, standing hat in hand as the car moved away. Leone noted that she had some regrets of her own. She couldn't help wonder in what manner she would relinquish his fine wholesome friendship and leave the least sting.

Arriving home without incident, she found all her sisters awake and earnestly trying to minimize the alarm they had felt for her safety. The huge electric storm had shaken the city and there had been alarm for all craft out on the water.

When she crept safely into her cozy bed, she thought about Bernie who must report for work soon with scarcely time for a refreshing breakfast. Then he would have to keep the train's engine hot throughout what would surely be a very long day.

Chapter 36
VISIT FROM MAYOR OF AUGRES

Helen was the one to answer a call on the telephone that produced a delightful quandary for the Neely sisters. The connection was cut off before Leone could reach the instrument. Helen said she could not be sure, but she thought the call was from James Grimore, the Mayor of AuGres. I think I heard that he and his wife, Jennie Grimore, were in Chicago and were on their way over for a visit.

If this was the case, it was exciting news for the Neely girls. Their friendship with the lovely Jennie Grimore during their early childhood years stood out for them. And everybody loved the smiling, kindly James.

The Grimores arrived in due time. Marie answered their ring of the doorbell. Nostalgia swept over her as Jennie put a familiar, friendly arm about her and said warmly, "Is this little Marie? I would not have known you if we met on the street!"

The rest of the girls came quickly to exchange greetings and to set about having an old-time visit. There are times in the life of each individual when just to sit and talk is a most satisfying sensation. It is brought about by some forerunner, present circumstance or aftermath. This moment seemed to be the combination of all three. The group talked of the marriages and some of them that had produced broken lives. One case in point embraced the future of Lea Peary, the man with the generous spirit and heart of gold. Everyone thought he was destined to remain a bachelor. He was now a Benedict. Lea's brother passed away, leaving a blind wife who was dependent on him. Lea went at once to the town in Canada where his brother and wife lived. In a short time he married this poor woman who found life so difficult. Lea's greatest happiness had always seemed to be helping others. Perhaps his new life requiring more from his heart than average would bring true happiness. This was the wish that followed him into his new life from many friends in AuGres.

When James and Jennie were taking their leave, it was with the promise of more visitors. Jennie's two brothers, both valiant sailors on the Great Lakes, were ships' officers, each in charge of a ship. The brothers plied their way into Chicago ports throughout the warm months and would also be stopping for a visit to renew former friendships.

James also assured the Neely girls that he personally would see that their name be entered onto a subscription list for the *Arenac Independent*, the local newspaper published in Standish.

Marked "Subscription Paid," a copy of this paper put in an appearance very soon and proved to be a welcome visitor at the home of the Neely girls for many months.

The Drexel Building where the girls lived was located near the old World Fair Grounds. The city's Fire Department flooded this area for the enjoyment of winter sports. When the girls went walking, they saw the ice forming on the chilled earth, mute evidence that winter was at hand. Rowboats had all been taken from the lake and lay in a well-ordered row, their sides shimmering in the cold sunshine.

The Neely girls welcomed each season. They loved the winter sports, and winter meant more social life. The girls had taken membership in a Social Club, and this meant dancing for them. Henrietta's eyes shown as she did a few dance steps on her dainty toes. She remarked, "Dancing's one thing we inherited from Dad. I don't believe mother cared so much for dancing."

Marie looked at her sister soberly, "There was no opportunity in our mother's life to develop youthful tendencies. Always there were babies and a continuous need to make a living for them."

Henrietta responded, "Yes, you're right. She spent many anxious hours wondering how we would make out. I hope she knows how happy and all right we are now."

"Oh yes, she knows," Marie replied confidently. "She had such explicit faith."

Christmas season came bringing with it all the traditional splendor and also extra seasonal business for the Neely Sisters Dress and Hat Shop. The girls worked fast and happily until Christmas Eve. Then they hung five stockings from the mantel near the fireplace. "It is more like back home that way," Laura said reminiscing.

Leone smiled, "We are rather grown up for that, you will agree."

Laura responded, "Oh, we're big enough, but not too old for the sentiment to strike a responsive cord. I think it was you who did a little gumshoe activity one night and caught Santa at work, bringing out the fact things were not so different even then."

"Yes," said Leone. "I recall that it was a revealing moment and I did not think even at that early age that it was very clever. But I talked it over with Marie, and we decided that there were times when silence is golden."

Laura's tinkling laugh followed this tact admission. "That is my sentiment, too."

Referring to an old euphemism and continuing to laugh, she added, "Whom shall we appoint as Santy?"

Leone studied a moment and then offered, "I think we will disregard holding anyone responsible. If Santa fails in his duties, it will be our hard luck."

Laura said in a conclusive manner, "What are you doing about Bernie? Will you consider his gift?"

Leone quickly responded, "Dear, no. I could not do that. The ruling we have is to accept only gifts that may be used by the entire family originated with me. I could not break the rule."

Laura lifted her gaze, looking ruefully at her sister. "My sympathy is with Bernie. He is a good guy."

"I can see your point of view," offered Leone. "However, there is nothing to be gained by conforming to his wishes. A gift he would buy me would be something expensive, when a towel would be a very nice gift for the family."

Laura let out her charming little laugh again and interjected, "And a forty-nine-cent one at that. I guess you are right, Leone; when you cannot marry the guy, no sense in letting him spend his money."

The weather modified somewhat for Christmas Day. The girls prepared a nice little Christmas dinner, timed for two o'clock, giving them an opportunity to attend church, prepare the dinner, and permit the small number of guests time to arrive. Santa had found the stockings without difficulty, as evidenced by their bulging sizes. Dinner over, they adjourned to the parlor to unwrap gifts. From a large window overlooking Drexel Avenue could be seen three men carrying a large box. One would conclude by their efforts that the contents were of considerable weight as they moved along closer to the Drexel Building. The girls suddenly recognized them as young men from their own circle of friends. The fellows had apparently engaged in the interesting prospect of delivering a Christmas present to the Neely sisters. When the doorbell rang, Helen lost no time appearing in the doorway. After laboriously carrying in the gift and exchanging greetings, the young men did not linger. Helen was all eagerness to open the box, and Laura went to her assistance. When they went to work, they immediately called out in delight. The two girls could lift the box with one hand. It was found to contain mostly paper. However, in the midst of this tissue was a beautiful copper teakettle with a little stove that burned alcohol. It was a very nice family gift and something popular with a hostess of that period.

There were also other nice and useful family gifts. All in all, it was a wonderful Christmas filled with peace and happiness.

The Neely sisters drifted into the new year, conscious that they had reached their first objective of having a home alive with love and cheer, a home where laughter was welcomed.

There were no gaps in their busy life schedule. The girls had special courses in studies to be kept up. Their place of business was requiring more time each day. There was also the fun of some winter sports and they enjoyed the social life furnished by the Dance Club. The winter passed pleasantly and smoothly, and, yes, it was a good winter.

Now spring was in the air. Orders were coming in plenty fast enough to the dress shop. Business was the barometer by which the Neely girls instinctively measured everything. If business should suddenly become suspended, the rosy glow on their horizon would have taken on a grayish tint. However, they were in no danger of such calamity. The Neely girls attended to business much too carefully for that to happen.

Chapter 37
BOARDER EMILY DALL

The girls had taken a few moments off of their busy morning for a little exchange of confidence. Leone told them how difficult further friendship with Bernie would be.

The girls looked at her searchingly.

Marie, who was always the one to regard their problems seriously, asked gravely, "And you, Leone. Is your heart involved?"

"I'm fond of Bernie," she answered frankly. "But not in that way."

"It better not be that way," Marie said roguishly. "After all, your sisters are not off your hands yet."

Leone continued. "That brings us around to the most involved and important part of the problem. Bernie's argument was that the older girls would marry in the not too distant future, thus minimizing our complexities."

Marie and Henrietta laughed humorously while the other girls contented themselves with a smile. Henrietta interjected, "Poor Bernie. He is so profound."

"Yet, we must face up to the facts: the natural way of life does revolve around marriage, and there is no future in marriage here," Leone declared.

Henrietta shrugged impishly and offered, "Leone means, "Hurrah for the West."

There was an intangible something about the confidential little chats with her sisters that revived Leone's confidence in herself. Her sister's affection, cheer and, reliance gave her the moral stamina to go on to try to shape their destiny in a manner that would bring the greatest return of happiness.

That same evening Fredrick Dall came excitingly to their door with two letters clasped in his hand. Mr. Dall was not a large man, perhaps a little smaller than medium. But this was a man of whom any woman would be proud. He had fine, sensitive features, and he was handsome to look at in his military uniform. However, the best thing about Fred was his philosophy about accepting life as you lived it. Further, he also had an admirable devotion to his little family.

Today, their friend displayed none of his usual calm matter-of-fact manner as he thrust the letters before the girls and said, "Just read this."

The Neely sisters found one letter contained a notification of transfer of employment for Fredrick Dall from Chicago to Portland, Oregon. The other one verified that the company would furnish his transportation.

Something in Mr. Dall's excited manner seemed to convey the feeling that he was not entirely happy with his good fortune. So, Leone inquired anxiously, "It is just what you wished. Is anything wrong?"

"Everything is wrong," was the answer. "I cannot take advantage of this opportunity."

The Neely sisters looked aghast. "I do not understand," Leone said in a puzzled tone.

"Poverty," he confessed bitterly. "The one word, 'poverty,' tells all the story."

"Maybe we could do something about your dilemma, if we concentrate a little," Leone offered soothingly. "You have your job and transportation with a nice boost in salary. Just what is lacking?"

"The balance of my salary that I collect here will just pay my expenses. I have a wife and baby to think of first."

The girls were greatly relieved when they heard his concern. "Your wife and son will just have to come and stay with us until you can get enough money to send for them," Leone told him warmly.

Tears of gratitude glistened in Mr. Dall's eyes. "Do you really think you can do it?" he asked.

"Sure we can."

"Perhaps you can sell our furniture and get a little money to help pay you for your trouble. I have to go at once if I go at all."

"I will figure out something on the furniture," Leone said.

"I must go and tell Emily," Fred said excitedly as he hurried away.

The Neely sisters promptly went into a huddle about what could be made of the furniture. Earlier that year Leone had gone to help her oldest sister, Margaret, when Margaret's second daughter was born. Margaret and Norman had recently moved into a nice new home, but it was very sparsely furnished. Margaret was quite determined not to incur indebtedness for house furnishings.

While her sisters admired this attitude of saving to help provide a future for their children, it troubled her sisters as they thought of those empty rooms. A few times they had gone into one of their customary little conferences over their concern. They ended up with conflicting thoughts without arriving at any conclusive solution to the puzzling problem.

There was no dissenting voice now as they discussed how the Dall furniture could be moved to Margaret's home. This was not the age of fast motors.

Fred Dall appeared at their door within a short time accompanied by his wife and baby son. Emily's brown eyes were shining through tears of gratitude after learning what the girls wanted to do with the furniture. "I regret that there is still nineteen dollars due on the contract for the furniture," Fred told them in an abashed tone.

"We will pay that. You are free to go whenever you wish," the girls assured him.

Fred was humble in his gratitude. There was in his background a family pride to be maintained as he came of honorable English lineage. There was a time in every man's life when pride and humility went hand in hand. He had arrived at this time in his life. He was proud to be the recipient of the kindness of the Neely sisters.

Since fate had decreed that he must be separated from his family for some weeks, it was gratifying to know they would be among friends.

Emily insisted upon staying close by her husband to the very last moment of the remainder of his stay in Chicago. And her young husband was happy to have her near.

The Neely girls agreed they would accompany them to the depot to see that she got back safely with her small son. When the question arose as to which of the Neely girls would accompany Emily and her son, it was found that they were all quite willing to go. Fred was jubilant, "Come on, let's all go!"

Smiles were prevalent, but there was an undercurrent of hysteria with a natural fear that family and close-knit friends who did not separate every day would.

"Do you want to acquire a reputation as the much married man appearing in public with six ladies in tow?" Henrietta asked with a grin.

"Quite the opposite. I will appear a hero of stage and screen surrounded by a group of admiring females," boasted Fred.

"Well, I like that! Females indeed," Henrietta repeated defensively, "but possibly not admirers."

However, when evening came and train time drew near, the group became serious. The train that would bear Fred away from his precious little family to the great unknown West soon arrived.

When he waved his final good-bye from the moving coach, all five of the Neely sisters were grouped about Emily and little Edmond. They all leaned intensely forward, close to the iron grille that separated them as they smiled through their tears. Their gaze was clinging to the young adventurer. It was the last time the Neelys were destined to see Frederick Dall.

Chapter 38
SISTER MARGARET'S FAMILY

Marie let her work fall to her lap in a listless fashion. Her eyes smiling upon the window, where a tempting day bathed in spring sunshine sparkled. Throughout the day's alluring challenge, Marie's smile deepened to a low guilty little laugh. She raised her hands past the olive and pink of her sweet young face in a large stretch. "Girls, I have about decided to go to market and buy groceries and not just have something for dinner, but a feast. I am half starved. We have not had a decent meal since we started on that bridal outfit. Now that it is safely out of the way, I think we will get back to normal faster if we start out with a good dinner." This brought smiles of approval from her sisters.

"Don't let anything weaken your resolve, woman," said the vivacious Henrietta. "This grabbing a bite and rushing back to work is grinding. We must deliver this other order today, or I would go with you. Have Helen and Laura help you. Leone and I will finish the order and live for the moment in which you announce the banquet. Now be off with you." Marie put her work away.

"Do you think it is a good plan, Leone?"

"Yes, darling, but do not expect any help from me. I am so absorbed in this job, I am unable to be of any assistance."

"Oh, you will not need to help. The two little girls are the best help in the world."

With this extravagant, but confident assertion, she hurried away. In a surprisingly short time a grocery wagon stopped at the back gate, and Marie opened the door to admit the delivery boy. The two little girls arrived home from school about this time, and things began to happen. Dishes clattered while girlish voices and giggles and the most welcome savory aroma floated from the kitchen. Presently Marie appeared in the hallway off the shop and called to Leone, "I don't like to bother you, but have we any flour?"

"Sure. We have it in a paper sack just as it came from the grocery last week."

"I do not seem to find it."

"The paper hangers probably took it for paste," suggested Leone. "Look again to be sure."

In a short time Marie, having investigated further, was again in the hallway holding a paper bag in her hand. "I found it all right, but it has a queer look and doesn't feel like flour."

Leone did not raise her eyes from the work that was engrossing all her attention as she answered, "Don't be alarmed. It is bulk flour unless we buy twenty-five pounds. That is the way we must take it. They probably sweep the bin once in a while and put that in if they are short. It will be well when the law demands that food be properly packaged. The grocers would welcome such a change I think."

"What are you making?" asked Henrietta.

"I am making berry pie. I intended to surprise you with it--strawberries, the first this year."

"Wonderful! You would not need to make pie. Have strawberries and cream."

"If you want the menu light and wonderful, you will have to go out to dine. Our banquet will be heavy and bountiful with roast chicken and pie." With a big grin she again departed for the realms of the kitchen, appearing later with an enormous uncooked pie in her hands.

"That is strange flour. It even felt queer when I mixed it, and it doesn't look right now."

Leone steadfastly remained with eyes only for the work to be finished on the order in her hands. "It is my guess that you are too fussy," she said soothingly.

Marie smiled as her glance met the light of amusement shining in the eyes of Henrietta.

"Indeed!" she said scornfully. "Two boxes of berries for sixty cents for one pie. It better be good. I ate one berry. It will have the proper degree of flavor, and I hope the crust doesn't let us down."

The medley of voices, giggles, and clinking of pots and pans with the most pleasing accompaniment of basting chicken continued as Leone and Henrietta contentedly applied themselves with needle and scissors. The goods were all nicely packed and marked for delivery when the banquet was announced amid more ripples of laughter and amusing small talk as the sisters gathered about a table laden with plenty of nicely prepared food. Leone sank wearily into her chair. "Marie, you are a genius. This is just what we needed most."

"That was what I thought. But to be perfectly frank, I felt a little bit guilty on account of the other order."

"Oh no, Marie, you did the right thing. We worked twice as fast after you started the dinner. You know the Neelys always have a weakness for the dinner table."

"Tell us who doesn't have that weakness?"

When the time came to serve the pie, Marie was anxious. "It is going to pain my frugal soul if I wasted that sixty cents. I am suspicious of that pie. It also did not brown as it should."

Leone's eyes turned to her plate as her serving was placed there. "It does look queer," she agreed casually. Taking a small portion on her fork, she set her teeth into it and as quickly took them out,

202

removing the offending pie with her napkin. She assured them hastily, "Do not eat it until we look into the matter. I don't believe it was flour you found. The painters have a lot of weird junk on that pantry shelf. Let me see what you thought was flour." Marie hastily produced it, and her sister as quickly pronounced it as "plaster-of-paris!" Leone added, "It was sheer luck that we did not eat any of it."

They gathered at the table for a sip of coffee and an improvised dessert. It was then Leone noticed how pale and shaken Helen appeared, and then she saw that her serving of the ill-fated pie was not on her plate. "Heleny dear, did you eat some of that pie?" The small child nodded. A hasty survey disclosed that she had partaken sparingly of the crust; most of it was hidden by her plate. Poor Marie worked so hard at that old pie that she had tried to eat it.

Leone responded, "The fault is all mine, Helen. I should have looked. I will talk to the doctor right now." In a very few minutes she rejoined the anxious group. "Don't worry. The doctor assures me that Helen will have little, if any discomfort. The fat in the shortening and baking process will prevent any tendency the plaster would have to set. Under those conditions, a small amount could be expected to do little, if any harm."

The Neely sisters were enjoying their nice old parlor, the evening was cool, and a small flame played about a gas log on the grate. Marie was seated on the broad arm of a chair in which Henrietta lounged. Henrietta was excitedly perusing an opened letter in her hand. "If I had known you were in receipt of such tremendous news as this, I would have bolted from the fashion show and rushed home to read it," she said laughing.

"It is well you did not know it," Laura made the amused reply. "Margaret is not coming until Thursday, and this is only Monday. Norman said they would be moving about now. I don't know what there is about the news that we find so upsetting."

"Oh well," Leone said soothingly. "Margaret is our sister, and the time has been long since she has been with us. And there are also those darling little children."

Henrietta aroused herself as though from a reverie. She sat up straight, looking accusingly at the others. "How many kids has she now? Four?"

"Yes, four," Leone answered mildly surprised.

Henrietta laughed in a relieved sort of way. "We must see to it all the little guys don't call us aunt. We are also a crowd. The neighbors will conclude that this is an ant hill!"

"You think of the most absurd jokes," Helen exclaimed. "I am glad summer is here and the weather nice and warm. We can take them to the park. I wonder how long they will stay. I hope a few days."

"They will not take very kindly to Chicago, coming from Gladwin," injected Leone.

"That's right, Leone. You did see Gladwin." Marie turned, and her smile moved into a thoughtful expression. "I made one trip to visit Margaret. It was only a short distance from AuGres. We had horses. However, you and I, Leone, were the only members of the family to see Gladwin. Aunt Rita's family lived there a long time, too. We surely had a cramped existence while we lived at AuGres."

Margaret's charming family arrived at the time stated in her letter. Leone went down to the Twelfth Street station to welcome them. She had followed the maneuvers of her family so many times of late that it had ceased to be a novelty. Leone sat on the observation car of the old Cottage Grove as it jogged along. The cable went grinding and clanging on its way. Leone smiled to herself as she recalled how important the throbbing old conveyance proved in her life, marking many of the major events and now the coming of Margaret.

Margaret's husband Norman was a quiet young man taking life calmly. He marshaled the little group of startled, curious youngsters along like veterans. The girls overwhelmed the children with loving attention when the little ones finally reached their embraces. The visit was planned to extend over Sunday to allow work at the dress shop to be laid aside. However, there was plenty to occupy the attention and energy of everyone concerned. Helen took over the entertainment of the little visitors, Laura the kitchen, while the three older girls concentrated their efforts on fitting a sample ensemble topped by the latest in hats to the tall graceful form of their sister. "You must not do this," Margaret protested. "You are too generous."

"Now, who is the best judge of that?" asked the smiling Henrietta.

"I insist," repeated Margaret steadfastly.

Marie appealed to Norman in her quiet, humorous way, "What do you think?" she asked. "You will be obliged to hold your wife's hand when she wears this costume to prevent her from throwing it off. Are you up to it?"

"When do I start?" he asked, his eyes twinkling.

"You see, Margaret? You have not a leg left to stand on," Henrietta said proceeding with a fitting.

"I yield under protest," Margaret responded. She permitted herself to enter the humor of the situation, although rather stiffly.

Together they began a survey of the programs that were then playing at the numerous theaters. Several suggestions had been made, when someone asked, "Margaret, what one would you prefer?"

She took the question under careful scrutiny for a moment, but then remarked, "You girls decide. Just so that it is not a leg show."

"And why not a leg show?" Henrietta asked audaciously.

"Norman does not care for them," Margaret answered primly.

Henrietta retorted, "Certainly a theater of dubious character could not exist in Gladwin." And with that response, the fun-loving Neely girls all tried rather vainly to control their amusement.

"Speak for yourself, Norman," Leone offered.

Norman made a funny little grimace that Margaret could not see, indicating his resignation and kept a grinning silence. The girls all enjoyed the exchange with their amiable "big brother."

When they parted at the end of a few days, it was with many promises of meeting more often. Earnest promises prodded this as did the warmth of family love. However, the promise was not destined to be fulfilled.

Chapter 39
ABOARD CAPTAIN MARKHAM'S BOAT

The morning meal that Monday brought a nice letter from their friend, Captain Bill Markham. Marie opened it. She beamed delightfully, "We are all invited to have dinner with the Captain on his ship on Wednesday of this week!"

"That will be a novel experience," Henrietta exclaimed.

Laura decisively interjected, "We could not shut up our shop."

Henrietta laughed outright. "But he would not expect more than two of us anyway."

"I cannot go on Wednesday," remarked Marie. "I have that order going out that will require my individual attention. Leone and Henrietta should go."

The two young ladies mentioned had no objections to this charming arrangement.

Come Wednesday, Leone and Henrietta looked forward eagerly to the dinner engagement with Captain William Markham aboard his boat. A modern conveyance, but not the clanking old Cottage Grove car, would make a brief trip of the distance they must travel to the ship's moorage. There was no crowd to soften the glow of the late summer sun that still had the power to reflect a rather torrid glare from the city streets. As the beautiful ship lay at anchor, she seemed awaiting them. The waters of the great lake shone green and brilliant with little choppy waves. The girls welcomed the boat's cool comfort as they arrived to be greeted most cordially by the Captain. A masculine replica of his lovely mother's beautiful smile lighted Captain Bill's handsome bronze features. It was a smile that had relieved the tension of many grievous moments in the troubled past of the Neely children. They would always have a warm place in their heart for the friends of that period.

Amid the girls' gay banter, he led the way to a portion of the deck that was quite obviously reserved as the Captain's own. The small group of guests had already put in an appearance and was rather silently sipping cool drinks. An attractive blonde girl lifted smoothly arched brows and gazed curiously at the newcomers, while the two young men arose being telepathically advised of a humorous hour in store. They met the girls with a broad smile. Introductions over, the Captain said pointedly, "I'm informed the Cubs will win today" as he sipped cool fruitade, and everyone laughed.

"Them fellows from down below?" asked one young man named Gene Danvers.

"Absolutely the same," Captain Williams answered.

"That is a good one," Gene added dismally. "I put my money on them when the season opened. I am always committing some folly."

"Your venture will pay off this time," Henrietta said confidently.

Ripples of laughter followed this assertion.

206

"I prefer to agree with the ladies," Gene asserted humbly. "But this is going too far." He looked straight at Henrietta with twinkling eyes. "When will this extraordinary winning streak start?"

"With today's game," she answered blandly amid much laughter and amusing quips.

They proceeded to the dining saloon where the Captain's table simply arranged with art and good taste awaited them. Except for an occasional glimpse of a crewman as they silently passed by on the outer decks, the boat seemed rather deserted. The Captain's party of cheerful young people were the only guests dining.

A slight lull occurred in the ripples of light laughter and gay witticisms. The Captain appeared to be waiting for just such an opening. Turning a searching gaze on the two sisters, he asked pointedly, "What is this I hear about the Neelys getting wild ideas about going West?"

"Why not?" Henrietta asked jestingly. "See the world while you're young."

"You will need all of your young strength if you go West," he said dryly.

"At least we are about to have a first hand report on the West," Leone remarked. She went on to tell him of Frederick Dall and further that he could be counted upon to send back a correct report.

"It is beyond me how you girls ever come by the notion of going West. You have earned an enviable place in the art of women's apparel. It provides you with a good living. What more could the West provide?"

"We could earn a living in the West," Henrietta retorted confidently.

"Yes, " he said a little scornfully. "At the chambermaid's art."

"That's a good occupation," she replied teasingly.

"Yes," he agreed readily. "No criticism intended, but young women who have reached high places in the creative arts simply would not be happy in that line."

Leone said soberly, "If ever I have to get a job caring for rooms, I'm going to remember you warned me. You may be right. But when I think of the jump from AuGres to Chicago with all it entailed, a move from Chicago to Alberta for experienced, self-reliant women seems but a step."

"Yes, but a very serious step," Captain Bill gravely warned.

"We have thought of all the dangers, but the lure of the West is too strong to be resisted," asserted Leone.

Conversations shifted to other subjects then, and when dinner was over, the group moved to lounge in the cool deck chairs enjoying the gentle breeze. Gene was missing for a short time, and then he reappeared looking complacent and displaying the blandest smile he could muster. Captain William looked at him with a slow grin. "Gene has plans to lure us into asking a lot of questions," he said confidently.

"Merciless I would say when he can see we are all languishing with curiosity," Henrietta chided in an indolent tone.

Gene placed a hand on the back of a tall, restful looking chair and paused a moment impressively. "I went to a telephone," he confessed. "The Cubs are winning."

"The Cubs are winning!" they repeated simultaneously.

"There is still plenty of time for them to lose yet," the petite blonde girl remarked pessimistically.

"I think they have a sufficient lead now to sew up the game," remarked Henrietta. "That is, unless they blow up under pressure."

There was frequently plenty of small talk about the games throughout the summer. The Neely sisters, enjoying the fruits of success, had not forgotten the bitterness of defeat. They had always instinctively defended the side that was down, and often in jest. They championed any apparently lost cause, and it was this defensive instinct that prompted their attitude now with assumed solemnity.

Staring, Gene queried Henrietta, "Will you please explain how you came into advance information of such importance?"

"I am psychic," she said demurely.

He joined the merriment that followed, but an expression of something between doubt and perplexity shadowed his countenance. "I hope they continue to win," he added.

"They will," she assured him confidently.

"I also hope you are not fooling us," retorted Gene.

"Time will tell," Henrietta replied sagely.

Leone and Henrietta made a polite exit a short while later and hurried home to share all of the evening's events with their sisters.

Almost before the Neely girls could expect, Emily had received a letter from Fredrick Dall. His first communication related that he was lonesome already for his precious little family. He wrote long and affectionately with the greater part of the letter describing the beautiful country, wonderful beyond his dreams. All it lacked for him was the presence of Emily and little Edmond. He also wrote that a letter would follow in a few days that would be directed to Leone. She knew the letter would contain direct evidence of what was waiting in the West. Further, Leone knew that when Emily and Fred established their new home in the Northwest, continued dependable information would be forthcoming. Powers responsible for advertising in the Midwest had continued to represent the Northwest as a wonderful land of promise, sunshine and flowers. The pamphlets slowly filtered into the city of Chicago and reached the waiting eyes of the Neely sisters. While they did not place much faith in this biased effort, the girls did not turn a deaf ear to the stories, which were not confined to the Puget Sound country, but embraced Oregon and Canada as well.

Fred's next letter followed promptly. He told the Neely girls about the flowers, forests, and mountains of the great West. Fred further wrote, "Leone, when you come West, I hope you will be better provided with cash than I am. You will know why I did not address this letter directly to Emily. I know she has no money, and my pocketbook is about empty. My paycheck will not come soon enough to save me from a harrowing debt by the starvation route unless some kind friend extends a welcome hand with cash in it."

While Fred had written in a humorous vein, Leone knew how deadly in earnest you can be when far away from home and friends.

She emptied her purse and promptly dispatched thirty dollars. That was the amount Fred said he deemed necessary to tide him over until that all important first paycheck would put in a welcome appearance. Emily remained with the girls for seven weeks. Fred's letters came with unfailing regularity. He seemed never to tire of sharing information about the West. His wife was pleased over this, "I think Fred is making good his promise to you girls to send a complete report."

"He has been very thorough and convincing," Leone replied thoughtfully.

"Do you think you will go West?" Emily asked dreamily with a faraway look in her eyes.

"Oh, yes. We are quite decided," was Leone's response.

"I will have moments of anxiety when I think of you girls giving up your fine business on the advice of my husband."

"You will need to take a different view of Fred's interest in this idea of going West. He had at no time advised us to sell our business. He has kindly described what he has seen and learned about the West, and that is all. When we sell, it will be on our own responsibility."

Emily inquired, "Will it be difficult to sell?"

"No, it will not," was Leone's reply. "Madame Marilyn has agreed to take over the business at any time. She is a very capable person and well fitted for such a post. What interests me more is our new life. We will perhaps have to take employment for a time until we can assume our proper bearings."

"But you will not take very kindly to that after running your own shop," offered Emily.

"I would consider such a move a long time," responded Leone. "I am weighing the present in balance with the future." She continued, "Emily, if the future was not at stake, the decision would be a minor one. One of the things that intrigues me most is the bold claim that men out West are paid better salaries than the Midwest has to offer. This continues to be an ever-present problem to the young men on our list of friends. My sisters are growing up and will be considering marriage in a few years. Getting married would be something quite out of the question here where the average young man earns such a meager wage. This factor does not apply to all of the young men of our acquaintance as several do hold important, high-salaried positions." Leone then admitted to Emily that she had found herself maneuvering at frequent intervals to nip an impending romance in the bud. "Two of my sisters have budding romances now with men who have no money. It also seems to be true that those with the least money bear the greatest charm. Even if it entails a little hardship to move, I truly believe a move will be best."

Emily's eyes grew dreamy. "I am glad my fortune is made."

"Yes," agreed Leone. "Fred is a prince among men and already established in the West. You have a wonderful little son. If the new baby is a girl, your cup of bliss will be running over."

A few days later history repeated itself. The girls mounted the Cottage Grove car trundling slowly to the Twelfth Street station, accompanying Emily and little Edmond to where they would embark from their former haunts for all time. Tears glistened in blue eyes and brown eyes. Too many months of pleasant association were terminated as the dainty young wife, clinging firmly to her sturdy

210

little son, ascended the coach steps. From the doorway she turned for a last farewell look to the devoted friends.

The Neely girls began the following day to work upon their own plans for an early departure for the West. Family ties were strangely woven in the Neely household. Their father and brother were still residents of Alberta, Canada. Edmonton was a capitol city, and women there must dress accordingly. They had decided that they would try that part of the West first. Preparations were quickly put into motion. However, it did take more time than they had anticipated putting final touches on all the orders the girls had started. Once they had completed the orders, they turned to disposing of their business and household effects.

Leone couldn't help recall Captain Markham's conversation as she went about preparing for their departure. She hunted out a rather pensive looking picture of herself and arranged it on the back of a fancy little tray of glass to be left for Bernie. He had asked for this gesture of friendship, popular at the time, and she had not refused him. Many conflicting thoughts passed through her busy brain as she worked over the trinket. She had already decided to leave it with Madam Marilyn for delivery.

They packed their personal belongings as baggage. Then they set about packing the big box that had come as freight from the farm and had been a family possession throughout their lifetime. Sentiment would not allow giving up such a family heirloom. The first item to be packed in the box was the sewing machine purchased for them by their father. Only the set of fine china and the sewing machine were placed inside. Then household linens and blankets were tightly packed in the huge box. The cautious Leone entrusted the task of packing the china to no hands but her own. Every piece was most carefully placed and safely wedged in the box. It was a family treasure that she wanted to arrive safely.

Another letter came from Fredrick Dall, and this one contained the money he had borrowed. The missive was couched in his usual humorous style with an undercurrent of embarrassment. He concluded his letter with sincere gratitude to the Neely girls.

Captain William was a caller that evening when preparations for the girls' departure had about reached a successful climax. This time he was very enthusiastic and offered them encouraging comments for a successful future.

Part IV

The Move West

Edmonton, Vancouver B.C.,
and Seattle

1907 to 1910

Chapter 40
MOVE TO EDMONTON

Just a few short weeks before if someone had told Leone that the Neely sisters would sell out their well-established business where they were reasonably sure of a nice living and purchase tickets for some point outside of their homeland, she would have expressed a prompt denial of any such possibility. And now they had done just that, although Leone did have some misgivings on the subject. It was true that they were fairly well provided with money, and a wealth of experience lay in their background in comparison with the timid, inexperienced little girl that first went forth to face the world. She was alone then with just one dinner to buy and one night's lodging to pay for, or if need be, she would be alone to experience any discomfort. Now they had decided to all pull up by their roots together and move out West.

The evening of their departure, the girls said a solemn farewell to the old neighborhood that had been the scene of happiness and good fortune for them during their time there. Even the squeaks of the Cottage Grove cable car did not sound as harsh as it faithfully performed a last duty for the Neely sisters and landed them safely at the Twelfth Street station. They were soon aboard the westbound train when the weird blast of the locomotive whistled a lonesome sound. The sound was similar to the one that could be heard every day as it reached them through the green woods from Omer to AuGres. It was nearly forgotten in the dimming past, and this one was calling them now to the new Great World. The sound brought with it a wave of nostalgia and perhaps some regret. The Neely girls had come and had seen and had succeeded beyond their fondest dreams. Were they throwing security aside and chasing a rainbow now?

While these thoughts passed, Leone found that it was most comforting to have her sisters with her, and to hear their laughter coming from the adjoining seat was sweet music to her ears. It was not until she parted company with the amount of cash required to pay for five railway fares from Chicago to Edmonton, Alberta, that Leone gave serious thought to the possible financial hazards of their situation. She was well aware from past experience that the eagerly looked forward to reunion with their father would not yield any financial assistance. True, their brother would share with them, but he would not have any money. Bill was still very young. However, no matter what fate held in store for them, there was no retracting now. The future was cast, and Leone was glad they had tackled a youth-loving adventure. They would manage somehow.

It was dark when the train passed through St. Paul. Leone looked earnestly from the window on the beautiful sleeping, snow-clad city. Memories of being with Mrs. Jacobus and her family passed through her mind.

The girls were traveling in an accommodation coach. There were not too many comforts at hand. However, it saved them money, and they must expect to find life a little rugged now. Time drifted slowly but happily by as the heavy engine tooted, puffed, and blew its way. The engine threw cinders without discrimination in the performance of its task of hauling the long train through the fields of sparkling snow and interesting stops.

The days seemed endless, and the nights also dragged a little. The Neely girls were accustomed to plenty of activity. Reading, knitting, and artwork would focus their attention for a part of the daylight hours. Then gradually they would become interested in lighthearted conversation. The passing scenery was very attractive in places. Groups of small trees and brush were blanketed in glistening snow, and frost greeted the eye. However, the glare of the sun on the snow had to be taken into consideration, so the scenery could not hold their attention too long.

When they finally reached Winnipeg, Manitoba, they were shocked by the sub-zero weather. The train was scheduled to remain there for one day. With the exception of the extremely cold walk to get to the hotel, it was a welcome change for the girls. The Neely girls were used to snow and frosty winters, but nothing approaching the blood chilling effect to be found in Winnipeg! Adding to the bitter weather was a slight wind that would quickly kick up. Their journey came to a close as such trips do, and so did the tiresome sound of the engine. The train finally pulled to a stop at Edmonton, Alberta. And the Neely sisters would remember their first days in Canada for a long time.

The shades of night were falling, but it was not too dark to have a most discouraging effect on the rather silent girls. They could not see very much of the struggling little city in the semi-darkness. They could see enough, however, to convince them that there was very little to see.

Marie was the first to speak, "So, this is Edmonton!"

Laura giggled through chattering teeth, "Is this Edmonton? I would say it's the Klondike!"

The reply to this was frozen smiles as they hugged their heavy wraps tightly about their shivering bodies and climbed to a place in a rather high stage that was bound for the St. James Hotel. Arriving there, the girls welcomed the real beds and steaming radiators that looked good after the long journey. The girls stretched out their tired young limbs in welcome repose. They awoke with the sunbeams the next day. Leone set forth at an early hour in search of rooms that would allow them more freedom and save on expenses.

This effort proved a most disappointing experience. The Neely girls checked out of the hotel deciding in favor of looking for one with lower rates. Late afternoon found them still on the earth burdened with grips and darkness falling at an early hour. Having separated into two search parties, they met back on a path crossing a vacant lot. Smiling, but getting a little worried, Leone observed sagely, "We will need to move along with more briskness if the darkness isn't to catch us."

Laura was silently but rather closely observing the top of the drab skyline. "Do you girls see what I see?" she asked. "I am afraid to laugh for fear my face might freeze that way."

Her sisters turned their attention to her line of vision.

"Do you mean the Temperance Hotel sign?" Henrietta queried.

"Yes, I do. Don't you think it looks promising?"

"But this is no laughing matter. Our situation is serious," remarked Leone as she led the way. Five pairs of feet scuffed rapidly through the frost and snow in the bitter cold, and soon the group was at their destination. The hotel proprietor met them most cordially. He told them that his establishment was a little crowded, but five young ladies was something very unusual. "If you will wait in the lobby, I will see if I can make satisfactory arrangements."

"We could wait in the dining room," Marie remarked. "A good dinner might restore our confidence."

The proprietor, a gentleman built on generous proportions, smiled broadly, "If you need confidence in this town, then eat heartily; we want you girls to like this town. Edmonton needs feminine influence. There is such a preponderance of men here. I am scarcely ever honored by a lady guest." As he talked, he led the way to the dining room. The tables were crowded, and dinner was

215

about to be served. It was just then that their congenial host found them a table. Turning to the dining room full of young men, he announced in his clear and hearty voice, "Gentlemen, presenting the Neely sisters from Chicago." The room full of men all arose in smiling acknowledgment. The girls found the friendly, informal atmosphere stimulating after the tedious experience of the afternoon.

Dark-haired Mike McDonald was generous. He had been the first to volunteer to vacate his room and take an improvised space with some other boys. Additional quarters were made available through chivalry of other young gentlemen they did not know either. The Neely sisters were unaware until a later date that such strategy plans had been resorted to in order to provide them a place to sleep that night. The sisters never did learn the identity of all the donors of the friendly favors, but they were nonetheless grateful.

A flat was found the next day, in fact, a large flat. And it actually had more rooms than they required.

"Let's take it!" Henrietta declared. "We can close up the rooms we are not using."

"I think it will give us an opportunity to get our bearings," offered Leone. "Yes, we can stop long enough to get a regular home-cooked meal and take a sight on the town. I might even do some potential invention in a place as large as this," Leone added with a rather thin little smile.

"And just what form would your invention take?" Marie asked.

Leone's smile broadened, "A patent kicker to kick me all the way back to Chicago."

All of the Neely sisters except Henrietta had arrived at the top of the long stairway at that moment and joined in the laughter.

"Sounds like the best laugh we've had since we left home," remarked Henrietta curiously. "What is it all about?"

"Leone is about to invent a kicker," responded Marie, which renewed the laughter.

"No need yet, anyway," Laura chimed in. "I think that little job can be left safely to circumstance."

"I quite agree with that," Marie said in her usual serious manner. "Things look bad, but let's try to make the best of it."

"Yes," Leone agreed. "We must figure out some way to make a living. There are so many men here; there should be some social life."

"I wish this flat was on the first floor," complained Henrietta. "It would be easier to heat. Store buildings on the ground floor make it higher, too, and it is of such light construction."

Marie laughed. "Well, that is a presumptuous speech coming from you! By the way, did you happen to notice how cheap coal is here?"

"Is coal so cheap? How did you learn that?"

"Leone and I crossed the market square and saw many tons of coal," responded Marie. "It was being loaded on farm wagons with high looking boxes. Different grades and different prices, but all of it very cheap."

"I don't know if that is good news. It doesn't sound prosperous," retorted Henrietta.

Marie put on her gloomy air, "It may be some time before we are prosperous. We will appreciate the poor price on coal just now."

The man in charge of the building put in an appearance at that moment, and the girls gave him payment for the rooms.

"Leone and Marie have been doing most of the pacing around in the cold today. They should stay and get the rooms warm, while we three scamper over to the Temperance Hotel for the grips," suggested Henrietta.

"I don't mind," agreed Leone. "If the stove is full of ashes, I still wouldn't mind."

As it turned out, two young men who worked for the manager of the Temperance Hotel aided the girls in carrying the grips. The enterprising young men learned the whereabouts of a horse and wagon they could borrow and with that brought the girls their baggage.

By the time evening came, the flat had assumed a lot of home-like atmosphere for the Neely girls. There was company for dinner. Gay, youthful laughter rang through the rooms, and the girls began to feel a little like home.

A few days had passed when Marie awakened Leone very early one morning. Marie whispered, "It is 2:00 a.m., and I think somebody is delivering coal."

"Delivering coal at 2:00 a.m.?" was Leone's doubtful response.

"Listen," answered Marie, "you will hear a succession of sounds as they load and then a great racket as it is emptied. If they are delivering coal here in the night, we should do something about it. The sounds are becoming more persistent."

217

There was then a great crashing noise that sounded like a pack of coal had been dropped from the top of the creaky old stairway to the bottom.

"Well now, this is something!" Leone whispered as she hastily arose. "Did I sleep through such a racket as that?"

"Yes, two of them. I waited for the second one before I was convinced that the sounds were connected with this building," replied Marie.

The two girls ventured forth keeping close to one another as they cautiously entered the kitchen. They were tiptoeing toward the stairway when Marie whispered, "Should we arouse the other girls?"

"Not until we learn what it is," was Leone's response.

Carefully opening the basement door, the two girls peered skeptically down into the depths of the darkness below. There was a faint shaft of light from somewhere, but they could discern nothing. Leone stooped, brushing her hand lightly over the stair steps.

"What are you doing?" queried Marie.

"Trying to find out if anything was dumped here," said Leone. "Shh, I hear something. Listen, there is something making the scraping sounds we thought was coal being loaded, and it is on the stairway." Leone continued, "Goodness me, the plot thickens. Let's turn on the light. Whatever it is must have spotted us by this time," she quipped as she lit a gas taper.

While it didn't prove very useful, they could see rather dimly the outline of a rather large dark object about at the turn of the basement stairway. Both girls gazed long and earnestly.

"Could it be a man?" ventured Leone.

Marie turned to her with a crooked smile, "Incredulously, it not only could be, but it is! How could a man get in here after we carefully locked the door? Strange!"

"Not so strange," was Leone's assertion. "Men are so numerous around here. Someone tossed him in a window just to get rid of him. And I believe we are confronted with that difficulty right now ourselves. But there is something wrong with this man. Perhaps it was him falling down the stairs that made all that ruckus. He must crave punishment if he fell down stairs three times. He is either hurt or drunk."

Marie agreed. "Let's venture down closer to him. He looks harmless."

Both girls began a cautious descent, closely watching the prone figure on the stairway. Leone tried to speak to him. The reply she received convinced them that the fellow was intoxicated. But there was something vaguely familiar about the man's voice.

This brought Marie a step nearer, "Why the poor fellow. It is Mr. Arter, the landlord of this building. His clothing is torn, and he is in a definite fix."

"You are right, Marie. It is Mr. Arter," Leone concurred.

Just then the man arose to a half-standing position and remained teetering on the edge of a step, trying vainly to regain his balance. The girls watched with suppressed breath. The suspense of the situation was shortened as he toppled backward and thumped soundly step by step back to the bottom of the stairs!

Leone turned comfortingly to Marie. "You are pale as ashes, Sis. Don't be so concerned. He should not get himself in such a dither."

"It got me when he was trying to stand on the edge of that step," replied Marie.

"He may have been standing on the edge of eternity," Leone answered gravely. "Let's go and see."

When both girls moved down to the aid of the once again fallen man, they were puzzled for a solution to the bizarre situation. His incoherent reply to questions was of little assistance. He appeared nearly frozen, and certainly if they turned him out into the sub-zero weather in his condition, he would inevitably freeze to death.

Leone looked appealingly to her sister. "Do you think we could persuade him to try to stand? We might get him up to the warm rooms by keeping him from falling."

Marie grinned. "I must say I am quite inexperienced with drunks, but I can try to help. I pity the poor creature if he is feeling only half as bad as he looks. But if we succeed in getting him upstairs, what will we do with him?" Marie asked.

"We will put him in a spare room," Leone replied, "and then lock him up until morning."

Marie couldn't refrain from a little giggle. "You sound like we are super human."

Listening carefully to Mr. Arter's muttering, they found to their dismay that he had as a result of his repeated defeats become satisfied with remaining where he was until he could walk away like a decent man. Both girls tried their most persuasive powers but to no avail--even when they told him he would perish in the basement's freezing temperature.

"We will all freeze here," Leone said dismally between chattering teeth. "Shall we give up?"

"Oh, not yet," firmly stated Marie. "But what can we do when he will not move?"

Leone suggested, "We could try forcing him to stand up, and he might become interested. He is so near frozen now that I think it would finish him to leave him here. Calling the police is the only other alternative, and we have no phone."

Taking him firmly by the arms, the girls lifted with all their strength. Trying to use a tone of authority, Leone scolded and was surprised to find some response from the figure. The man was making a clumsy effort to adjust his weight to his feet, which he finally succeeded in doing. After repeated urging, he began lifting his feet in an awkward fashion. The girls remained firmly aiding the man, and in this manner the trio finally reached the safety of the kitchen. Once Leone removed Mr. Arter's shoes, they saw that he was wearing heavy wool socks. The girls removed his socks and found his feet were not yet frozen but were so cold the girls declared they never would be warm again. He managed to get to the bedside and tumbled in. The sisters put a hot water bottle to the chilled feet, added plenty of blankets to the bed, and then shut and locked the door. They even put on an additional safety catch, although the man appeared harmless enough.

Leone awoke early the next morning. Their unwelcome guest had retained enough of his normal senses to say he must leave at an early hour, and the girls were only too anxious for his departure. Leone sewed up the rips in his otherwise nice overcoat and then brewed some strong black coffee before she called him. Mr. Arter appeared promptly, quite sobered up, and humbly thankful for the nice way she had fixed his coat and more than grateful for the generous care they had given him. He said he may have lost his life without their kindness. He explained that in his befuddled state he was under the impression he was going to his own room. When the apartment was vacant, he had remained there at night to keep the rooms warm and prevent damage from frost. Before he took his departure, he begged them not to give the incident any publicity.

"He didn't need to worry about that," Laura proclaimed as she and Leone breathed a big sigh of relief at his being gone. "One thing we learned is that we'll need to lock our door the next time in such a way that his key will be useless."

The rest of the Neely sisters arose about this time and emerged from their rooms rather cautiously.

"What was the cause of all the excitement around here last night?" said Henrietta curiously.

Leone and Marie tried to look mysterious.

"I could hear you girls pussy footing around and whispering," continued Henrietta. "And then making an awful racket at times. I could not imagine what on earth was taking place."

"But you were not sufficiently interested to come to our assistance?" Marie answered demurely.

"Oh, you always try to be funny!" Henrietta responded impatiently. "I did not get out of my nice warm bed because I was too cowardly to face this Alberta cold. Moreover I knew you girls would call us if it was anything requiring our assistance. You tell us, Leone."

"The truth is we were rescuing a man," offered Leone blandly.

"Rescuing a man?" Laura repeated in a horrified tone. "I thought I heard a man's voice. What did you rescue him from?"

"The cold," was Leone's simple answer.

Henrietta continued her inquiry, "And you brought him in here? Was that him just leaving?"

When Leone nodded, the three sisters who had been asleep stood in disbelief.

Marie laughed loudly. "That was him all right. But he was under lock and key. We saw to the lock."

Leone then proceeded to explain in detail. Her sisters listened intently.

"Well, the old goose. I for one gave him credit for having better sense," Laura declared.

Her satiric remark seemed an ample reply to the unforgettable incident.

Chapter 41
GUEST HOUSE/HOTEL OWNERSHIP

The girls enjoyed skating in the afternoon. But they looked about the town every day in the morning trying to discern what the town had to offer in the way of a livelihood.

As the days passed, it slowly became apparent to the Neely sisters that the principal reason for the existence of Edmonton was the traveling public. Hotels and rooming houses were numerous and all crowded with prosperous guests.

"If we stay in this part of the world, we will find it necessary to follow our friend's predictions and start waiting on the public," Leone remarked to her sisters at a time when they were all puzzling about their future.

"Do you mean to go into the hotel business?" Marie asked amusingly.

"And why not?" Henrietta responded. "That is the best idea I have heard yet."

"We would not have enough money to go in very deep," Marie added dubiously.

"And we have not a bit of experience," Henrietta continued. "Let's you and I take the job in the Hotel Vermilion that was offered to us. It is a leading hotel. We would learn a lot about the business. Leone could take a small place and with the aid of Laura and Helen succeed in running it. We might get into a real hotel later, if we decide to stay here."

"That is just the way I have been thinking," Leone answered. A few days sufficed to make another change in the lives of the Neely sisters. The girls had decided it was best if they separated as they'd earlier discussed. Marie and Henrietta went back along the seemingly endless snow-clad roads, miles to the town of Vermilion to work in a hotel. Leone, Helen, and Laura took on a small place already established. Their first guests would be the landlord and his family.

The establishment was a neat little place. The three girls did all the work, even shoveling the tons and tons of coal required for stoking the big furnace to a red-hot glow necessary to keep them comfortable.

Evenings there was plenty of amusement. Mike was a frequent visitor, accompanied by other attractive young men. The friendships were casual and sincere. The girls had many pleasant evenings at home augmented by the guests from their own lodge. There were also other happy times skating and dancing to the accompaniment of quaint musical selections rendered by a little orchestra that showed considerable talent.

One day in midwinter when a cold sun sent its golden rays adding charm to the hard frost and clinging to everything exposed to the bitter cold, Robert Neely walked in. His children were surprised and delighted to see him. He still wore the beard, and this day it was loaded with particles of ice and was white with frost adornments that he had acquired on his way from the depot. Time seemed disposed to treat him gently. He did not appear any older, and his perfect crown of dark hair showed no signs of gray.

The girls hovered around him. Laura prepared a nice lunch while they considered the bewildering problem of where he would room. Their popular little place was filled with guests, and there was no place for their father. The Neely girls did not favor the thought of asking a guest to move, as the income from each one was important. A temporary solution was offered later when a generous young man said he would share his room.

All this put a new thought in Leone's busy brain. She promptly went about counting her assets and expenses. Robert had given her forty dollars, but kept five for himself stating that this was all the money he possessed until he could find work. Leone believed him. It was an old story she had heard before. But she also knew he could not get a job until spring. With this added expense, she must do a little planning.

Marie and Henrietta on each payday had sent the greater part of their salary to Leone, who had managed judicially the varied income and hoped to acquire a larger hotel. After a few days' concentration and quite a few more of hard work, the Neelys were established in a much larger hotel. As before, the first guest there was their landlord. While he was a nice old man, he was in feeble health. There were some guests already, and under the new management of the Neelys, the house soon filled.

The three Neely girls were rather proud of this latest achievement. It was a small hotel as hotels go, but it was several times larger than the first one. A lady's parlor on the second floor was an attractive feature. There was a rotunda and office on the main floor along with a room and pleasant dining room.

In the weeks to come the three girls had numerous reasons to recall the kindly admonishes of their friend, Captain Williams. Not only must they excel in the chambermaid art, but they must cook, waitress, and clean up as well. Only excellent workmen could have accomplished what they succeeded in doing.

Helen and Laura also both took on a cheerful and dependable manner. Just barely out of childhood years, they helped Leone work out a system whereby no moment was lost. There even was one thing their father could and would do: he served as a receptionist clerk of sorts and thus saved valuable time for the girls.

The Neelys continued to take time for recreation. This included mostly skating or dancing on some few occasions. They also attended church as usual.

The month of March arrived. It was not a blustery March, but just the same it had a hard, still cold with frost glistening in the air. This March marked the arrival of their brother, Bill, who was now a young man. The scar on his face was much improved, and he still was the same cheerful, irrepressible Bill. He took over the care of the big furnace, shoveling the large pile of coal and clinkers necessary to heat the big building. He also relieved the girls of many other tasks while whistling softly as he worked. Bill helped solve some of the problems that had confronted Leone. However, there always were others. It was as though a new one seemed to appear each day.

One morning Leone was called to the aid of one of the guests. A rash had made an appearance on his skin. Leone promptly called a physician. The scare turned out to be nothing worse than the three-day measles. But the local physician, Dr. McDonnell, declared that the case must be isolated, or it would sweep through their establishment and cause an epidemic. The doctor asked Leone, "Can you handle it?"

"Very well," was the cheerful response. "I have a very remote room downstairs. I can arrange for this case."

"But there could be more," said the doctor raising his hand to his forehead as if preparing to meditate. "Put the patient in a small room, and one room may take care of the situation."

When he had gone, Leone slipped into the dining room for a little refreshment before undertaking this rather heavy assignment. There were two late diners in the dining room, Bill and Mr. Cross, an old gentleman of reputedly great wealth, who had been a guest for the past week. The two men were carrying on an animated conversation concerning matrimony. Bill, full of his usual mischief, was arguing against marriage. Leone took a place at their table. Mr. Cross was well groomed and a man of evident refinement and had a good command of the English language. On the other hand, Bill was not well groomed or refined, but he could keep up an easy flow of words. Mr. Cross seemed to be pleased by Leone's appearance.

"I've been trying to convince your brother that he should marry young," was Mr. Cross's opening comment.

Bill scoffed, "He wants to see some poor girl starve to death."

"I am quite in earnest," the elderly man remarked. "You will not find it such a joke if you reach my age. I am eighty-one in June and still single. I have no family of any sort and am wondering what I will do with my wealth."

"You could leave it to me," Bill said grinning.

"I would much rather leave it to your sister. She is a self-sacrificing young woman of unusual business ability," he offered as he looked admiringly at Leone.

He continued and asked Leone, "I was in hopes that you might see fit to marry me and take over the business management of my property. I say this with all due respect to your youth. It would be managing my property, an easy task for a woman of your ability. It would be a marriage of convenience. And since I would not be around to bother you very long, I could pass on secure in the thought that I was leaving my property in good hands."

A slow flush mounted to Leone's sensitive face. "I appreciate the honor you do me," she said gently, "but I must decline."

"Are you sure this would be your final answer if you took more time to consider?" the elderly gentleman urged.

"Quite sure," Leone replied. There could be no other answer.

Bill sat silent. Leone could see without looking that he was ready to burst a blood vessel from repressed amusement. She was glad to be able to make a kindly withdrawal from the scene and plunge into the important task of the moment of transferring what had been a storeroom into an isolation ward. She went rapidly to work clearing out everything stored there. Just as she had the room looking its worst, she was joined by her brother who was beaming a huge smile. Bill looked about inquisitively, "Gosh, what's up, Leone. Did you change your mind?"

"What do you mean, change my mind?" Leone retorted.

225

"Well, it struck me that you might be preparing the bridal chamber!"

"Bill, aren't you the most ridiculous person!"

"Well, of course, I didn't know," he said modestly. "Just teasing, Leone."

Once he'd had his fun, Bill helped Leone scrub the room to a shining example, and the two installed the patient there. In a few days, even that problem had ceased to be one.

Time passed. The hard, relentless cold of winter loosened its grip, but then the rains started. The Neely sisters had seen rainfall before, but not such torrents as this. Marie and Henrietta came home, and the sisters were together once more. Henrietta had accepted a position in a nice lady's wear shop on Jasper Avenue. It was decided that Marie would help her sisters in their larger hotel. This arrangement was very comforting for all the Neely girls. It gave them more time and energy to spend in recreation and feel the gladness of their youthfulness.

Later that spring the girls were given a fair offer to sell their leasehold on the hotel. Such a transaction would enable them to take on another hotel at a more desirable location in the area, and this they then resolved to do. Both deals went through without a hitch, and within a week the Neely sisters were established in the hotel of better class. As Henrietta described the hotel, "It is larger and swankier and will pay a little better." Mike McDonald remained a good friend of the girls. He had done his share to help them in lifting and tugging on the many boxes, barrels, and odd pieces of furniture that they had to get moved. Mike always had an amusing quip to offer. His cheery voice rang out, or, if he was not talking, he was laughing. Robert Neely declared that his tongue was installed on a swivel and worked from both ends. Robert had not, however, intended the comment as unkind criticism. He liked the cheerful fellow, and all of his daughters did also.

It was about this time that Mike confessed to Leone that he cared deeply for Helen. Mike told Leone of the incident that had occurred at a recent party when he had felt slighted by Helen. Leone attempted to soothe his wounded vanity by her response, "You know Helen is only fourteen years of age. She is unconscious that any man would honor her with his affection. She is not even out of childhood yet. And you are very young yourself, Mike. And I think you would prefer that she be allowed to grow up unaware of this?"

"Oh, yes, yes," Mike quickly answered. "But she is perfect."

And so it was that Leone learned of Helen's future.

That spring a dramatic club was organized. Henrietta was chosen as the leading lady. The girl had a natural aptitude for dramatic art, and she also had natural expressiveness. Rehearsals were begun shortly. Most of the responsibility for the production went to the Neely sisters as they were willing workers and had previous experience with productions.

The Neely sisters continued to run true to form, all busy as the proverbial bee. The hotel stayed filled with guests. Leone found that one important bit of work never seemed to ease, and that was collecting the money. The guests were nice people and from everywhere. But some of them were not too well supplied with funds, and collecting was a difficult job.

On rare occasions the Neely girls were left with a grip piece well filled with masculine apparel in lieu of a small bill. Another time, an old English butler who had been in that service most of his life appeared at the desk with a rifle in his hands. "Is the mahster in?" he drawled. The man was addressing Helen who had no idea what was meant by his remark. After repeating "Is the mahster in?" several more times in a nasal tone, the old gentleman stood there apparently at his wit's end. Leone came in just then and offered, "I think he wants to see Dad," as she turned to the quaint guest. This proved to be the case. He was checking out and wished to leave his gun in their care. Such odd characters they were and strange to the way of life that the Neely sisters were accustomed.

Most of the girls were in the upper hall one afternoon hurriedly putting two rooms that had just been vacated to right when Marie tiptoed in looking very pale and in evident state of alarm. "Girls, girls," she whispered hoarsely.

Her sisters turned to her anxiously eager to know what the trouble was. "A man is in my room," she answered "and, asleep in my bed. He must be drunk."

Marie led the way downstairs to the family quarters, and sure enough a man in a suit of dark gray check was lying face down. His head was almost buried in the pillows; he was apparently fast asleep. Fred Hastings, a frequent escort of Marie's of late, arrived about this time. Seeing the figure on the bed, Fred signified his willingness to take the intruder by the neck and throw him out. However, Leone advised caution. Approaching closer, she placed a hand on the fellow's shoulder and shook him gently. "Sir," she demanded, "What does this mean? You are intruding. Do you want me to call the police?" The fellow did not move except for his shoulders. He even seemed to be shaking slightly. Fred eyed him scornfully and announced, "He is drunk all right!" As Henrietta reached and lifted the pillow, the figure sat up and let out a burst of laughter. It was Laura! She had found a man's suit in one of the grips they were holding in lieu of collections and decided to play a prank on Marie. Their wonderful sense of humor always had a way of lightening the days for the Neely sisters.

The season moved along to mid-summer. The days were dream days--long and shining golden, tinted with reflections from the Alberta sun. The morning seemed to begin a few hours after midnight and then lingered the drawing of the curtain of night. One evening Leone went into the fragrant twilight and seated herself upon a boulder, which lay half-hidden some distance from the hotel. Groups of traditional willows lent attraction to the scene, and the eerie rays of the aurora borealis cast a soft brilliance about her like a pool of lamplight. She sat appreciating in silence until a few moments later when Marie came to sit down by her side. Smiling, Marie greeted her, "It is lovely out here this hour. Mike just arrived, and they are all coming out."

"Is Dad in the lobby?" Leone inquired.

"Yes, he is blarneying with some old gentleman. Good to last two hours anyway."

"And where is Freddie this evening?" came the teasing note in Leone's voice.

"He will be a little late tonight. Among all the other things he does for his firm, he collects the slow accounts and must see a man tonight who is not available in the day time."

"I was thinking when you came." Leone continued, her words trailing uncertainly after one another, "Your remarks dovetail right into my thoughts."

"Yes, I believe I know what you're thinking. This is small-town stuff. And what are we lingering around here for? I have asked myself the same question. However, since I met Fred, I will admit the question is not so pertinent."

Leone looked squarely at her sister. "You like him; don't you?"

Marie looked happily confused. "He likes me," she said. "No puzzle about that."

Their sisters accompanied by Mike and Fred could be seen coming toward them.

"Did you read the letter from Bill?" Marie asked.

"Yes, I did," answered Leone. "And I believe he thinks more of his range-riding and his horses than he does of his sisters."

Marie laughed and then responded, "Perhaps, but he does have a living to make. It is well that he is happy about it."

"I think so, too," Leone agreed.

The group of young people then gaily approached. They were all gazing with interest at the numerous waving shafts of an aurora borealis, which completely covered the visible heavens. While this was a common occurrence in the region, this evening's display was extraordinarily vivid.

"I have some alarming news," Marie gravely remarked.

The members of the group all turned to her, and the smiles died away.

"What do you mean?" asked Laura anxiously.

"Leone is considering going on to the coast," replied Marie.

They all turned to the older sister, and it was Henrietta who asked, "Are you thinking of selling our leasehold on the inn?"

"No," replied Leone. "I thought it would be a better plan to go first by myself and see how the land lays."

"You can go without me," Helen sharply interjected.

Leone gave her a tender smile. "No, dear, I need you to go with me." She then turned to Mike knowing he would be concerned. "What do you think of the plan?" she queried.

"I have never been to the coast," he replied thoughtfully. "But I intend to go. This pioneering stuff does not have the appeal for me."

Leone continued, "I have spent time and money in obtaining an education and training to fit me for other lines of endeavor that there is no possible use for here. However, Seattle and Vancouver are both among the larger cities where there is need of my skill."

The group listened carefully, but remained silent. Leone added, "There is one thing I don't like about going though. It seems like breaking up our home. And I wonder if we will resume our lives together."

"Oh, yes you will," Mike hastened to reply.

Fred beamed and offered, "You will all marry before many years and then, of course, have separate homes."

All the objections were set aside as simply as that.

Chapter 42
NURSING HOME MANAGEMENT

A few days later Leone and Helen found themselves aboard a train for Vancouver heading for the new life that awaited them in the Canadian Rockies. Having lived thus far in level country where little rolling ground would be the only excuse for a hill that could be seen, it was indeed a revelation to see the glamorous mountains dressed in all their dramatic grandeur.

The train was not crowded. Many seats were vacant and could be changed at will to afford the girls a better view. There were several friends on the train, among them two young men. The two were just good friends, not at all the romantic type as so many others the girls had met in this new country.

Before they had reached Vancouver, the gruesome news had leaked out that the hangman from Ontario was a passenger aboard their train. Three men would pay the extreme penalty of their lives at the New Westminster prison during the coming week. This dreadful news, so haunting in character, got around. All the passengers promptly decided to have at least one look at this marked man. He remained in seclusion most of the time, but many of the passengers got the coveted peek at him, including Leone and Helen. While they were not happy about this, it certainly made the trip more memorable.

The two Neely sisters liked living in Vancouver from the first. They missed the other members of the family, but tried to look bravely to the time when they would all be together once more.

Leone procured employment in a tailoring department of a leading store of the city. They had taken some nice rooms, and Helen found a housekeeper position.   A small group of friends, mostly people from Edmonton, allowed for frequent callers. Everything seemed to be running smoothly.

Then one evening when Leone was looking so very tired, Helen remarked about it to her.

Leone answered, "Yes, we pushed hard on the work today with special orders for people going to Europe."

"But Leone dear, you are as pale as a ghost."

"Well, for the special orders, we had even to work on them at home to get them done," Leone responded.

"Do you like your job?" Helen asked.

230

"Oh, it is all right, as jobs go. But I do not like my salary," offered Leone.

"But the place you are working should be paying the best wages in town."

"I think they do," Leone replied thoughtfully, and added, "but, I have a profession."

Helen grimaced at her response. "I should know," she said. "Let's have dinner. It will rest you. Then we will consult the ads section of the evening paper."

The girls watched that same ad section of the *Vancouver World* for two weeks before they saw what could be what they wanted: a nurse to take charge of a rest home. The nurse in charge at present planned to go to California for a change.

Leone presented her credentials and secured the appointment. In a few days she and Helen were in full command of the situation, which included a real efficient Japanese houseboy called Hari. There were a few rest cases always with them, but the babies with their respective mothers came and went in successive numbers. When all the rooms were occupied, the girls found the work overwhelming. But again, the strong Neely girls had proven their ability and willingness on many occasions. Helen was a quick and efficient assistant, and they were grateful to a kind Providence for giving them fortitude and a natural cheerful disposition. And at last, but not least, help was appreciated from the silent and efficient Hari. He seemed to know by instinct what would be required of him when a contingency arose. He had the happy faculty of remaining a nonentity himself.

If the rooms remained filled to capacity, the girls would have been forced to increase the number on their staff, but that was not the way things went. There were times when they had ample opportunity to become rested and enjoy their friends. And Mike was certainly one of those friends. He had spent long days with them coming from his hotel at an early hour each day. Mike enjoyed the weather to be found on the coast and promised the girls he would surely join them in Seattle in the spring. They missed him when he was gone. The pleasure and excitement his coming brought into their lives vanished with him when he left in January. The beds were once more filled with patients, and the girls were too busy for proper rest. Ultimately, however, the two women were determined to go on to Seattle when relieved of their obligations. The move would require money. The boat fare was but a trivial sum, yet there were other expenses of unknown quantity that must be reckoned with. This circumstance prompted them to work longer hours with greater effort.

After reading a letter from Marie one morning, Helen hurried to find Leone. "Marie and Fred are about to be married!" she exclaimed excitedly.

Leone was in the act of sliding a pillow into a fresh slip preparing to place it on a freshly made-up bed. She sat weakly down on the bed, the pillow in her arms. "Is the letter from Marie herself?" Leone inquired as her voice faltered.

"Yes, and they plan on a quick marriage with the family as scattered as we are." Helen added, "And Fred is away from all his family, too."

"It makes me sad," Leone finally commented. "I had always planned on a nice wedding for the girls."

"But it can be a nice wedding even though there is no fanfare," offered Helen.

Leone gave a rather weak little laugh. "Fanfare is scarcely the word. Will they live in Edmonton?"

"No. She says that Fred has a better job in Calgary, so they will go directly there."

Leone looked dreamily at Helen. "And Henrietta will be next on the list of newlyweds. And then two of the Neely girls will make their home in Canada."

"It's a fine country, and we all love it," Helen replied staunchly.

"You are right, dear, and it was Mother's country. But I feel…well, you know I cannot explain, but sort of beaten," answered Leone.

"You had us kids on your hands so long, we seemed permanent. When we begin adding beaus to the picture, it gives you a feeling you cannot identify. I know I feel like crying myself because I had planned on being a bridesmaid at the first wedding."

"Never mind, darling. You can be my bridesmaid," Leone promised.

Both girls looked at each other then and laughed. Helen replied, "You have to find a man yet!"

"Yes, and a man that will have me!"

"You will not have to look very far for one to fit that description and a nice man, too," the younger sister suggested.

232

"If you are referring to our neighbor, he has no charm for me," Leone said ruefully.

Helen continued, "He is good looking and rich. I am just stating facts, not pleading his case."

"Your remarks even to the untutored ear sound suspicious. When I marry, it will be for love," stated Leone emphatically.

The two girls then quieted to listen to voices in the lower hall. A few of Hari's words reached them, "... and, the two young missies are very busy."

The reply was in a masculine voice with a distinctly audible British accent, "But I must see Miss Cindy."

Leone smothered a laugh and whispered softly to Helen, "That fake English Lord nut!"

Hari's meek voice floated up again, "Missie Helen say, 'Very busy. Do not disturb!'"

The Brit grew impatient and tapped on the stair banister with a folded newspaper and called out, "Miss Cindy."

Leone peered coldly at him over the railing. "My sister asked to be excused. We have work to do," and with this she turned abruptly away.

However, the clever young man remained obstinately at the bottom of the banister.

"Cinderella," he called. "Just one glance from your beautiful eyes is all I am pleading for. Cindy, I will place the world at your feet," as he symbolically tossed the *Vancouver World* newspaper on the stairway. Hesitantly, he then allowed Hari to show him out.

Helen watched his form retreating from a window as the Brit walked away. "I wonder how that oaf got the notion of calling me Cindy?"

Leone replied, "You have the dainty foot of Cinderella," according to him. "And he is a handsome chap, as well as a member of British aristocracy."

Helen looked demurely at her sister, "So he says," she countered. "Strange such a sophisticated man would notice me," she said doubtfully. "When I marry, I shall also marry for love."

Leone smiled tenderly at her youngest sister. Baby Helen is growing up, she thought to herself. She responded, "Men jaded by society find youth delightfully refreshing. You will do well to avoid them. You and Mike will marry some day and perhaps too soon."

Helen replied, "Not so soon. I resolve to wait until I am twenty-two years of age."

"Words of wisdom," responded Leone.

"Yes, and I can see how you always had a different outlook on life than most girls. You have seen life as it is lived."

"I find it does not weaken my appreciation of family ties to have witnessed many things that have taken place here. But it has made me think love's young dream is a normal as well as fascinating part of life. I think we can have that and also have our youth and that each comes in its own good time," advised Leone.

In the early autumn following that busy summer, Leone and Helen were seated on a pleasant little side porch that overlooked their quiet street. They were enjoying a short reprieve from their arduous duties. The postman coming by on his rounds smiled and handed them two letters. One proved to be from the nurse for whom they were substituting. In the letter she informed them that she was returning and planned to resume her duties. The other letter was from Laura to let them know that their sisters were disposing of the lease on their hotel in Edmonton. Laura planned to start for the coast in a few days; Marie and Fred had gotten married and were in Calgary, and Henrietta was leaving for Winnipeg.

These changes meant that prompt preparations must be made to move. The two hoped that Laura would reach Vancouver in time to take the boat trip with them to Seattle. They told Hari, the houseboy, of their upcoming plans. Hari was packing his humble belongings for departure when Leone touched the bell and called him to come quickly. She needed him to assist her in lifting a patient who appeared to be fainting. Later when she saw Hari in the hallway, he was standing stoically and unsmiling looking into space with all his processes at work.

"Why so sober, Hari?" she asked.

Hari turned his face, which lighted up with the customary little grin. He said laboriously, "You are a doctor Vomin."

"No," responded Leone. "We have explained nurse to you so many times!"

Later when he was leaving, he came and placed his neat little grip at Leone's side and stepped back, arms folded and waited.

"You go now, Hari," she said. "But why are you giving me the grip?"

"Search," he said in a stoical way.

"Search your grip, Hari? Whatever for?"

"Silver," was the reply.

Leone patted Hari gently on the shoulder. "Faithful little Hari. I do not need to search your grip."

Hari understood and smiled gratefully as he picked up his grip and departed.

That day's mail brought another letter from Laura to advise that her trip to the coast was unavoidably delayed.

"Shall we wait for her?" Helen asked Leone.

"No, darling, we will not," was the response. "It is a tempting prospect, but we would have to go to a hotel, and her exact time of arrival is indefinite. I think it best that we go and do our waiting in Seattle."

Chapter 43
FINAL DESTINATION

There were scattered clouds and pale sunshine with one little shower on the boat trip to Seattle. On board the girls met a couple, also returning to Seattle, who were natives of the Pacific Northwest. They found the couple both charming and interesting. The couple knew much about climatic conditions, shrubs, and flowers as well as businesses of the city. The Neely girls listened with rapt attention to the two.

As it had been a long time in reaching this destination, the two Neely girls were determined to remain in Seattle. Without incident they were quickly established in a nice little apartment. And it was not that long before Laura joined them. The reunion of the three Neely sisters and the return to their homeland was such a monumental accomplishment for them. It proved to be a time long remembered by the girls. Their lives had been so closely interwoven that the many months of separation seemed long indeed to them. But it was also in reality an auspicious time. It was too soon after the Christmas holidays for businesses to have returned to normalcy. It required considerable study in the ad section of the daily papers for them to secure work.

Leone was able to resume her nurse status and went about caring for a critical case of a little woman she had been directed to through a friend in Vancouver. Both Laura and Helen after a time got work on a staff in the tailoring industry. Their faith enabled the girls to also take other unpleasant incidents and trials in their stride.

This time of their lives did not prove to be at all dull or uninteresting. Too many of the passing glimpses of life around them were strange and new. Roses and other summer flowers displaying beautiful blooms in the cooler months thrilled them. This strange, new climate controlled many other admirable things that affected their daily life and kept their interests high. Their laughing voices, like a spring breeze, seemed always ready to bubble forth at will.

There were other incidents that touched their daily life more closely but were less cheery. One was Leone's salary. She had been anxious concerning this important matter. She came home one evening and informed the girls that she was not to have a payday. The husband of the patient she had been caring for was out of work and about out of money.

Laura's pretty little face took on a shadow as she dryly commented, "Now isn't that just something?"

Helen was sympathetic, "You can scarcely be fair with your conscience and leave her flat."

Leone concurred, "At least not until after the baby comes, if she even lives through the ordeal. The doctors say she has no chance, and that only a miracle will save her. She cannot go to a hospital as a Canadian citizen without money. I will have to stand by the ship. If I announced that I was leaving, the blow would be a fatal one. There are also the three children to consider. However, their home is nice, and she can have good care as long as I contribute it."

Her two sisters smilingly agreed with Leone. Laura added, "Let's just hope it will not be too long."

Helen added, "And that they will have the money sometime soon."

Two weeks passed before the girls saw Leone again. The time had been filled with tragedy and triumph for the valiant little mother who was to have fulfilled the age-old obligation of womanhood. While the infant died, the doctor, a man of medicine, did not claim any of the credit for saving the woman's life. He proclaimed that only faith could have done that.

Leone's work was not finished for some weeks. Tender buds were already thrusting forth in the first signs of early spring. The curtains at the window waved softly against a billowing breeze pouring through the open sash when Leone came home. Her sisters greeted her warmly. Laura noted Leone's grip, and almost reluctantly inquired, "Well, are you released from that case?"

"Yes, the poor little woman feels she is sufficiently recovered to get along by herself," Leone responded.

"What a blessing," Helen said fervently. "We were just sitting here speaking of our circumstance. Laura and I have a notion to move, and we want you to like the plan."

Laura jumped in to explain, "We have found a little cottage close to the water's edge. We have never lived near salt water. I think it will be nice."

"You mean Puget Sound?" Leone inquired dubiously. "Is it distant?"

"Oh no," Laura responded. "Right here in the city."

Helen continued, "At Interbay there is a small cottage. We have not had the opportunity to see the place yet. We just found an address in the ad section of today's paper. We were going to go about seeing it this evening."

"I would love that," Leone agreed, her eyes sparkling. "I feel as though I have just secured my freedom from jail and must make use of my liberty."

"Well, come on then," Laura said. "It is only 6:30 p. m. now, and we have a long evening."

"Leone is tired, too, no doubt," Helen observed.

Quick to respond, Leone replied, "I shall not mind. I will rest on the streetcar."

The girls were soon changing cars downtown for the Interbay trip, swinging aboard the high steps of the none too modernistic streetcar which went clanging noisily along its way. The girls gazed through the open window looking out at the alluring waters of Puget Sound as they noted the balmy spring breeze was getting a little cooler. They could see both large and small boats. The last slanting rays of a setting sun found its resting place on little white sail steamers and chugging crafts alike. Some of the crafts were secured to a wharf while others were attempting to make their way through placid waves. The streetcar tracks were actually built for some distance upon a trestle where the tide washed some depths beneath. This was truly a novelty to see for the Neely sisters. The girls disembarked from the streetcar at Smith Street and then preceded downhill to the Sound.

After dabbling their feet in the salt water for a time, the girls retraced their steps to the cottage. Laura had the key, and they entered a gloomy atmosphere of musty, repelling, harsh, and torn wallpaper disfiguring the snug little rooms. But the waves splashing idly, the incoming tide, and prospects of possibly finding a geoduck were all too magnetic to resist. The girls decided in favor of taking the little cottage.

Within a week the Neely girls were moving in and promptly went about polishing and wallpapering. The little cottage was soon shining clean and had freshly papered walls. Pretty window curtains were added, and their little pieces of furniture were attractively placed in position. The cottage very soon reflected an appreciable change.

Leone went back to her work and in her profession again. This time she found employment in the home of a member of a wealthy pioneer family. She worked there through the lovely spring and mellow summer that followed.

The girls loved the temperate weather and never tired of going down to the water when the tide was out to run barefoot, prospecting for clams. They did find clams, but never found the much sought after geoducks. If time allowed, they lingered to watch the tide come swirling in over the pebbly bottom.

The season was about spent when the man who owned the little cottage stopped by to chat a moment one evening. After explaining his appreciation of them as tenants, he assured them he intended to improve the house by moving it to a more desirable place on the lot. With visions of torn wallpaper and attended disorders, the girls hastened to assure him that the house suited them just as it was. The owner, however, was quite persistent about the matter. He had already engaged an expert to do the job and promised it would go smoothly. He assured them they would be quite unaware that the house was even being moved.

The Neely girls conceded but were quite skeptical of his promise knowing the water supply would have to be cut off for an indefinite period of time. Laura decided to remain at home to do the family wash and make a few other preparations for the upheaval as the girls called it. In this way, they figured they would be prepared for any inconvenience. The situation was not destined to be peaceful, in spite of their careful plans.

The moving equipment and crew arrived at eight o'clock that morning and set to work at once. However, each effort they made to accomplish their mission intensified with their inability to get it accomplished. The little house was built in such a fashion that the wing portion soon began to sag away from its moorings, and daylight was apparent through a wide crack in the wall.

Inside the cottage, Laura scrambled around on a floor that was tipping dangerously. She managed to salvage the coffee urn, toaster, and pieces of furniture. Then with a great splitting and creaking, nails gave way, and the wing fell in a great heap. Laura had managed to spring clear of the wreckage and reach the dubious protection of the main portion of the cottage before the wing collapsed. Peeking through the opening in the debris, the man in charge could see her standing in a doorway, her eyes blazing with righteous indignation.

"Are you hurt, Miss?" he called anxiously.

"No," Laura answered acidly, "I am not even surprised!"

The indignant Laura headed to the city center where she knew of another cottage located at Mercer Street, a few blocks from the Sound. After looking at the cottage, she secured the services of a moving van. With the help of the moving crew, all possessions of the three Neely girls were rescued from the wrecked cottage and were relocated into the new little cottage on Mercer Street.

When Leone and Helen arrived home that evening, the still indignant Laura was standing on the walk in front of the wreckage. The girls stopped the next streetcar and climbed rather gloomily aboard. They managed to laugh a little, too, when Laura launched into her description of the events leading up to the ludicrous proceedings that wrecked their home. Laura, however, could not join the laughter.

The Neely sisters were soon comfortable in their new home on Mercer Street. Even though it was not located on the water, they could see boats passing on the beautiful waters of Puget Sound. Leone was able to get employment in the business district. The ride to work for all of them was scarcely half the distance it had been. This fact was greatly appreciated since shorter, cooler days of fall had crept upon them. Overall, the Neely sisters were once again busy and happy as usual.

Chapter 44
THE FUTURE?

Helen had met a young woman employed at the same firm where she worked, and a friendship had formalized. The two girls appeared together frequently at lunch. After a time Helen invited her friend, Dell Scheff, to come home with her. Leone, Helen, and Dell were having a lively topic of conversation when Laura broke in, "When I arrived home a half hour ago, the real estate agent was showing buyers through the house."

Leone inquired, "He admitted himself and a group of strange people to our home without the courtesy of asking our permission?"

"They were here when I came and they had a dog running through our rooms," accused Laura.

Helen giggled and proclaimed, "I am in favor of buying a moving van."

"Why a van?" Leone asked.

"It could come in handy in moving so often," was the reply.

"That is a possible solution of the matter," Leone agreed. "But I for one, am tired of moving."

At this point, Laura had taken over the role of hostess, as she always fell naturally into this position. Dell, who was petite and blonde, was quite the opposite in appearance of Laura. However, they grew to be good friends in rapid order thanks to the way paved for them by Helen. Dell's friendship had been followed by the introduction of an attractive young man named Lue Berg. He was a nice looking chap, not too tall, hair thick and dark and slightly unruly. The mischief never seemed to go out of his eyes, and his pleasant laugh always lurked near. He was devoted to Dell and made a pleasant addition to their small circle of friends.

The Neely sisters reluctantly agreed they would need to relocate their home. They went about it deliberately in an attempt to eradicate any oversights. They located a home in Ballard, a suburb of Seattle that filled all their requirements. The house was big and roomy, well furnished, and they were soon comfortably ensconced in their latest habitation.

One evening Leone answered a ring at the doorbell and was both surprised and pleased to find there the courageous little mother she had nursed back to health after losing her baby. The woman announced that her family was leaving the city and that all their furniture was being seized by law to cover past debts. However, she did own one piece of furniture that was not included in the transaction, a sewing machine. She advised Leone to send for it as some payment for the nursing care she had provided. The woman also regretted that the item could possibly be all she would ever receive for her efforts. The following day the girls acquired the sewing machine.

The season was soon slipping into a nice soft but not too slushy winter. For a brief period after the Christmas holidays, Lue and Dell discontinued their regular visits. However, when the excitement brought about by the holiday season wore away, the visits were resumed. One evening Lue raised his voice in a manner he occasionally employed when wishing to command attention, "When are you going to have me bring my cousin, Bill Mayouck, out here to spend an evening, Leone?"

"I believe it is up to you and your cousin Bill," she replied. "I assured you sometime ago when you first proposed presenting your cousin that he would be welcome."

Lue's good-natured face took on a look of embarrassment. The truth is I told him and promised him he would enjoy the evening. We always have a jolly time here. I bragged the subject to him again later, but he had some excuse. Lue sat there looking so uncomfortable and frustrated that all the girls joined in laughter. Laura patted him on the shoulder in a comforting manner and predicted, "Bill is evidently discriminatory, and he doesn't trust you to choose his friends."

"Bill can't do this to me. I am going to bring that fellow out here if I have to put him in irons," asserted Lue.

Leone laughed, but she had a feeling of disapproval for this type of levity.

Early in February Lue made good his boast. Accompanying him and Dell one Sunday evening was an impressive young man who stood quietly in the background, a half-smile illuminating his fine features. Lue was obviously exhilarated with his success of bringing about a meeting between Leone and Bill. But Lue, who was even more exuberant in spirit than usual, wasn't about to accept Bill's quiet presence. Assisted by the attractive and amusing Dell, they had Bill out of the background and into the foreground in one minute flat. Leone and Laura in their roles as hostesses also quietly assumed the limelight. Mike, having met Bill on former occasions

241

through fraternal affiliations, was also flanked beside him. Lue, with a feeling of chagrin, raised a bold stand in deference of his attitude, "Bill can take a joke. He's no sissy."

The girls, who were endeavoring to be subtle, turned smilingly to the irresistible Lue.

Leone protested sweetly, "You have overlooked the fact that you have known Bill all your life while he is a stranger to us."

"And we must not allow our guests to gain the impression they are being hazed," Laura added just as sweetly.

The amiable Lue, not in the least abashed, chose to subside meekly for the moment.

After this meeting, time passed. Leone developed a light case of The Grippe. When the malady had made its departure, there remained a slight bronchial annoyance that aggravated into a cough at times. Leone went back to work, but the condition persisted. Her sisters worried. "I don't like that nasty little honk you have, Leone," Helen remarked anxiously. "What did the doctor think about it?"

Leone smiled slowly in a meditative fashion. "I don't know what he thought really, but he prescribed that stuff I am taking and said the honk would wear away."

Helen continued, "You should not have it in the first place. After all we are a hardy people from the Michigan lumber region."

Leone laughed more lightly this time. "I thought you had Michigan in mind when you used the word honk. The great flocks of wild geese there that winged their way overhead with an occasional weird call will always remain in our memory. People are beginning to associate that word with automobile horns here, but I guess it will always remind the Neelys of AuGres and wild geese."

Laura entered the room then and seated herself on the cushioned arm of Helen's chair. The girls were in a reminiscent mood. "We have come a long way since we watched the wild fowl heading for their resting grounds at Mudd Lake," Laura commented.

"Yes," Leone agreed. "I have thought sometimes of bringing up the subject of regret. I wonder if we were wise to come West."

A charming flush surfaced on Helen's little face, and her eyes shined. "I would never have met Mike if we had remained in Chicago."

"There is much other compensation well worthwhile," chimed in Laura.

242

the table alone. Bill expressed his pleasure on meeting her there. "My mother is here!" he said proudly. "Can I take you to her?" he asked.

Leone arose with a smile, and together, deep in animated conversation, they were jostled about in the crowd but did not notice. The two moved slowly as there seemed to be so much to talk about. Then Leone met Margaret Mayouck for the first time, and a link was forged in friendship destined to last throughout the years. Bill's mother was a beautiful woman with a perfect complexion and fine eyes that glowed with a mother's pride. Bill's mother was tall and cordial. Leone, seated by her side, listened to her gentle voice filled with friendship and charm. Bill departed momentarily, but returned smiling. A lottery ticket he had purchased for Leone proved to be the lucky number. He announced that she was now the owner of a dinner set. Agreeing to claim this prize for Leone, Margaret Mayouck took the lucky ticket and gazed happily after Leone and her son as they made their way slowly to the exit.

In the weeks that followed their long ride to Ballard that evening, the two young people met frequently. Having come to the city as a small boy, Bill had lived most of his life in Seattle. Leone loved to listen as he related interesting stories of Seattle's early history.

Leone's health was not at its best, but Bill brought delicacies for her that he hoped would aid in rebuilding her naturally strong physic.

"Can I come tomorrow?" he asked on seeing her home one Saturday.

"Of course. Why not?" Leone answered with a smile.

He took her hands and pressed them gently in his warm clasp. "I do not wish to intrude."

Leone drew a hand from his light caressing finger and grasped his arm impulsively,

"Why, Bill," she said. "What a thought." She then paused a moment to make an appraisal of this cheerful, unobtrusive young man who had quietly become so important in her life. There flashed through her thoughts in retrospect the times when he had appeared in an old suit and put their fuel safely under cover or raked the yard. He was at all times a comforting guest who could enjoy a book or a paper, if she was busy. "The spring days have become warm and smiley," he said. "Shall I come with Prince and we can drive until sundown?" Leone was delighted, and her heart raced with the prospect. Prince was a high-stepping sorrel gelding who would be hitched to a smart turnout that Bill drove on occasion.

The next day the weather was heavenly, and Leone ran out to greet Bill as he drew Prince up to the gate. Prince was decked out in a new spring outfit, and his spirit matched the new outfit. Bill's eyes glowed happily as he helped Leone to a seat by his side. Prince seemed to swing out with a spirit in tune with the glorious day, his hoofs beating a rhythmic sound on the pavement as he trotted along keeping his own pace.

"I do not have the usual overpowering impulse to take the reins," Leone remarked grinning.

"You would enjoy driving Prince," replied Bill. "He is not shy and does not have any tricks."

"Nevertheless, I shall be content just to ride today," answered Leone. "Automobiles are becoming more numerous every day," she added while watching the cars glide past.

"Yes," Bill replied. "But there will always be a place for horses. It will just not be in passenger service. You will note that nearly all the horses we've seen are general purpose horses."

As they neared the big city's center, Bill inquired, "Shall we drive around by the waterfront where you can see our wholesale district?" There was a note of civic pride in his voice as he spoke. "And incidentally, see a glimpse of Puget Sound and the boats there?"

"Oh yes, one of my favorite pastimes," offered Leone.

After they had explored the waterfront, Bill turned Prince's head to the south. He asked, "Are you hungry?"

"Famished!" was her answer.

Bill quickly announced, "Well, I know the most perfect spot in Rainier Valley where they serve substantial food to travelers like us and as it should be served. Even Prince can have a hitching post there, a little water and a feed bag."

"Sounds wonderful," responded Leone.

They arrived at the attractive little inn. There they enjoyed the atmosphere and lingered over the delicious dinner that was served. Once they'd finished, Bill checked to see that Prince had been readied to travel, and they boarded the turnout once again. The sun was shimmering on Lake Washington, and Bill headed Prince toward the sinking sun. The glad hours drifted by as they enjoyed the setting.

Bill turned to Leone and said, "We should be going. It is a long way to Ballard."

Having been entranced with the lure of the wonderful day they'd had, Leone looked pensively at Bill. "Poor Prince," she murmured. "He must be tired. He has contributed his share to our pleasure today. But I must admit, I am reluctant to go."

"We could turn Prince in at his stable in town and go home on the streetcar," suggested Bill.

"Would you like that?" she asked.

Bill turned to her and earnestly answered, "I would like that very much."

He tied up Prince, and the shadows lengthened as they wandered on a woodland path to the shoreline of Lake Washington. The lush beauty and fragrance of the hour cast the spell, forming an arbor of intimacy all their own. They noted how tall and straight the reeds grew as they looked across to the departing sun with its last rays lighting a gorgeous sky.

Wild waterfowl squawked as they coaxed their young, and the lonesome sound of a cowbell reached them from afar. A soft breeze made a faint ripple on the usually placid surface of the lake. "This moment is ours," Bill proclaimed. "The spring, the sun, the soft whisper of the water and us."

It was then the two young people confessed to each other that they had fallen in love.

Part V

Epilogue

It seemed important to me to share a short overview of the rest of the story for the Neelys. So, here is what happened to each of them:

LEONE NEELY (1885-1955):

In February of 1910 Leone met Bill Mayouck. He continued courting her. As she acknowledged in her last chapter, the couple professed their love for each other. Plans were begun soon after that for a large wedding celebration. Grandma was twenty-five and had fulfilled the charge her mother gave her to "carry out my most cherished wishes of seeing the children raised." She married my grandfather in St. James Cathedral in Seattle in June of 1910. She wore the beautiful wedding gown that is pictured on the cover. And as she had promised, Helen, her youngest sister, was her bridesmaid. Laura served as her maid of honor.

It wasn't until 1917 that their only child was born--my mother, Willina. Grandpa Bill continued working as a fireman in the Seattle Fire Department. In 1923 he was disabled when a horse he was shoeing at work fell on him. He was hospitalized for a dislocated vertebra. The injury led to his being medically discharged.

My grandparents then moved to Marysville, Washington, where they owned and operated Mayouck's Grocery for twenty-three years. Here Grandma Leone resumed her love of gardening. I remember her snowball bush, white calla lilies, and especially the beautiful and fragrant pink climbing roses.

My father, Lloyd Eisenman, as a young man delivered fresh meat and cold cuts to Mayouck's Grocery. That is where he met my mother, Willina, who was working for her parents in the grocery store. Following a year's courtship, my Mother and Father married in St. Mary's Catholic Church in Marysville in June of 1939. Grandma Leone and Grandpa Bill hosted the reception. I clearly recall and still enjoy looking at the pictures taken outside in Grandma's gardens on that day. When her health worsened in 1947, Grandma and Grandpa retired from their very successful grocery business.

My brother Jim and sisters Pam and Barbara and I all fondly

remember receiving cards, letters, and photographs from Arizona from Grandma Leone or "Ommi" as she affectionately liked to be called. During the hot Arizona summers, my grandparents would return to Washington. They parked their trailer at our home in East Everett where Grandma continued work on her memoirs. She died in Mesa, Arizona, in January of 1955 at the age of seventy. Grandpa Bill accompanied her back home on an appropriate last railway journey for funeral services in Marysville.

HELEN NEELY (1893-1961):

Helen did marry Mike McDonald, the long time love of her life in Seattle in 1912. Mike was the last of true, old-time type blacksmiths. He had been apprenticed at eleven years of age and ran blacksmithing shops in Edmonton and Seattle before coming to Victoria in 1910. At one time he had fourteen blacksmiths in his shop and became known all over Victoria Island for his work. He was a "smithy" for sixty-five years-- fifty of them in Victoria.

Helen and Mike had six children. Three daughters--Patricia, Helen, and Myrna remained in Victoria and so did one son, Bill. Two other sons moved: Jack to Calgary and Gerry to Vancouver. The three girls recall that their mother would sometimes make the same "moon potatoes" that she and her sisters made back on the farm in AuGres. The girls also recall coming down to Marysville, Washington, during summers and helping out their Aunt Leone at the grocery store.

In spite of raising six children, Helen continued to assist others in need. Her daughters recall that she often cared for elderly neighbors who were not well. She also passed required first aid tests to qualify for being "on call" with St. John's Ambulance Company in Victoria. If there were large events scheduled, she was hired to assist with any needed medical emergencies that might occur. Additionally, she was one of the founding members of the Catholic Women's League of Victoria and remained very active in the group. She was sixty-eight when she died in 1961.

LAURA NEELY (1891-1963):

Laura did move to Seattle to join Leone and Helen there in 1910. However, she had left her heart back in Canada. So she returned to Calgary and joined Henrietta. She remained in Calgary one summer through a winter and again into the following year's summer. While she was not pleased with the bitter cold winters nor the many mosquitoes that summer brought, she was happy when she became engaged. World War I broke out shortly afterwards, however, and her fiancé went into one of the branches of the Canadian services. Laura returned to Seattle and went to work as a tailor in a dry-cleaning shop. It was there she met Joe Steiner, whom she later married at Sacred Heart Church on Denny Hill in Seattle in August of 1916.

Joe and Laura later opened their own business, the Denny Way Dye Works and Cleaners. Joe did the dry-cleaning and deliveries; Laura did the alterations and pressing.

Laura was thirty-eight when their first daughter, Julie, was born. Laura chose to be a stay-at-home mom at that point, but she did take in tailoring and sewing projects at home. A second daughter, Clara, was born a little over two years later.

Some of my favorite memories are of trips my mother and we children made to Seattle to visit Aunt Laura and Uncle Joe. There were beautiful flowers in the yard. Uncle Joe repaired clocks, so we all recall the "ticking" sounds in the house and, of course, the wonderful aromas of Aunt Laura's cooking. We were usually treated with a warm bowl of soup always followed by a delicious bakery item she had picked out especially for us at the nearby Van de Kamp's Bakery. In 1963 Aunt Laura died of a stroke at seventy-two years of age.

MARIE NEELY (1887-1978):

When Leone and Helen left for Vancouver, British Columbia, Marie remained behind with Laura and Henrietta. The three Neely girls continued managing their hotel in Edmonton, Alberta. However, it was not long before Fred proposed to Marie, and they decided to get married. The young couple then moved to Calgary where better work was available for Fred. In 1909 Leone, Laura, and Helen received a letter from Lethbridge, Alberta, that a new baby had arrived. Marie and Fred were proud parents of a new little son, Ronald. Their second child, Ruth, was born in May of 1911; this time the letter came from an area near Winnipeg, Manitoba. The young family was also living in Winnipeg when Fred enlisted as a foot soldier; World War I had begun at the time. Fred was killed following the assault on Vimey Ridge in April of 1917. As was the case then, all soldiers killed were buried where they fell. Fred is buried in a cemetery near Vimey, France.

When World War I ended in December 1918, Marie left Winnipeg with her two children to stay with her brother in Chinook, Montana. Bill had returned ill from his Army service, and Marie went to nurse him back to a healthy condition.

About the time Bill recovered, the Canadian government was offering 320 acres of land free for homesteading to both soldiers returning from the War and war widows. Once families lived on the property for three years, they were given ownership. Bill urged Marie to take advantage of the opportunity to homestead in Saskatchewan. Marie did return to Canada with her children and filed on a half section (320 acres) in south Saskatchewan near the border in a very small town called Vivora. The location was not that far across the border to Chinook. Marie had a Model-T and would drive down with her family for visits.

Marie hired help to plant and harvest wheat that grew well on the prairie soil. She had a small house moved onto the property. With the pension checks she received and raising cows, horses, and chickens, the family survived. Conditions were harsh, especially in winter when they were forced to go to the more northern town of Shaunavon. Even the one-room schoolhouse the children attended had to close when winter snows arrived. Not enough money to pay for hired hands and the harsh winter conditions drove the family to abandon the farm. In 1934 they moved to Vancouver, British Columbia, where Marie took over a boarding house. When her daughter married in 1936, Marie gave up the business. My family always looked forward to visits from Aunt Marie. We had a fifteen-acre farm in East Everett, Washington, when I grew up. There was a large fruit tree orchard, and we raised cows, chickens, pigs, and rabbits, as well as all of our own vegetables. Now that I know she survived on a farm as a young widow, I think it was nostalgic for her to come for visits. She had a dry sense of humor and a memorable chuckle. Marie lived to be ninety-three years old; she died in a nursing home in 1978.

BILL NEELY (1888-1964):

Bill did leave Chicago to join his father in the border town of Portal, North Dakota. Bill and his father traveled across the border into Canada. Both took jobs in the lumber industry, and it was here that Bill ended up with the axe mark on the right side of his face.

He returned to Chicago and joined his sisters for a time helping them with their guesthouse. However, restlessness drew him back out West where he homesteaded 160 acres in Canada. When severe drought conditions forced him out, he moved across the border into Montana. Bill was hired as part of a wheat threshing crew. The crew moved from farm to farm working the wheat fields for farmers in northern Montana.

Bill arrived unexpectedly in Edmonton to again assist his sisters; this time it was with running a hotel. After a short period, he went back again to the area that he loved.

In March of 1918 Bill enlisted in the U.S. Army. He served through the middle of December when World War I ended and he was discharged. In April of 1919 he married Alice Fitzsimmons in Chinook, Montana. Like his father, Bill married a bride ten years his junior; Alice was 18. Marie made Alice's gown for the wedding.

Bill and Alice had seven children. Two infants died; the other children were John, Julie, Bob, Bill, and Pat. The couple stayed in northern Montana. They lived in both Harlem and Chinook where Bill drove road graders. He is credited with inventing the first motorized road grader in Montana. His living relatives have told me our Washington relatives probably never got to meet him as they considered him to be a person who liked being home. Alice died in January of 1964, and Bill died in April of the same year at the age of seventy-six.

HENRIETTA NEELY (1889-1943):

Henrietta, Laura, and Marie all stayed in Edmonton to run the hotel when Grandma Leone left with Helen for Vancouver. When

Marie married Fred and moved to Calgary and Laura returned to Seattle, Henrietta moved to Calgary. Laura came back to join her there for a time.

Family recall that Henrietta dated a railroad executive for a number of years, but as it turned out, she later married Brian MacDonald. They had two children: a son, Bill, and a daughter, Patricia. The couple later divorced.

A talented seamstress, one of the things Henrietta did was make baby comforters, which were filled with feathers. Making one of these comforters involved a great amount of work, as the feather plumes were hand stripped from the spine of the feathers. Family members recall that a friend either had or was expecting a baby. Deciding to make a comforter as a gift for the baby, Henrietta drove out to a farm to get the needed feathers. On the return trip, the car was hit by an army truck and unfortunately Henrietta was killed in the crash; she was fifty-four. I never knew Aunt Henrietta; I was only one year old when she was killed.

MARGARET NEELY (1879-1954):

Margaret was the first Neely daughter to marry; it was two years after her mother died. In 1898, she married Norman Curl; she was nineteen years old. Her father insisted that she and her new husband remain in the household to assist him with the farm work. They remained through the winter and then left for Gladwin, Michigan.

Margaret and Norman had four children. They stayed in Michigan and ended up in Albion. I remember visits from Aunt Margaret; she had a very gentle presence and a warm smile. She died at seventy-five in 1954.

Bill Mayouck Working for Seattle Fire Department

Bill on Motorbike in Seattle

Leone and Bill Mayouck on Their Wedding day in June 1910

Helen and Mike McDonald Standing Up for Bill and Leone

Helen and Mike McDonald on Their Wedding Day in June 1912

Henrietta and Laura Visit Helen in Victoria

Henrietta with Her Father Robert

Laura and Joe Steiner on Their Wedding Day in August 1916

Bill and Alice Neely on Their Wedding Day in April 1919

Marie's Homestead in Saskatchewan

Laura in Seattle Tailor Shop

Margaret with Her Husband Norman Curl
(Married in March 1898)

Marie Visits Margaret and Her Four Children

Norman and Margaret Curl in Albion, Michigan

Leone with Only Grandson Jim in 1941

Leone and Granddaughter Pam on a Trip to Canada in 1948

Leone Shopping in Seattle

Bill and Leone Mayouck's Grocery Store in Marysville, Washington

Leone with Grandchildren Jim, Paula, and Pam

266

Leone in Arizona

Leone and Bill Visit Daughter Willina Eisenman, and Her Family

Appendix A – **LIST OF BOOK'S MAIN CHARACTERS**

FAMILY MEMBERS

Robert Neely:	Father
Julia Neely:	Mother
Margaret Neely:	Daughter
Leone Neely:	Daughter
Marie Neely:	Daughter
Bill Neely:	Son
Henrietta Neely:	Daughter
Laura Neely:	Daughter
Helen Neely:	Daughter
Minnie Tallon Neely:	Stepmother
Norman Curl:	Margaret Neely's Beau/Husband
Fred Hastings:	Marie Neely's Beau/Husband
Mike McDonald:	Helen Neely's Beau/Husband
Bill Mayouck:	Leone Neely's Beau/Husband

OTHERS

Cleo Ramsdale:	Leone's Chicago Friend
Jackoline O'Donnel:	Close Chicago Friend of Neely Sisters
Katherine Curray:	Close Chicago Friend of Neely Sisters
James Grimore:	Mayor of AuGres

NAME IN THIS BOOK	GIVEN NAME	NICKNAMES*
Margaret	Margaret Ann	Ann
Leone	Sarah Jane	Sallie, Sharrei
Marie	Mary Theresa	Mollie
Bill	William George	George
Henrietta	Elizabeth Henrietta	Becky, Liz, Liza
Laura	Laura Josephine	Jo, Josephine
Helen	Ellen Ruth	Ella

* Names Grandma Leone used in her original manuscript.

IN MEMORY OF JULIA NEELY
(Died February 28, 1896)

Mrs. Neely, the deceased, was born in Canada in 1860 and came to Michigan in 1881, where she and her husband located on a farm on which she resided, and here she raised her family respectable and respected until her demise. In all her transactions she was noted for her honor and integrity and a more agreeable lady was seldom met; her correct habits, generosity, sociability and all those traits of character, which raise a lady to the higher grade of human progression, made her loved and respected by her friends and neighbors and esteemed by all who made her acquaintance, as she counted many friends amongst those who knew her best. She was a devoted member of the Catholic church, whose teachings she followed to the letter; also being liberal to all religious and moral societies; charitable to her less fortunate neighbors; ever careful and attending to the wants of her family. Her life was such, that when the time came that she should prepare to meet her Maker, she died with a clear conscience and an honest conviction that she was at peace with the world and with her God. She passed peacefully away blessing her husband and children and her many friends, who cherish her memory and regret her demise. The writer of this piece has had the acquaintance of Mrs. Neely for fifteen years and never knew another who was possessed with more kindly and beautiful traits of character, and can safely say that a good woman has died; a devoted wife and mother and a tender, unselfish and faithful friend, universally beloved and respected. She leaves a husband, one son and six daughters to mourn her loss. She was honored with having one of the largest funerals ever held in AuGres.

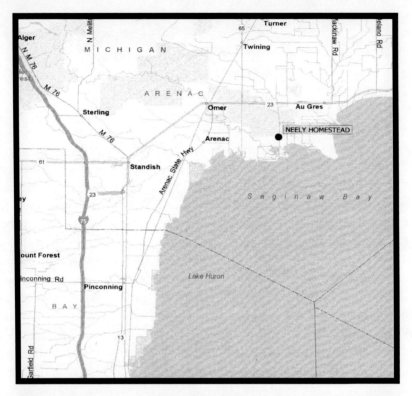

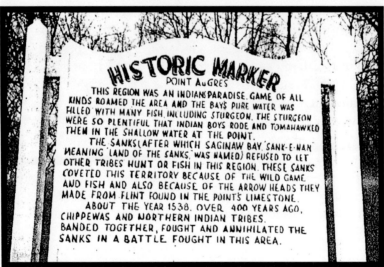

(Courtesy of Arenac County Historical Museum)

Appendix D – SETTLEMENT OF HOMESTEAD (1903)

QUIT-CLAIM DEED—SHORT—(6) Arenac County.

Liber 30

Minnie Neely
TO
Robt Neely

Received for Record, the 6th *day of* Feby *A. D.* 1903, *at* 8 *o'clock* A.M.

W R Chamberlain *Register of Deeds.*

This Indenture, Made the 4th day of February in the year of our Lord one thousand nine hundred and three

Between Minnie Neely of the Township of Au Gres, Arenac County, Michigan, wife of second party of the first part, and Robert Neely of the same place, husband of first party of the second part;

Witnesseth, That the said party of the first part, for and in consideration of the sum of One Hundred and Twenty five Dollars and other valuable considerations to her in hand paid by the said party of the second part, the receipt whereof is hereby confessed and acknowledged, do es by these presents, grant, bargain, sell, remise, release, and forever QUIT-CLAIM unto the said party of the second part, and to his heirs and assigns, FOREVER, ALL that certain piece or parcel of land situated in the Township of Au Gres in Arenac County, and State of Michigan, known and described as follows:

The north half (½) of north West (¼) of Section thirty three (33) Town nineteen north of Range Six (6) East, the South East quarter (¼) of South East (¼) of Section Twenty nine (29) and the South west quarter (¼) of South West quarter (¼) Section Twenty eight (28) both in Township nineteen (19) north of Range Six East.

This deed is given by first party, with a view of releasing all right title and interest she has or might obtain thereto by reason of their marriage contract which exists between them, and hereby release her dower interest or any other interest or title which she may have in the above described premises.

Together with all and Singular, The hereditaments and appurtenances thereunto belonging or in anywise appertaining: To Have and to Hold the said Robert Neely Minnie Neely to the said party of the second part, and to his heirs and assigns, to the sole and only proper use, benefit and behoof of the said party of the second part, his heirs and assigns, FOREVER.

In Witness Whereof, The said party of the first part has hereunto set her hand and seal the day and year first above written.

Signed, Sealed and Delivered in Presence of

C. H. Macomber
O. L. Marr

Minnie Neely [SEAL.]

[SEAL.]

[SEAL.]

[SEAL.]

State of Michigan, County of Arenac } ss.

On this 4th day of February in the year one thousand nine hundred and three before me, the subscriber a Notary Public in and for said County, personally appeared Minnie Neely to me known to be the same person described in and who executed the within instrument, who acknowledged the same to be her free act and deed.

Clarence H. Macomber
Notary Public

Clarence H. Macomber Notary Public Arenac Co. Mich

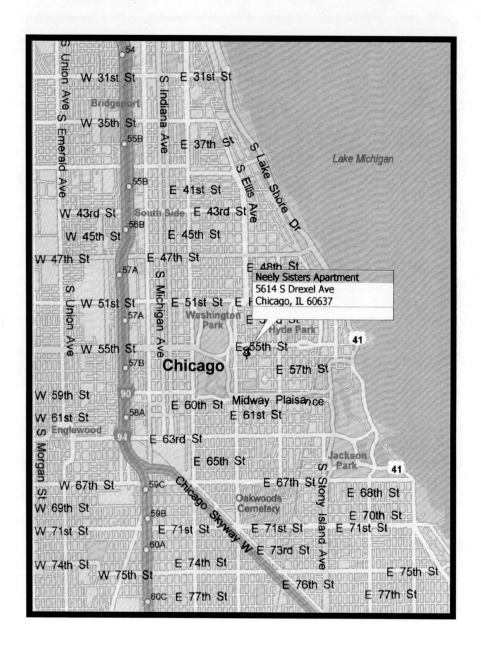

Neely Sisters Apartment
5614 S Drexel Ave
Chicago, IL 60637

The honor of your presence is requested at the

marriage of

Miss Leone Jennette Neely

to

Mr. William James Mayouck

on the morning of June twenty ninth

nineteen hundred and ten

seven o'clock

in St. James Cathedral

Seattle, Washington

At Home

after July tenth

1210 East Howell Street

PLEASE OMIT GIFTS

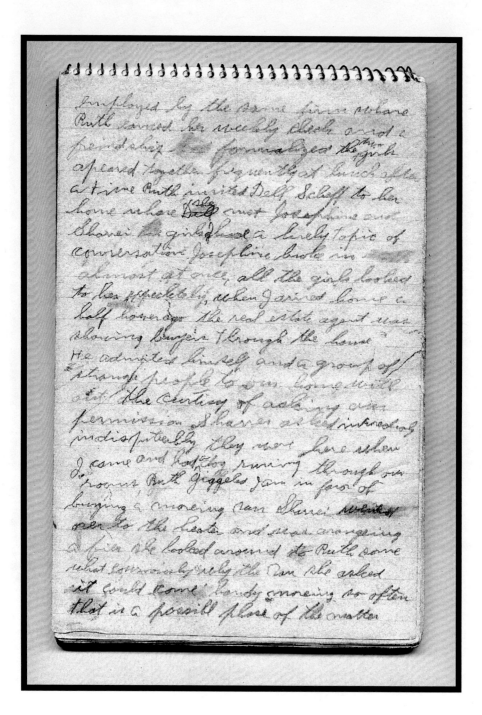

Editor, Arenac County Independent
P. O. Box 699
Standish, Michigan 48658

LETTER TO THE EDITOR:

We would like to express our sincere appreciation to a number of local area residents. Recently we came to town in search of our great-grandmother and great-grandfather's 100-year-old homestead. With all your generous help and information, we succeeded in our search. The homestead property is located off Saginaw Bay in the early French Canadian settlement outside of Omer.

Our personal thanks to: Kieth Ososki, Helen Eichstead, Pat Killingbeck and her staff, Mayor La Verne Dittenber, Gene Howard, Annabelle Goodman, Lester Selle, Horatio Davis (all in AuGres), members of the Historical Museum staff in Bay City, Ricky Rockwell and his staff in Vital Statistics, the Land and Deeds staff members, and Norma Curcio in the Office of Equalization at the Arenac County Courthouse in Standish.

We couldn't have done it without all of you!

Pam & Irvin Snow of Milton, Wisconsin and
Paula Pascoe of Fox Island, Washington

Appendix I – **ACKNOWLEDGEMENTS**

Family and friends have offered me much encouragement during the process of preparing Grandma Leone's manuscript pages. I greatly appreciated the support of my brother, Jim Eisenman and his family; my sister, Pam Snow and her family; and my youngest sister, Barbara Keefe and her family. Special thanks goes to Aunt Laura's daughter and my cousin, Julie Elftmann, in Arlington, Washington. Julie was the keeper of old address books, letters and photographs that were most helpful. Our numerous phone conversations helped me determine Grandma's book was truly an autobiography. Aunt Helen's daughters, my Victoria, British Columbia cousins, Pat Sedger, Helen Campbell and Myrna Dorras, each gave early on and continued encouragement throughout the project. Additional photos and information were obtained when I located two of Aunt Marie's grandchildren: Ellen Leonard of Victoria B.C. and Jim Walsh of Orillia in Ontario, Canada. Also, John Neely of Indianapolis, Indiana and, grandson of Bill Neely, stopped by during a trip to the Seattle area. Each cousin contributed photographs, family records and/or shared recollections of stories from their respective parent or grandparent.

Of great value to me was a trip my sister, Pam and her husband Irvin made with me in 2000 to AuGres, Michigan in search of the Neely homestead. We found the homestead site located off Saginaw Bay in the early French Canadian settlement area. On a second trip in 2002 we found the location of the Drexel Street apartment in Chicago. Today the University of Chicago owns the property.

Lance DuBois of Belgrade, Montana, did artwork for the divider sections of *Grandma Leone's Memoirs*. Lance is a fourth generation Montana artist who also does work for *Montana Magazine*.

I am sincerely thankful for my good friend Georgia McDade's assistance with editing. She honored my request to retain Grandma's expressions and phraseology as much as possible.

Finally, most grateful appreciation goes to my husband, Roy Davis, who has been there for me through every step in this project. Just the time alone to get the entire book set up page-by-page to be press-ready for printing was huge. Your contributions were truly a gift from the heart, and I will be forever thankful. Without your initial and continued support, Grandma's book would not have become a reality.

With the project of preparing this manuscript, I have developed such a deepened respect for Grandma Leone. I had never heard about the hard life she had experienced. Further, I had no idea that her mother on her deathbed, charged twelve-year-old Grandma to see that the Neely children got raised properly. It is incredible to me that Grandma had both the courage and faith as a child to succeed in her plan to make enough money in three years to provide for her younger sisters and brother. When the Neely sisters were on their own in Chicago, even the Mayor of AuGres and his wife came to visit because they had heard of the Neely sisters' successful tailor and dress shop business. I marvel that the girls not only again owned and operated a guest house once they moved to Edmonton, but then they took on managing several hotels! Finally, Grandma managed and with the help of her youngest sister and operated a nursing home in Vancouver, British Columbia. It was not typical to find such successful businesswomen in the early 1900's!

We know about at least three resident homes that Grandma designed. My grandparents made their first home in one of them; it was located at 1210 East Howell Street in Seattle.

Powdered paint with gold flecks in it was an invention credited to Grandma. It was packaged similarly to seed packets and when mixed with a can of paint would make a fluorescent look for "dressing up" walls and ceilings. Grandma's paint invention was used in the ceiling of the Seattle Fifth Avenue Theater.

Another Seattle theater was looking for words to come up on the movie screen before the main feature to spotlight short news clips, so they sponsored a contest. Grandma's entry "THE EYES AND EARS OF THE WORLD" won the contest! These words would come up on the movie theater screens before the news update and credited my grandmother.

My grandmother continued her nursing skills throughout her life. My brother and I were born at home, and Grandma Leone assisted at both of our deliveries.

Deja vu best names the feeling I had when I began working on the chapters of this book and learned that I have walked in my grandmother's shoes! In my semi-retirement I have owned and operated a bed and breakfast, just as she owned and operated a "guest house." My grandfather was a firefighter employed with the

Seattle Fire Department; my husband in his semi-retirement was employed as a firefighter with the Tacoma Fire Department. Finally, I worked to enter these chapters on our laptop computer while in our motorhome, just as Grandma had worked on her memoirs in her trailer. I feel privileged that this granddaughter was the one asked by her mother to finish this book.

Paula with Grandma Leone's Underwood Typewriter

IT IS WITH GREAT PRIDE THAT I PAY PERSONAL TRIBUTE TO GRANDMA LEONE...AN AMAZING EARLY PIONEER BUSINESS WOMAN WHO WAS AHEAD OF HER TIME.

PAULA EISENMAN PASCOE